MW00474699

The Essential Guide to Writing History Essays

The Essential Guide to Writing History Essays

KATHERINE PICKERING ANTONOVA

OXFORD

UNIVERSITY PRESS

OXFORD
UNIVERSITY PRESS

Oxford University Press is a department of the University of Oxford. It furthers
the University's objective of excellence in research, scholarship, and education
by publishing worldwide. Oxford is a registered trade mark of Oxford University
Press in the UK and certain other countries.

Published in the United States of America by Oxford University Press
198 Madison Avenue, New York, NY 10016, United States of America.

© Oxford University Press 2020

All rights reserved. No part of this publication may be reproduced, stored in
a retrieval system, or transmitted, in any form or by any means, without the
prior permission in writing of Oxford University Press, or as expressly permitted
by law, by license, or under terms agreed with the appropriate reproduction
rights organization. Inquiries concerning reproduction outside the scope of the
above should be sent to the Rights Department, Oxford University Press, at the
address above.

You must not circulate this work in any other form
and you must impose this same condition on any acquirer.

CIP data is on file at the Library of Congress
ISBN 978–0–19–027116–9 (pbk.)
ISBN 978–0–19–027115–2 (hbk.)

For my students: past, present, and future.

Contents

About the Companion Website

Additional resources for instructors are available at
www.oup.com/us/writinghistoryessays

Note to Instructors

History is as much a writing field as literature, yet few historians are trained in how to teach writing, as graduate students in literature usually are. Most required composition courses are taught by English departments and are explicitly interdisciplinary. This often leaves history instructors scrambling to find ways to address writing in our own discipline-specific ways with little direct training or curriculum space devoted to it. This book is intended to help fill this gap. It is the product of nineteen years of classroom experimentation and student feedback, informed throughout by evidence-based practices developed by composition studies researchers and educators.

No book can help students, however, if students don't read it. To make this book work for you and your students, specific references to chapters and sections could be integrated into your syllabus, assignments, and feedback. The detailed table of contents and index should aid you in quickly finding the right references to incorporate into your course materials. In addition, the accompanying website (www.oup.com/us/writinghistoryessays) for instructors provides sample syllabi, assignments, and rubrics already filled out with references to relevant book sections, as well as additional exercises and examples for classroom use where time allows, an FAQ covering common teaching concerns, and suggestions on how the book might be integrated into different levels or types of courses.

This book is informed by several core concepts developed by composition studies researchers: plain-language vocabulary (offered alongside the most commonly used synonyms); goal-oriented instruction, which offers students tools to meet the varying purposes of each assignment rather than idealized models to copy; "scaffolding," which means breaking assignments down into steps that build on each other; academic writing presented as a "conversation," in which we each contribute with reference to the ongoing contributions of others; and an understanding of the writing process as a translation from writer-directed drafts to reader-directed revisions.

"Writing in the Disciplines" (WID) is a term from composition studies that refers to the specialized norms students encounter within their majors that should build on introductory composition instruction. "Writing Across the Curriculum" (WAC) refers to the effort to continue writing instruction throughout a student's degree program. These specialized terms may serve as an entry into the extensive research literature in composition studies for those instructors who would like to explore further.

This book is also informed by the "Tuning" assessment project of the American Historical Association, which strives to articulate the defining goals, methods, and skills of historical scholarship. A wealth of information and resources assembled by that project are available at https://www.historians.org/teaching-and-learning/tuning-the-history-discipline.

1

Orientation

This guide teaches goal-oriented writing skills. That is, its underlying assumption is that there is no ideal form of essay that students should strive to imitate. Instead, the book encourages you to identify specific goals for each assignment and provides a variety of tools to reach those goals in your own way. It explains the expectations for the most typical written assignment types and then offers tools, habits, and strategies to meet them, along with exercises and examples. It explains the assumptions, conventions, and purposes that are often left unspoken. Rather than giving traditional advice to "be clear," this book shows what clarity looks like and why some sentences are clear to readers, while others are not.

The book is intended for students completing formal writing assignments in history courses and is based on typical North American university-level history coursework. It is intended to be accessible to anyone, regardless of preparation or previous experience with history. If you are new to history or have struggled with the subject, you should find the book a complete guide. If you have taken some history classes and currently work haphazardly—relying primarily on habits and guesses—this book will help you develop consistency and a toolbox of methods for approaching any assignment successfully. If you have been able to succeed in history coursework so far, you will learn to become self-aware about why and how your current strategies are successful and develop a vocabulary for talking about writing and history that will help you to take your skills to the next level.

Undergraduate history majors will find a roadmap to the writing you will do throughout the major. Non-majors taking only one or two history courses will also find the book useful, because it fills in many of the unspoken assumptions that history majors usually gather over time. Many high school courses, especially advanced placement and honors courses, may engage with history in similar ways, and precocious high school students in any program may be challenged by this book. Students who come late to a history major or graduate students in history who did not major in history as undergraduates will find the expectations, skills, and language that are usually taken for granted in the practice of history at these more advanced levels.

Students working on a master's degree in history will find chapters 8 to 11 most closely relevant to your coursework, but you will need to refer to earlier chapters, where terms and skills are first defined, as guided by internal references or the index. Students of history at the doctoral level may find this book useful to fill the occasional gap but primarily as an aid to teaching, by expanding your ability to isolate and explain rhetorical moves that you may have learned through imitation or intuition. For your own research, doctoral students should consult a more advanced text such as *From Reliable Sources: An Introduction to Historical Methods* by Martha Howell and Walter Prevenier (Ithaca, NY: Cornell University Press, 2001) as well as *The Craft of Research* by Wayne Booth, Gregory Colomb, and Joseph Williams, one of the excellent Chicago Guides to Writing, Editing, and Publishing (Chicago: University of Chicago Press, 2008), and Jean Bolker's *Writing Your Dissertation in Fifteen Minutes a Day* (New York: Owl Books, 1998).

Outside the United States, many university systems are encouraging formal standards of argumentative, academic writing modeled on the American academy. This book may also serve as a guide to what American academic history is. History teachers at the secondary level as well as school boards and other K–12 decision-makers could similarly find it useful as an overview of the expectations of tertiary education in history.

Any casual reader interested in the methods, assumptions, and goals of scholarly historical writing, such as writers of popular history and reviewers of history books as well as journalists and researchers in adjacent fields like literary studies and digital humanities, will find chapters 2 and 3 and much of chapters 8 and 9 particularly useful, but also sections 4.5 (on historical significance), 5.2 (on reading academic history), 6.5–6.6 (on historical claims about causality), 6.9 (on logic), and 11.4 (on types of historical argument).

The Essential Guide is intended for students working in any historical period or region. Some forms of history overlap with other disciplines; if you are concentrating in those areas, you may find that the common disciplinary assumptions covered here are less central to your work. For example, the study of ancient history shares assumptions, methods, and sources with classics and archaeology, while digital historians use some tools and methods more common to scholars in library and computer sciences than in traditional history, and cultural and area studies combine perspectives from anthropology, psychology, sociology, political science, economics, folklore, art history, and literature as well as history. While most historians primarily work with texts, and therefore most of the examples in this book reflect such work, some historians focus on visual sources or physical objects, sometimes sharing methods with art historians or anthropologists. Others incorporate economics and statistics into quantitative history. Historians working on contemporary subjects often use sources or data from political scientists, economists, or sociologists, and may create their own sources through interviews with living subjects (known as oral history). This book aims to distill the methods and assumptions common to typical history coursework without forgetting the many ways that history borrows from other disciplines. Appendix 2 provides references to sources specializing in some of these areas that may provide a useful supplement to this text for students with special interest in those areas.

1.1. How to Use This Book

If you read this book from beginning to end, you will take a tour through the expectations and practices of academic history. This will provide a useful understanding of what historians do as well as a practical guide to doing it yourself. But reading in sequence is not necessarily the most efficient way to use the book. As you should for any nonfiction book, start by studying the table of contents and index to understand what is covered and how the book is organized. The book is structured by assignment type because primary source essays, for example, have different goals than response papers or research essays. Every choice you make as a writer should serve the goal of what you are trying to communicate. The book is designed so that you can jump straight to a chapter that matches an assignment you have right now. Concepts are introduced as they become necessary, in order from the simplest to the most complex assignment. Because some skills and concepts are relevant to more than one genre of writing, you will sometimes need to refer to the definitions of key terms or review earlier passages as they become relevant, using internal references.

Chapters 1–3 provide a broad background to college-level expectations and the principles that guide this book as well as to academic writing and history, so they are a good place for everyone to start. All readers should use the index to find explanations of common terms that may turn up in any form of coursework or research, and be ready to refer as needed to sections 5.10, 6.6, 6.9, 8.5, 9.2–9.5, 9.8–9.9, and 9.11, which focus on various types of specialized historical vocabulary, presented at the point where they are most likely to be needed. Most undergraduates should next determine which of the assignment categories provided here most closely matches their next assignment by browsing the descriptions at the beginning of each chapter. Work through the relevant chapter as you plan and write your essay, skipping sections that do not apply. A multistep assignment may involve more than one chapter.

Whether you ever write a response paper, all history students would benefit from consulting the sections in that chapter on reading secondary sources (section 5.2), annotating readings (sections 5.3–5.4), and making word choices (section 5.10), as well as section 5.7 on how to structure a short essay that is not argument based. Similarly, every history student should contemplate sections 6.5–6.6 and 6.9 about historical thinking.

Reading this book in addition to your other course readings may seem to require more time than you have. But as you begin to master these skills, you will find you can work more efficiently while getting better results. Using the book may sometimes feel uncomfortable, because it may ask you to set aside habits that have worked well enough so far and push you instead to think beyond what to do, to discover *why*. It is best approached with playful openness to the unexpected.

1.2. How to Interpret Instructions

Beyond the practical need to figure out which chapter of this book most closely relates to your next assignment, you must of course read or listen to your professor's specific instructions. Don't skim instructions looking for the topic and page length. The topic of an assignment is less important than its *goal*.

Knowing your goal tells you what kind of essay you are expected to produce, what preparation you need, and what skills you need to demonstrate. Do you need to show that you have memorized a set of facts? That you fully understood a text? That you have thought through an important historical problem? That you can distinguish between a useful source and those that are irrelevant for your purpose? That you can formulate a workable research question? That you can weigh evidence and compose a convincing answer to a historical question? These questions represent a list of very different skills that each require different preparation and writing choices.

The verbs your instructor chooses are usually the best clue to what is expected from you. Most assignments, even relatively short ones, ask you to take several actions, expressed as verbs, and it will help you to consider each one. The following list of common assignment verbs explains how each matches up with expectations for the work you will do. If anything your instructor tells you contradicts something written here, you must of course follow your instructor's instructions. But in many cases, your instructor may be using a synonym for what is described in this book: if you are in doubt, ask your professor.

- **Read.** Scholarly reading does not mean you force your eyes to hover over a certain number of pages before you release yourself to do something more interesting. It requires your active, thoughtful attention and often is not best done straight through from beginning to end. See sections 4.2, 5.2–5.4, 6.3, 7.3, 8.2, and 9.6–9.7 on active reading and note-taking.
- **Describe.** To describe is to list the relevant characteristics of something. To know what's relevant, you first have to think about the purpose of the assignment and the nature of whatever it is you're describing. Then you need

to painstakingly notice and put into words each feature, in the most concrete possible words.

- **Summarize / put in your own words / distill.** When you summarize, you briefly describe an overall theme, choosing just a few details to represent the whole. A summary is what you do when you tell your friend about a movie: you mention only the most important bits that drive the story along and maybe a little background about which actors are in it or who directed it. Some instructors will describe this using the more precise terms "distillation" or "to distill." In a distillation or selective summary you make active, thoughtful choices about what details to explain, what to mention only in passing, and what to exclude. Be careful not to confuse a selective summary of key points with simplifying a text (it is the difference between explaining the major characters and plot points of *Game of Thrones* versus saying, "It's a show where a lot of people die").

- **Explain.** To explain is to unravel the "how" or "why" about something. You tell how it happened (a chain of causes and effects), why it is complicated, and why it matters. Explaining is the opposite of simplifying or generalizing from a single case into a pattern. To explain is to explore the unique causes and consequences of a given case, distinguishing it from others.

- **Identify (ID).** To "identify" is to find, name, and explain some thing and to tell us what matters about it. If you are asked to "identify" the author of a text, you should find that person's name and provide it, but also explain what is important about that person. If asked to identify, say, the author of a certain diary about a small town in Maine shortly after the American Revolution, you should answer "Martha Ballard," but also add that Ballard was a midwife who recorded her work in her diary, leaving us a record of medical care and women's roles in local economies. That added description tells us how Martha Ballard's diary relates to historically significant questions.

- **Define.** To define is to explain how a term or concept is used and what it signifies. Historians also "define" terms in new ways or invent new terms in order to explain or categorize some phenomenon we discover in our sources. A historical definition should be as specific as possible about where, when, and to what people it does and does not apply.

- **Think about / consider / discuss / explore.** To explore is to find your way around a new subject by trying things out. When you explore, you ask questions and attempt answers, which will necessarily be somewhat speculative (but not arbitrary: stick as closely as possible to available evidence). When asked to "explore" a historical document, for example, you are invited to ask questions that may not be fully answerable but can still help us to discover more about the document than we would know otherwise. You would then explain the reasoning behind each of these possible answers, weigh how convincing each of them is, and come to some tentative conclusion. Perhaps you will conclude that the answer is no more certain than it was when you started, but you will have identified the range of possible answers.

- **Respond.** When you are asked to respond to a text, you are being asked to show that you read and understood it *and* that you have thought critically about it. A critical "response" does not include your personal taste or feelings, nor is it necessarily negative. A "response" is a thoughtful exploration of the dilemmas, confusions, problems, or questions inherent in any complex text. In other words, when you "respond" you are first identifying questions or problems in the text and then suggesting possible answers or resolutions.

- **Interpret / examine / analyze.** To interpret a piece of evidence from the past is to look at it closely and ask questions about what is there ("text") and what is not there directly ("subtext") as well as how it relates to the time, place, and people it comes from (its "context"). By "examine" or "analyze" we mean that you need to identify and explain your subject and also go one big step further to pose questions and suggest answers about what can be learned from this process. Analyzing or interpreting is the opposite of summarizing. When you analyze, you examine each detail, look for patterns, inconsistencies, questions, problems, and assumptions, and try to explain them. An analysis of a text must by definition be longer than the text being analyzed, since it is a process of untangling, questioning, and explaining each part of the source text.

- **Criticize / critique.** In a scholarly context, criticizing does not just mean finding flaws, and a "critical" reading of a text is not necessarily negative. To critique a text is to test its evidence and reasoning and to ask questions about its methods or scope with the aim of verifying the text's claims or finding additional or more effective approaches.

- **Argue / come to a conclusion / take a stand.** An argument is series of claims supported by evidence and reasoning. When you "take a stand" or "come to a conclusion," you are arguing for a certain interpretation or analysis and supporting that position by lining up all the evidence and reasons that make you find it convincing. When you state your position most clearly, we call that a "thesis statement" or "main claim." An argument is what motivates most scholarly essays: the main purpose is to articulate a position and support it with evidence and reasoning. Arguing in a scholarly context is not about hostility. It is a process of suggesting, defending, and criticizing various positions in order for the scholarly community as a whole to get closer to truth.

1.3. What's Different about College History

It will be useful to consider the habits of writing and thinking that you may have brought with you from high school or other previous experiences, and how you will build on or develop those habits as you tackle more complicated assignments.

In most cases the chief difference between high school and college is that high school education aims to give you broad knowledge of the world and introduce you to the main fields of inquiry (mathematics, science, social science, humanities, the arts), whereas the goal in college is to train you to think critically about where knowledge comes from, to analyze, to find and sort through new information effectively, and to apply lessons from one sphere to another. Most college coursework will be housed within a specific discipline, and taught by active, expert practitioners of that research field. Each discipline uses different methods to think critically about the world, and you are meant to familiarize yourself with these varying methods as you take courses in different departments, but the overall goal of higher education is to train you in critical thinking.

In high school history courses most students acquire the basic knowledge of their own and the world's history that helps them to be good citizens. In college, you are expected to act as an apprentice historian in order to understand how professional historians generate knowledge about our past and to ask deeper questions about the nature and uses of history and how history influences our society. There is of course great variation from one classroom to another, but one rough way of highlighting the distinction between secondary and higher history education is that in high school you encounter stories and discuss their meanings; in college you are also invited to discover how stories are written, to try writing some yourself, and to discuss what this process reveals from many points of view.

1.3.1. Developing the Five-Paragraph Essay

Many American students are taught to write analytical essays according to the "five-paragraph essay model." This model represents the basic outline of argument-driven scholarly writing: an introduction that sets up a problem and proposes a resolution, a series of points of evidence supporting the resolution, and a conclusion that summarizes the case made and connects it to broader implications. This basic structure is still expected in some formal college essays. But naturally not every argument in the real world relies on three points of evidence, and not every introduction or conclusion can best be articulated in one paragraph each. Moreover, many essays are not argument-driven; the structure of an essay should reflect its goal, which varies from one genre to the next. The rigidity of the five paragraphs can safely be left behind now as you focus on content and learn different genres of writing.

This difference implies something very important about how your writing process in college should be different than it might have been in high school. If your goal was simply to copy a model until its structure became second nature, you started with an outline and then filled it in. But that process allows you only to record what you already know, or can look up, rather than to discover new knowledge. Writing should become a process of sorting through complex information, understanding it better, figuring out what it might mean or how it might be applied in new ways, and then deciding how your conclusions can be best made clear to a reader. To do this properly, you must write multiple drafts. Plan more time for writing the same number of pages compared to what you may have done before. Even when you write an argument-driven essay, you may find it helpful to rename the parts of the five-paragraph model to be more specific:

Introduction = problem + resolution
Body = evidence + reasoning
Conclusion = implications

1.3.2. Don't Quote the Dictionary

"According to Webster's dictionary . . ." is a famed rhetorical move in student essays. At first we need to pay attention to dictionary definitions and distinctions between them in order to build vocabulary and ground essays in concrete, well-defined terms. You should now be encountering words that take on specialized meanings in a certain context, however: words that are invented to describe new understandings or phenomena and words with meanings that are still debated. At this point both author and readers should be familiar with dictionary definitions, so quoting the dictionary is unnecessary. But it is still important to define your terms. As a student, you will likely draw definitions of important terms from readings (attributing them to their authors; see sections 5.9 and 11.7), or perhaps you will stake out and defend a new term or specialized meaning as a way of explaining a phenomenon you are studying (section 11.10).

1.3.3. Do the Reading at Home

You not only have to do the reading outside of class, but you have to do it whether or not it's being discussed or even mentioned in class. College courses are structured so that a full load should be approximately forty hours a week, or the equivalent of a full-time job. Expect to work an average of two to four hours at home for each hour you spend in class (you will find that you'll spend less time in some weeks and more in other weeks). Ideally, class time is concentrated on bringing together key points from the material, asking questions about it, and learning how to identify patterns in it. For that time to be worthwhile, you and your classmates must come prepared. Your success in writing assignments will also depend on how much you incorporate course readings into your writing. College is like a gym membership: you pay for access to the facilities and trainers who can figure out what you need, push you along, show you the most efficient methods, and keep you from hurting yourself. But you still have to do the work, or you'll never get in shape.

1.3.4. Assignments Have Higher Stakes

College history courses typically require you to master a large amount of material for each writing assignment, and each grade carries considerable weight in your final course grade, with few or no opportunities to make up missing or unsuccessful work. Final exams may ask you to synthesize material from the entire semester to enable you to make important connections among widely separated places and periods. For this reason, studying cannot mean memorizing a list of details just long enough to pass a test. Think about the material as it comes, asking yourself how each piece connects to others and why it matters. Essays may be longer and will have more specific goals than "writing on a topic." Approach each essay assignment with attention to these variations.

1.3.5. Understanding Feedback

Feedback may be infrequent and focused on what you need to do differently next time. Feedback is never about you as a person, but about the written work you turned in. Don't take it personally, but do consider it a guide to how to approach your next assignment, even if that is in another course. If you don't understand the feedback you're getting or it isn't enough, talk to your professor. Professors who don't hear from you will assume you know what you're doing. See sections 8.10 and 11.12.

1.3.6. What We Expect You to Know

The traditional four-year college program in North America is a unique stage when most students are being treated as adults for the first time, often far from home. You are also exposed to new information and asked to perform new skills at a higher level than before, with much greater variety and at a faster pace than you are likely to face anywhere else, including the workplace after graduation. Simultaneously, traditional-aged students are still completing their cognitive development into adulthood. Many students are also the first in their families to go through this experience, with little exposure to the many assumptions and unspoken expectations of the university. This is a challenging environment, but also one that is full of opportunities to explore, to make and learn from mistakes, to build relationships with a broad diversity of people, and to begin real mastery of at least one main subject of study. If you take advantage of these unique opportunities, you will carry a strong set of skills, knowledge, and connections through the rest of your life.

The most important skill as you enter the university is self-regulation. You will be expected to manage your time, stay focused on your goals, take responsibility for your mistakes, and ask for help when you need it. Many students are still struggling with some or all of these skills when they come to college; it may help just to acknowledge that this is not unusual. The following are assumptions your professors may have about what you can do and suggestions on where to look for help with them.

- **Use general knowledge.** It's much easier to remember new facts, concepts, and ideas if you already have a basic scaffolding, so that you can attach each piece of new information to an existing outline. Incoming college students are generally expected to know a rough chronological outline of the major historical periods, events, inventions, and ideas. For example, you should recognize that the date 950 C.E. is from the medieval period, that the French Revolution happened in the eighteenth century and World Wars I and II in the twentieth. You are expected to recognize the names of people like Hitler, Queen Elizabeth I, or Thomas Jefferson, and to know that television was not invented until the twentieth century.

  Normally high school provides this background, but if you do not yet have it, you might find history coursework easier to handle with a general reference work like the *Atlas of World History* (Patrick O'Brien, ed.) or by first reading a very brief overview such as an appropriate volume of the New Oxford World History series. In addition, basic geographical knowledge makes history courses easier to follow. Keep a map or Google Earth handy. The quickest way to familiarize yourself with a large-scale map is to first identify the bodies of water, starting with the largest, then follow these to the major cities (almost always located on or near bodies of water) and borders (which often follow bodies of water, mountain ranges, or other large geographical features).

- **Use word-processing software to produce a professional-looking essay.** You should be familiar with how to insert page breaks, page numbers, and footnotes; how to adjust margins, headers, fonts, and spacing; and how to convert a document to other formats, such as PDF. You should give appropriate titles to all documents (not "Paper1.docx" but "Lastname-PrimarySrcInterp.docx"). If you run into a specific problem while working on a document, use a general internet search: "how to [blank] in MS Word." For more complicated questions, consult your campus computing help desk, not your professor.

- **Back up your work.** Use a free automatic cloud backup service, or email a copy of your documents to yourself. Flash drives can also be useful for backups, but don't rely on them for your only copy of your work.

- **Write complete, grammatical sentences in correctly spelled formal English with appropriate formatting, punctuation, and capitalization.** Although some instructors may address these issues in some classes, these are skills you should already have by the time you begin college. If you know you have gaps in any of these areas, plan to spend quality time on your own with good reference works and perhaps consult appropriate campus services. Some students find it easier to say their ideas out loud, recording and transcribing them (or use campus resources to have them digitally transcribed), or using dictation software, and then revising that text (software will create its own errors). Built-in grammar and spellcheck functions in word processing software are reminders for those who understand the principles and can distinguish between correctly spelled homonyms. If you rely on those functions without this understanding, the result can be unreadable (or unintentionally funny, as when you write an essay about "pheasants" instead of "peasants"). Using translation software or synonym apps usually results in incomprehensible nonsense. A simple, clear essay will serve better than one full of words that are not used correctly. The best way to significantly improve both your grammar and vocabulary is to read widely and often. Notice how words, sentences, and paragraphs affect you as a reader.

- **Cite sources, consistently using one recognized citation style:** In most courses beyond your first semester, you will be expected to be able to cite appropriately and may be instructed only in the peculiarities of a particular citation style or unusual source type. Being able to trace where evidence or an argument comes from is one of the core principles of academic work, so to err in this way undermines everything else you do. At the same time, citation is one of the simplest tasks that will be asked of you—it is as simple as coloring by number. See section 10.10 on how and why to cite your sources.

- **Follow all instructions:** Take care of your syllabus and other handouts and read them carefully. Turn to these resources first, asking your professor only if something is unclear or absent from these instructions. The syllabus tells you all the most important information: the schedule of assignments (due dates!), the topic for each class day (the goal!), policies for what you can and can't do in class and with assignments, how to contact your instructor, and more. Assume that the assignment guidelines offer meaningful parameters, not arbitrary rules. For example, if your draft is significantly shorter than the length requirement given for the assignment, this likely means you are not working at a sufficient level of detail. If your draft is significantly longer than requirements, you have either taken on too broad an approach or may need to eliminate repetition or filler.

- **Attend class:** It is not always clear how one class day connects to your overall purpose in taking the course. But each part of a course is intended to build on others, to help you learn new skills. When you miss class you lose track of the threads that hold the course together. Class time provides you limited access to an expert practitioner of the field you're paying to study. If you miss a class, ask for a classmate's notes to copy rather than asking your instructor to recreate content just for you. If outside commitments or a lack of motivation are keeping you from attending class, consult an adviser or campus counselor to discuss balancing your goals and responsibilities.

- **Be on time and engaged:** Class is a collective social endeavor for adults, most of whom are paying for the privilege of being there. Be respectful of everyone's time, comfort, and concentration. And while you are in class and paying attention, take good notes (see section 4.2). Avoid electronic devices if they distract you or people around you.

- **Stay in touch:** If course management software (such as Blackboard, Moodle, or Canvas) is being used for your course, that is probably where you will find handouts, readings, grades, announcements about schedule changes, and more. Look for links to help tutorials or contact your campus computing help desk in the event of technical problems. Make sure you know what email address is registered by the software or that the instructor has for you, and check that mail regularly. Don't miss an email about a cancellation, deadline change, or notification of a problem with one of your assignments!

- **Manage your time and attention:** Perhaps for the first time in your life, you will determine how you spend most of your time, with only a few hours per week scheduled into class sessions and probably no one checking in on whether you are keeping up with your work. Set aside time for readings and extra time well in advance of large graded assignments for drafting and revising. You will need to read whole chapters, write whole drafts, and listen to whole lectures and discussions without letting your mind wander excessively. Train your brain to handle that kind of focus: concentrate for fifteen or twenty minutes, then take a five-minute break. There are timer apps to help you keep track. Gradually do more sets and adjust to longer periods between breaks.

Between work sessions, get exercise, fresh air, water, and balanced meals. When you have struggled with a problem for some time, exercise or a shower will cause your brain to work subconsciously on the problem, perhaps letting an answer pop up later. Use a calendar app to give yourself reminders in advance of due dates. During particularly busy times you may need to complete some work early or ask for an extension (in advance). Use apps or browser extensions to limit your internet usage during work times. Plan small rewards for starting work and for partial accomplishments. If you find that you're still not managing your time well, consult your campus counseling center or peer support services.

- **Read more:** By the time you enter college, you should be able to read long, dense texts and emerge with a basic comprehension of their main points. You will now work on expanding your vocabulary and reading for detail, subtlety, and subtext. College coursework should help you to identify when to scan, skim, read for comprehension, or read for analysis, and give you the tools to perform each of these kinds of reading effectively (see sections 4.2, 5.2–5.4, 6.3, 7.3, 8.2, and 9.6–9.7). If you are not yet accustomed to large amounts of reading, or you do not yet have sufficient vocabulary to get through a college-level text without constantly consulting a dictionary, plan extra time for reading assignments. When you look up an important new word, write its meaning in your own words and use it in a sentence. The more you read, the more easily and quickly you will be able to handle all assignments.

- **Be an active learner:** There is no incentive for professors to give you busywork. Assume your assignments were designed to make you practice a valuable, higher-order skill that cannot be done thoughtlessly. If the purpose of an assignment is not clear, ask, but as a rule attempting any task with goodwill makes you more likely to gain something from it. The work should feel hard and a little scary if you're doing it right. It is natural to fear you can't do the work or that others know more than you do (this feeling is so common it has a name: "impostor syndrome"). This is a normal part of the learning process as you confront how much you don't know and try out unfamiliar skills. It's much better than living with the "Dunning-Kruger effect," which is when having very little knowledge on a subject gives you the sense of being an expert only because you don't know how much you're missing.

- **Understand your grades:** You are graded on the words you turn in, not on who you are, how hard you worked, or what your instructor thinks about you. Your work is graded according to how closely it meets assignment expectations, usually relative to how closely your classmates met the same expectations (the differences among essays are usually much less subjective than you might imagine from seeing only your own paper). Grades tell others what skills and knowledge you have demonstrated under the formal conditions of an accredited classroom, as determined by a qualified instructor. You earn grades so far as you demonstrate specific knowledge and skills (you don't start with an A and have points taken away).

  Course grades are often weighted, meaning that some assignments count for a greater portion of the final course grade than others. To estimate how your grades are adding up during the semester, look for an online tutorial for "calculating weighted grades." Don't wait for a grade to reassess how you're engaging with the course or ask for help—you already have a sense of how clearly you understand course materials and how much effort you put into meeting assignment expectations.

  Grades are likely to have a greater or lesser effect on your future depending on whether you plan to apply for graduate programs or fellowships (most of which have a minimum grade point average requirement for admission). Having skills, knowledge, and experiences is more important than grades, but the things you need to do to acquire skills and knowledge are often the same things that result in good grades. Think of the skills and knowledge you acquire in the classroom as complementary to other experiences, from learning to manage your workload to doing internships to socializing with a variety of people. Your ability to demonstrate your skills, knowledge, and experience through writing—in the form of cover letters, résumés, and correspondence—will be essential to future academic and professional endeavors (see sections 2.8 and 3.5, and appendix 2).

- **Learn how to get your questions answered:** Part of being an adult and a critical thinker is knowing how to find answers to your questions efficiently and appropriately. Taking your professor's time to get answers you could easily find on your own is inefficient and rude. At the same time, being too shy to go to your professor with questions only she can best help you with is also costly. Advocate for yourself when you need help or resources beyond what has been provided for all students.

- **Ask questions about basic facts:** First try to find your answer in the materials provided for the course. The definitions of basic words might be in a dictionary (if they are not used in a specialized way) or encyclopedia (if they are specific to a field of study or a time and place). Specialized encyclopedias and other reference works like the Stanford Encyclopedia of

Philosophy will provide more useful answers than general encyclopedias like Wikipedia (see section 10.5). If you can't find your answer in these likely places and you think other students might have the same question, ask it in class (at the beginning, end, or when invited to do so). If you need an answer between class meetings or it is not relevant for other students, email your instructor.

- **Ask questions that require a conversation:** Professors are unlikely to be able to engage in long email exchanges. Those kinds of questions are best handled in person during your professor's office hours: announced times when you are invited to drop by. Most faculty are also able to set up an alternative appointment time on request, set aside specifically for you. Most professors' jobs are divided into teaching, research, and service responsibilities, so they are not usually in an office Monday through Friday 9:00 a.m. to 5:00 p.m. They may be working on research or attending meetings or doing other organizational work in other locations. "Adjunct" or contingent faculty who are paid by the course are in many cases not paid to hold office hours or given a space for meeting with students (many adjunct faculty do meet with students, but be aware they may be on their own time).

  Office hours are not only for "problem" students or situations! You should not feel shy about coming for any reason relevant to the course, but don't go just to put in "face time." You may also visit office hours for a faculty member who taught you previously to discuss recommendation letters or get advice about your future if it relates to the field that person teaches. General questions relating to the university are better addressed to a college adviser. If you have just a casual interest in the area of a professor's research or teaching, take a class, attend a lecture, or read her work rather than asking her to repeat that information for you personally in time that is allocated for other purposes.

- **Ask questions nicely:** Interacting with faculty is a good way of practicing professional manners in a setting where you can't get fired. Consider the difference between showing respect and deference. We should all strive to be respectful of others and respectful of knowledge. Think of your instructor as a facilitator and guide, not a boss or employee. Address instructors by correctly spelled name and title. Most faculty have PhDs and can therefore be addressed as "Dr. LastName," but "Professor Lastname" is usually safest, since (in North America) it is considered accurate for most people instructing a university-level course. For non-faculty use "Mr./Ms. Lastname" (not "Miss" or "Mrs."). Don't use first names for instructors or university staff unless invited to do so. Identify yourself and mention the course and section you're in—most instructors are teaching multiple courses. Use an email account with your real name on it (not sexybaby69@

yahoo.com). Compose your emails in full sentences, correctly spelled, and avoid slang. Start with a proper greeting such as "Dear Professor Lastname," not "Hey you"!

Don't ask your instructor to do your work for you, such as to formulate topics, locate sources, make copies or scans, check electronic submissions, or recreate material you missed. If you need to inform your instructor of any special circumstances such as illness; disability; religious, athletic, or military obligations; or a late or missing assignment; state the problem and present any documentation you have without personal details. You have a right to privacy under FERPA (the Family Educational Rights and Privacy Act). This also restricts your professor's ability to communicate with anyone but you about your situation.

• **If you feel you're drowning, ask for help!** Your campus may provide peer support services or counseling to help with juggling coursework in addition to other kinds of counseling. If you're having trouble keeping up in all your courses or you have spoken to a professor and he doesn't believe you or won't accommodate you, go to the dean of students or Academic Affairs office and ask for an appointment to discuss your situation. You may be referred to campus resources for help, and if accommodations are justified, this will be communicated to all your instructors through official channels.

The basic skills described in this chapter, as remote as some of them may seem from writing or history, are fundamental to succeeding in the more complicated tasks that come next. Making the most of your brief and intense experience in higher education requires curiosity, self-regulation, and the ability to find answers to questions as the need arises. These skills support your ability to think critically, write with scholarly rigor, and reason through causality and multiple perspectives as historians do.

2

What Is Academic Writing?

In any discipline, scholarly writing aims to identify and resolve complex problems through open-ended discussions among fellow scholars, based on independently vetted evidence. Your aim as a writer is not only to shed light on a particular problem through your analysis of sources, but also to relate that problem to similar ones that other scholars are working on, so that we—as a group—may better understand our whole field of inquiry.

Learning to write like an academic is similar to learning a foreign language. No one is born fluent in formal academic style, and no one really speaks it, though some who read and write scholarship may find it slipping into their speech. Some people have learned academic writing simply by reading a lot of scholarship, unconsciously absorbing its conventions. But anyone can learn it, regardless of how you speak or the ways you prefer to write in non-academic settings.

2.1. The Virtues of Academic Writing

Because the aim of scholarship is to develop new knowledge, our subject matter is by definition unfamiliar to readers, even fellow specialists. We address questions that cannot be answered in any easier way, or explain that which is usually taken for granted. This unfamiliarity and complexity requires that our writing be as simple and clear as possible, to not get in the way of the ideas. The goal of situating our ideas in relation to a wider public discussion, and basing our claims on evidence, requires that we refer to and analyze outside sources as an integral part of our own work. Because of these defining goals, most scholarly writing has the following features:

- A **thesis statement**, which resolves a **main problem** or question that motivates the text
- **Original claims** made by the author
- **References to the arguments of other scholars**, which situate the author's problem and main claim within a public discussion of wider issues and may also serve as support for some claims
- **References to evidence** (documents or objects produced at the time being studied as well as agreed-upon facts) that supports the author's claims

- **Analysis of sources**, in order to explain how they support claims or connect claims to other scholars' research
- **Definitions of specialized terms** so that the terms may be reliably used in the same way by other researchers, so they can be applied or adapted as necessary in new contexts, and so that the nuances of key concepts can be analyzed in detail
- **Style and structure** appropriate to the intended audience
- **Attention to rules of logic, evidence, citation, and intellectual property**

Readers of academic essays are fellow scholars who are looking for evidence and interpretations that will enrich or develop their own research and teaching. Readers of academic writing are not looking to it for simplified or summarized versions of what they already know or for entertainment or aesthetic gratification (that would be a bonus!). We don't want conclusions without reasoning or evidence to justify them, since scholars cannot evaluate other researchers' conclusions without knowing what they are based on. Therefore, the virtues of style and structure most often looked for in academic essays are clarity and brevity. We want to find what we're looking for, understand it, remember it, and apply it in new contexts. We want to do this as quickly and easily as possible without losing the complexity of the ideas. While this may result in writing that feels dry, the predictable form allows us to focus on the excitement of the ideas.

2.2. Academic Structure

Academic writing should allow a reader to navigate the text easily and not be in suspense about what the text contributes to broader discussions:

- **Introduction:** context, problem, proposed resolution
- **Body:** claims, evidence, reasoning, definition of terms, background information, and discussions of counterarguments
- **Conclusion:** fully articulated resolution, exploration of impact and future implications

From paragraph to paragraph, we aim for each point to flow from the one before and for each new piece of information to be introduced as the reader needs it. In other words, rather than recording our ideas as we develop them, we consciously revise to create a path for the reader from some point of common interest through the new ideas and evidence we are presenting, so that readers always understand what they are reading and the role of each piece in the overall project.

2.3. Academic Style

At the sentence level, we aim to be as clear and brief as possible, and we restrict ourselves to formal language (avoiding colloquialisms and abbreviations), so that our words can be understood in the same way by any reader. These stylistic goals are largely a matter of word choice and word order.

Word choice. Choose words that are accurate, specific, and economical:

- **Accurate.** Use the simplest word that best captures your meaning. If you are not completely sure what a word means, find out or choose a different word.
- **Specific.** Choose the narrowest possible word that covers what you need it to cover.
- **Economical.** It is not always possible to be brief and specific at the same time. But we can leave out any words that are not directly helping to meet goals. Choosing accurate and specific words also helps you to be concise in the long run, even when it sometimes means using a more accurate phrase in place of a single ambiguous word.

Word order is partly determined by the rules of English grammar, but within those rules we have choices. Readers understand sentences more easily when they are tightly organized around "who did what" (subject, verb, object) without distracting filler between those key elements. We also want to guide readers from what is already familiar to what is new, and we want to put our emphasis—at the ends of sentences and paragraphs—on the new ideas we are contributing to the larger conversation.

Here are some frequently asked questions about style:

- **"Can I use 'I'?"** You may have been told never to use the first-person singular "I" in an academic essay. This rule is often given in high schools to prevent students from filling their essays with "I believe . . ." or "I feel . . ." statements. Academic essays are not about your personal opinions or feelings; they are about asking and answering difficult questions using evidence and reasoning. "I" also suggests subjectivity, whereas academic writing is usually understood to aim for objectivity. More recently, however, scholars have realized that objectivity is not really possible (see section 3.2). The best we can do is to adhere to the rules of logic and evidence and be transparent about our motivations, methods, and assumptions, so that errors of subjectivity are easier to identify. For this reason, it has become more common to use "I" precisely because it helps you to be clear about where you are inserting yourself into your text. Statements beginning with

"I argue that . . ." or "For the purpose of this exercise, I assume . . ." are therefore welcomed by most instructors.

You may also have heard the rule not to use "we" in an academic essay. Authors sometimes use "we" metaphorically to refer to themselves as part of a larger scholarly endeavor ("We [scholars] have long pondered the question of . . ."), or they refer to the author and readers together, as in "Now we will begin an inquiry into . . ." These usages are often frowned upon because they can be unclear (which "we" is it?). The most common way you are likely to see it in recent academic writing is when the text has more than one author, where it is used in parallel to "I."

- **"But this is so formulaic—why can't I be creative?"** Academic writing is formulaic on purpose, since the most important goal is for other people to find what they need in it quickly and reliably. However, that does not mean scholarship is not creative. Our creativity is in our ideas, in the imaginative ways we approach problems and use sources. It is also possible to experiment with or subvert the expected formula while still fulfilling your key goals, but to do so without losing readers you must know the readers' expectations so well that you can guide them in your own, new directions. When you give readers something contrary to their expectations for no better reason than whimsy or rebellion, they are likely to be frustrated.

- **"Okay, but can I at least write beautifully? Does it have to be so stilted and boring?"** Beauty is a bonus, certainly welcome. A writer who can be graceful in addition to being accurate, specific, and economical about abstract ideas is an impressive beast. In an academic setting, if you are forced to choose between clarity and beauty, clarity must win (sorry). To learn more about writing gracefully, see Joseph Williams and Joseph Bizup, *Style: The Basics of Clarity and Grace* (University of Chicago Press, 2014).

2.4. The Writing Process

The main difference between novice and advanced writers is how much and how thoroughly they revise their work. Turning in an unrevised draft is like offering a plate of flour, sugar, and eggs and calling it cake. This is a sure way to avoid living up to your potential or learning new skills. Instead the writing process should consist of a series of separate, equally important steps. These steps tend to occur in something resembling the order given here, but writing is not a straight line from fewer words to more words, or from messy words to polished words. Writing should be a process of discovery that involves many twists, cuts, and fresh starts and that never completely "finishes" in the sense that there is no ideal text out there that you are trying to find. Instead, you hack away at a problem, trying it from many angles, until you have something that will serve your purpose. Each chapter of this book will consider how these steps look for a given assignment, but all the following steps are usually necessary.

- **Exploring** takes place long before you sit down to write a paper. Reading, research, and class time are not separate from the writing process. Course readings and in-class activities are meant in part to help you learn enough about a subject to identify interesting questions worth addressing in writing and enough about a scholarly conversation to contribute to it in your own essays.
- **Planning** should begin as soon as you receive an assignment, even if it is not due for a long time. Planning begins with thinking through the instructions and, if necessary, asking your instructor for more information. You may need to choose an area of focus or sources. You should look ahead at your commitments and make sure you have time allotted for all subsequent steps. Notice when relevant material comes up in class or in readings and think about how you can apply those materials in your assignment, while taking especially careful notes (see sections 4.2, 5.3–5.4, 6.3, 7.3, 9.7, 10.3 on note-taking for various kinds of readings).
- **Brainstorming** is the first stage of putting thoughts on paper. Let your brain be creative, throwing out ideas that may or may not be relevant to your goals. Some people like to brainstorm in lists or use mind maps (by hand or with software; see section 7.5). With experience, you may be able to do some steps in your head. Try different methods to discover what works best for you. Most importantly, push yourself to continue brainstorming long past the first idea that might be workable. The more ideas you have, the more you discover and the more effectively you can winnow down to a few of the strongest.
- **Drafting** is the first stage of writing down whole sentences. It should also begin as a creative, relaxed process, with the critical voice inside your head turned off. Let yourself write badly, incoherently, and ramblingly. Keep going further than you think you can go. Then go back and read your drafts and identify ideas or phrases that have potential. As you revise these, you will generate several new drafts. When instructors ask you to turn in a "draft" for comments, they do not mean a first draft that is still rambling or incoherent, nor a set of disconnected notes. Such assignments refer to a late, revised draft that is clean enough for others to read so you can get feedback.
- **Revising** is the stage when you put your judging hat back on and focus on your goals for the specific piece of writing in front of you. To "revise" means to see anew, and this stage is about seeing your work in a completely new way, not just once, but many times. The most effective writers will revise

early drafts several times just to discover what it is they want to say. They revise further to rearrange these ideas into a form easily understood by readers. They revise further to make sure they've included everything necessary and to remove what may now be repetitive or tangential. They revise even further to refine and clarify the writing on the sentence and word level. They go back and forth between these levels of revising, because each set of changes prompts other changes.

Every time you revise, you should have a clear sense of your goal for the finished piece and also a goal for that particular revision, such as "clarify what is most useful from my draft" or "put the whole draft into a logical order for the reader." Work on just one task during each revision to avoid getting distracted or overwhelmed. To free yourself to make significant changes, save your work periodically under a new file name with a number for each significant revision (for example: LastName-ResponsePaper1.doc, LastName-ResponsePaper2.doc, etc.) or work with software or a cloud backup service that automatically saves previous versions. In the later stages, revising is also a process of checking to see whether the ideas in your head are in fact reflected on the page. It is an amazing but common phenomenon to be sure you've made clear an idea that in fact is only hinted at on paper. Revising requires you to see your work from the reader's point of view.

- **Proofreading** means doing a final check for spelling or grammatical errors, typos, formatting problems, and other superficial mistakes.

2.5. The Vices of Academic Writing

As you already know if you have read even a few published academic texts, bad academic style happens often. Unfortunately, it is even sometimes rewarded in published works, or at least not discouraged. Academic writing that is so full of jargon or needlessly convoluted sentences that it becomes difficult to read, even for a specialist, is sometimes mistaken as a sign of complex ideas. Worse, bad style is sometimes approved as a way of keeping "outsiders" out, leaving only those with the most experience able to read it. Most often, academics simply spend so much time talking to each other in our specialized shorthand that we no longer notice the difference or don't have time to do better. Academic writing has been taught, and its standards discussed and criticized in a systematic way, only for the past few decades. This means that when you run across older academic texts (as you might often do studying history), the standards of structure and style may be quite different, making such texts more difficult to read.

When you are daunted by the difficult style of an academic text, it may be that it was written as clearly as possible but reflects complicated ideas that are new to you. In that case, use a dictionary and course materials to work your way through it slowly, knowing that it will get easier as you familiarize yourself with new words and ideas (see also section 5.2). The other possibility is that the author chose words that are needlessly complicated, hid their purpose in unexpected parts of the text, and failed to reorganize sentences and paragraphs to lead a reader from one thought to the next. As you become more self-aware about your own writing, a side benefit will be an increased ability to notice when a text is difficult because of the author's choices and an increased ability to navigate through such forests.

As a novice academic writer, you have no reason to imitate bad style. Happily, you are likely to encounter academic writing that is gracefully written as well as clear. Historians' writing, especially in book form, can be one of the best examples of academic writing that engages and entertains even while meeting its academic goals. That is what scholarship looks like at its best.

2.6. What Academic Writing Is Not

It may be easier to understand what academic writing is by contrasting it with other forms that may be more familiar. The following genres each have a different goal and therefore different expectations of content, style, and structure:

- **Writing that aims primarily to entertain or provide aesthetic gratification** (fiction, some memoirs). These kinds of writing may use literary devices to convey meaning (such as imagery, formal complexity, foreshadowing, juxtaposition, etc.), and they may emphasize expressionistic or impressionistic understanding over analytical methods. Structures and formal elements can vary infinitely.
- **Writing that aims only to convey information** (news journalism, professional reports, textbooks, technical writing). Writing that intends to inform rather than to persuade does not revolve around argument, as academic writing does. It is often structured with the most important information at the start and proceeds in decreasing order of importance. Part of the goal may be to accurately simplify ideas for the benefit of a non-specialist audience.
- **Writing that aims to direct future action or justify an action** (exhortatory or opinion-based journalism such as op-eds or editorials, grant proposals, legal briefs, certain kinds of professional research reports). In these cases an argument is an integral part of the structure, but the goal is to convince or inspire the reader toward a specific action rather than to contribute new knowledge for its own sake. Such pieces generally begin and end with a

statement of the action desired, and the body consists of evidence or reasoning. They may or may not emphasize a critique of alternative arguments
or points of view. Depending on the intended reader, they may simplify reasoning or evidence. Such works may also differ from traditional academic
writing in tone, style, conventions of evidence or reasoning, and the degree
to which they rely on outside sources or analysis of sources, and may have
different rules of citation and attribution.

- **Writing that tells a story based in fact** (biography, autobiography, memoir,
narrative / popular history, family histories, *New Yorker*–style essays). This
kind of writing generally avoids technicalities of argument and analysis of
sources (though it may be implicit in the narrative), and may employ literary devices. It is often chronologically organized or told through a series
of anecdotes, rather than organized around a series of claims and evidence.
Such writing may leave out or simplify citations and may make little or
no effort to communicate to the reader the exact source of facts, ideas, or
quotes.

Some popular history and biography does adhere closely to scholarly
rules of evidence and citation and may have an explicit, transparent argument or point of view about its subject. The main differences between such
works and scholarship are whether the text underwent peer review before
publication, the degree to which it explicitly frames its argument as part of
an existing scholarly conversation, and whether its focus is directed more
toward its subject (that is, the person or event it's about) than on how that
subject sheds light on larger questions of interpretation, such as the social,
cultural, political, or other context that the subject of a biography lived
through or represented, or the chain of causes and effects surrounding a
historical event and connecting it to others.

2.7. Who Is the Academic Reader?

You know your writing must be revised to suit the needs of your reader. Who
is that person? Your literal reader (your professor or a teaching assistant) is not
quite the same as the theoretical academic reader we write for professionally
and for whom you should practice writing in your assignments. Professional
historians write for fellow specialists, but also future specialists, scholars of related fields or disciplines who may use the work in new or unexpected ways, and
often "the educated public."

Because this diverse group of readers comes to our text with different background knowledge, we must explain our specialized terms and how our topics
connect to others. Because these readers ultimately want to use our writing for

some purpose of their own, we need to be clear about what original perspective, new evidence, or new interpretation we are offering, so they know whether they will find what they are looking for. These readers come to us for work, not pleasure. They do not want to invest their time only to be confused or misled, so we must tell them what we will do and follow through on our promises.

At the same time, since the ideas we write about are complex and specialized, we can safely assume that we don't need to worry about whether a child could understand it. By "an educated reader" we assume an adult with a college education or equivalent. This is why you, as a college student, are probably encountering such writing for the first time, so that by the time you graduate you have become that "educated reader" who is capable of approaching such texts successfully.

As a student writer, you are acting as an apprentice historian and doing what the professionals do by addressing that potential reader. At the same time, you are also writing for your professor or teaching assistant, who is looking to see whether you have demonstrated the knowledge and skills required by the course so your work can be evaluated. Your grader is also an academic reader, though—she reads a lot of scholarship for her own purposes—so these two kinds of readers are really not that different. You please your grader by appealing successfully to the metaphorical reader rather than by catering to what you imagine are the individual desires of the one person grading you.

Academic writing at its best is not so much about convincing readers to agree with you as it is about provoking new questions and pushing us all toward greater, deeper knowledge. The best way to win goodwill from academic readers is not to hammer your argument so hard you can be sure of convincing anyone, but rather to offer something interesting as efficiently and accurately as possible. Having something interesting to say is not dependent on skill or experience. It depends only on whether you're paying attention and actively thinking. You don't have to reinvent the wheel or outsmart the entire canon of published work in the field: just apply your own thinking to your own careful reading of the sources. The combination, if done sincerely, will be interesting.

2.8. Why Practice Academic Writing?

Most college students are never going to write academic essays for publication and therefore will never need to rely on exactly these skills for their living or in order to discover knowledge that others need. So why do we ask you to practice academic writing as one of the core activities in any college curriculum? The most common and correct answer is that academic writing teaches critical thinking, and critical thinking is necessary for everyone to solve problems effectively and to be a good citizen in a democracy. But what is critical thinking exactly and why is it so important?

Humans are problem-solvers. We have incredible brains that allow us to self-consciously observe and remember our experiences so that we can draw lessons from them. This innate ability has evolved for solving problems within our physical environment: we use our senses to know what is around us and hear what people we know have experienced, in order to improve our immediate circumstances. At the same time, we are social creatures who need to fit in and get along with others as much as we need food and shelter and physical comfort. So our brains are also good at intuiting what others want from us and adapting our sense of reality to compromise with theirs, so we can bond with each other and against others we identify as outsiders.

These are impressive skills that have allowed us to dominate our environments for millennia. However, we have become so dominant that we changed our world, to the point where the skills we are born with are no longer enough to keep us safe, sane, or comfortable, and the effect is accelerating. As technology has made it possible to travel and receive communications from all over the world with increasing speed, our world has expanded. The information we encounter now is more often abstract: something we cannot experience through our senses but must imagine. Our brains need to sort and prioritize information so we know what to care about most and what needs to be acted on quickly, but we make those choices based on assumptions that developed in an environment where we were more likely to be attacked by a predator than be threatened by identity theft, a medical emergency, a government policy, or news from the other side of the planet. Our social needs make us want to agree with others, sometimes more than we want to be right. Sometimes we need to feel we are right—if that reinforces our place in the groups we identify with—more than we want the truth. This can happen even when our security depends on getting the truth or when real belonging and community depends on getting along with people who are different from us.

Critical thinking is a method of training our brains to sort, prioritize, and solve problems based on abstract information. It is not something you're born with and is much more than the "common sense" anyone might develop with a little life experience. It is a way of handling information about things that we *cannot* experience.

Our instincts tell us that anything we experienced ourselves—which imprinted itself on our brains with the overwhelming power of our senses—is more real than anything we did not personally experience. We believe stories about people like us who sensed an experience first-hand more than we believe other information because of that overwhelming weight we give to sensory input and our relationships with others. Critical thinking teaches you to see information *despite* your own place in it. It forces you to systematically identify and set aside motivated reasoning and biases to see the world as it is rather than as it looks from your angle. This gives you a strategic advantage: it allows you to see more and to test whether your information is accurate. Critical thinking also teaches you how to reason from evidence to solutions. This is another strategic advantage: knowing the most and least likely outcomes in advance helps you make better decisions in an environment of uncertainty.

Picture a table in a room. There is a real table there—that's truth. But how do we know the truth? If there is a group of people in the room, each person sees some part of the table—just one angle—and perceives from that partial view that it is a table. If everyone in the room agrees that it is a table, it is likely that we are right. This example seems stupidly simple when we imagine we are all looking at a familiar physical object. But what if the thing we need to understand is an atom or a cell? What if it's an idea? What if it's an event, where everyone involved played a role that limited their view, colored their experience, and motivated the way they remember their experience? How then is it possible to identify what is true? If we all described the angle from which we saw the table and all of our descriptions aligned into a picture of a table except for one person's, and that person's account described a liquid instead of a solid object, what should we do with that information? We could dismiss it—we could say that person must be mistaken. But what if the truth in this case is that there was a puddle of water in the room and the majority of people were actually looking at an image of a table reflected in that water? What if we start again, but this time all of our accounts are widely different? How would we begin to sort among them to figure out what we're looking at? Is there a better way to sort the evidence from various observers than just assuming the majority is correct?

Critical thinking offers not only multiple perspectives, but objective rules and methods to sort through a variety of evidence so that we can give greater weight to evidence that is more likely to be true. Just as scientists measure and test a variety of samples and then mathematically assess results, other forms of critical thinking use rules and tests to compare different kinds of evidence. We make our best effort to question, undermine, and overturn the results to make sure they are reliable. We consider what can and cannot be known and find new ways to know. We navigate and manage uncertainty so that we can make better choices.

Critical thinking is a process, not a result. Getting initial results that don't stand up to testing is a sign that the process is working properly. The process should tell us when we go in a wrong direction and offer a systematic set of possible new directions. Scholarly knowledge is therefore not a truth in itself, but a way of finding truth and testing whether we are right through collective effort and debate. Our knowledge is cumulative—it accrues over time from the work of many—and it is self-correcting: while error is inevitable, the process is defined by finding and rejecting unsupported claims.

The rules and methods of critical thinking can be explained—and are explained throughout this book—but they can only be learned through practice within a community of other practitioners. No one can be a solitary critical thinker, because we need the criticism and questioning of others to test our results, expose our biases, and offer new ways of looking.

Academic writing, as done by professional researchers, is critical thinking in practice. When we ask students to practice writing as academics do it, we are asking you to practice critical thinking. The core form of academic writing—the argument—is defined as a series of claims supported by evidence and reasoning. In order to be supported, claims must be substantive, specific, and contestable. A claim is contestable if reasonable people can disagree with it. In other words: our purpose is to debate, and the source of our knowledge is the outcome of debate—questioning and testing—not the dominance of some voices over others or any inherent authority. The very nature of claims is that they can be debated. This means that every voice in an academic discussion (including those of students!) has an equal right to be considered. At the same time, equally strictly, the rules of evidence and logic must prevail over any claim, no matter whose. Claims that are unsupported, or unsupportable, by evidence and reasoning must be discarded no matter who posited them or how much we may want them to be true.

Critical thinking equips you for the world by teaching you the following:

- To see more than one or two "sides" to any issue
- To distinguish between small differences in meaning
- To understand meaning in context
- To get your ideas vetted, so you can rely on them
- To vet the ideas of others, so you can know whether to rely on them
- To distinguish between what we can and cannot know
- To notice the difference between following evidence and giving allegiance to authority
- To know how and where to find answers to knowable questions
- To know how much you don't know
- To be skeptical and open to learning at the same time
- To live with uncertainty
- To balance probabilities so as to make decisions with incomplete evidence
- To solve problems in the abstract before having to experience them personally
- To distinguish between evidence-based certainty and blind passion or conviction
- To separate fact from emotion (this does not make fact superior to emotion, but allows you to consider each as appropriate to your needs)

Academic reading and writing also teach you how to navigate long, dense, complicated texts and understand them accurately, which you need to do in most professional settings and as a citizen who participates in government and engages in legal contracts. It expands your vocabulary, which opens the doors to higher-order thinking and allows you to express your thoughts more effectively. It encourages you to find out what is already known before adding your voice, and then encourages you to articulate and defend your contribution convincingly. Writing an academic essay teaches you how to sort, rank, and organize information, analyze and present evidence, and compose it for a reader. These are skills required by many professions. Every adult needs them when they want to convince someone to agree with them or do what they want done, when they write a cover letter applying for a job, and when they communicate with superiors, clients, or funding agencies to ask for something. Reasoning in writing is a way of understanding, it can be a form of power, and it provides satisfaction in its own right, keeping us mentally fit and interested in the world around us.

3

What Is History?

"History" can refer to the many ways we think about the past or to the many things we do with what we know about the past. Some historical work is focused on "making history come alive" in order to help us understand it, remember it, or appreciate its lessons. Some is dedicated to figuring out what happened as nearly as possible. Some people use what we know about the past to weave stories that provide entertainment and perspective. You witness these kinds of history in museums, at historical landmarks, in documentaries, and in popular written history. These common interactions with public history may make the subject seem familiar. Many people assume they already know the general outlines of "what the history books say" and that the most difficult part of history coursework or scholarship is remembering a lot of names and dates.

However, these assumptions are mostly wrong. The history you do in a university classroom is an abbreviated version of the analytical work done by professional academic historians—the work that goes on before and behind a presentation for a public audience. Names and dates are incidental to larger goals. Stories exist only to be questioned. We do "make history come alive" in the sense that we are discovering and creating history by examining evidence and finding meaning in it, but it's more like an investigation than like reading a story, and the result is evidence-based interpretation, not objective truth.

Understanding the purposes and methods of professional academic historians will help you understand the goals and activities you'll meet in the classroom. Academic history can be defined most simply as the study of change over time: why and how changes have occurred. We begin with the most accurate or reliable sources we can find, and we have various methods to help us judge the reliability of sources and use some sources despite their limitations (since we can't create new data about the past by conducting surveys or interviews, as one might in other social sciences, and we can't experiment with or directly observe the past, as one does in the hard sciences). Part of the process of asking "why" is not only verifying known sources, but also discovering new sources and reinterpreting sources that people thought they understood.

Studying the past in all its complexity and observing it only through incomplete, unreliable evidence is inherently a messy job. We can't reduce it to patterns or define concepts in universally applicable terms without losing accuracy. We can't impose a narrative for the sake of a good story without doing injustice to a real past. Where other approaches, such as game theory, offer a way of studying causes by isolating key factors, history forces us to make sense of cause and effect within the chaos of lived reality. We seek to get as close to truth as possible, knowing that truth is complicated, contradictory, and many-sided.

Examining fragmentary evidence and received narratives in all the messiness of their original context may be intuitive for some, but most people will find that historical thinking feels impenetrable and at times even disturbing. This means that history is not objectively more or less difficult than any other field of knowledge. As in any other discipline, practice and effort will make concepts clearer and methods easier. Historical thinking is a learned skill.

History is unique in being considered both a social science and a humanities field, often depending on which university division has more office space or the inclinations of a particular department or individual historian. History began as a humanities field because from its origins in oral storytelling it was partly a literary exercise and therefore part of the humanistic tradition. Much of the work historians do today is still based on interpreting texts, and so we share many methods and assumptions with other modern humanities fields such as literary criticism and philosophy. However, historical scholarship became professionalized in the nineteenth century as part of a broader movement aiming to use objective data to understand human behavior. This movement was the origin of the modern social sciences, eventually evolving into sociology, anthropology, psychology, political science, economics, and related disciplines. Today's historians use empirical evidence, construct their interpretations within the constraints of logical argument, and often borrow methods and concepts from other social science fields.

In fact, as the study of everything that has happened in the past, history can be said to encompass all other disciplines. Historians rely on an exceptionally broad range of evidence types: we use written documents (public and private, statistical, official, informal) as well as fiction, film, popular culture, fine arts, objects, architecture, landscape, interviews, and demographic, climate, health, and economic data. What holds this broad field together is simply that we all study change over time. Historians of science may need to master many principles and methods of scientific inquiry, but their goal is to understand how it developed up to the present and why some directions have dominated over others, rather than to further new scientific knowledge.

Although historical arguments are sometimes grounded in theory or models (as in all academic disciplines), another way of distinguishing historians is that we tend to place unusually strong emphasis on *context*. Context is the specific time and place where something occurs, but also refers to cultural, social, intellectual, political, or other kinds of environments that limit, influence, inspire, or reflect human behavior. Other humanities fields often use context to better understand their subject (which might be a text, object, or person), but historians often use texts, objects, or people's lives in order to understand their context (a time, place, and social setting). Other social sciences usually aim to formulate models that apply accurately to many contexts, but historians mostly seek to distinguish each context from others. Rather than striving to identify workable rules, we look for singular causes and effects.

For example, where a literary scholar may examine how a writer described a certain region in order to understand his ideas about national identity because this enriches our reading of his text, a historian working on the same material is more likely to be interested in how the writer's ideas add to the ideas and experiences of other people to explain what regional and nationality identity meant in that time and place. A political scientist may seek to distill the common factors causing people to vote in a certain way, comparing voting patterns in a number of elections over time, so as to formulate a model about how voting works. But a historian is more likely to delve into the unique factors of each particular election in order to understand what caused one outcome that year but had different results in the next election. The historian's goal is to discover how particular contexts affect particular causes—that is, to identify unique causal factors and track how they affect other factors—rather than to directly predict future events or reduce particular phenomena to general principles. (Both approaches are valuable and informative, and each can balance the weaknesses of the other.)

All this is to say what makes history distinct. It is also worth noting what it has in common with other branches of critical inquiry. The categories of "social sciences" and "humanities" are relics of how branches of knowledge were formed in the eighteenth and nineteenth centuries. These categories became part of institutions—literally divided into buildings and divisions of administration and degree programs—and thus became difficult to change. But today the social sciences and humanities have in common the mission to analyze and interpret information. Our current digital age is an information age: we have more access to more information than we ever had before, and that challenges us to find better ways to sort, manage, understand, and apply all that information. Disciplines like political science, sociology, anthropology, philosophy, literature, art history, economics, linguistics, library sciences, and history all bring different methods and perspectives to the analysis of information, much as the so-called STEM fields (science, technology, engineering, and math) all bring methods and perspectives to observing, understanding, and using the world around us. Increasingly, information analysis fields use digital aids to reach our goals, so that computer science can be said to bridge both STEM and information analysis disciplines. As our world becomes as much about managing information as managing our physical environment, the traditional distinction between "applied" knowledge and "theoretical" knowledge breaks down.

In sum, historians ask questions of every kind of source from the past in order to "read" whatever it may have to tell us, directly or indirectly, intentionally or unintentionally. We seek to view each source as much as possible in its original context, to understand how it influenced or was influenced by this context, and how one context connects to larger questions relating to how change occurs over time. This form of inquiry is part of the effort to understand ourselves and our world, primarily using the logical analysis of information rather than direct observation or experiment.

3.1. Questions Historians Ask

Scholarly history can also be defined by the kinds of questions we ask. Our questions determine the kinds of arguments we make, and the kinds of writing professional historians do informs the kind of writing we assign to history students. Since we study change over time, the most important question we ask is always "Why?": why did a change occur? Another way to describe this is to say we focus on understanding *cause and effect*: what caused a change, with what results? All the names and dates—the content knowledge—is meant to help us sort out answers to these questions.

3.1.1. Why (Cause/Effect)

In the real world (as opposed to a controlled experiment), infinite factors play on each other simultaneously, causing cascades of changes large and small. Studying historical cause and effect is the art of separating one factor from another in complex systems or phenomena. Historians work to separate causes from effects, and to separate and name who, when, where, what, and how, so that we can compare the relative influence of different causal factors and examine how they interact with each other to create certain results.

Other disciplines such as sociology and psychology also try to untangle the causes of human behavior. Sociology uses data and observation to study present behaviors of social groups. Psychology attempts to understand present-day individuals from within, using clinical studies of our bodies as well as observations of what we do and say. Historians study people from the past both individually and in groups, and we look at evidence of what people did and said, evidence of what people (said they) believed. In addition, by reading between the lines we try to place individual behavior and mentalities in their contexts in an effort to find plausible explanations. Since we cannot test or prove whether an explanation is objectively true, we propose interpretations and critique each other's arguments in a collective attempt to find which explanations best fit all available evidence.

For example, historians ask questions such as "Was the British Empire profitable? When and for whom? How did it operate?" These questions ultimately aim at understanding why the British Empire was built and maintained. Initially, this might seem like a simple question, but the first problem we run into is that the answer is different depending on whom you ask. The justification given at the time of colonization was that the empire fulfilled a moral duty to offer British civilization to supposedly inferior peoples, as well as to bring valued goods to Europe. In retrospect, the empire may seem to reflect a simple desire to profit by controlling the terms of trade. Depending on their angle of interest, historians have argued that it was really about asserting Britain's dominance over rival European powers or primarily driven by Christian missions for reasons separate from both politics and economics. Taken separately, all the seemingly "obvious" explanations for the empire fail to fully explain its existence and longevity. The best explanations we have today derive from a systematic examination of multiple factors and how they interact, which results in a more complicated story of competing interests and unexpected consequences.

3.1.2. When (Continuity and Change)

Part of how we find out *why* a change happened involves first noticing when the change occurred, or conversely noticing the absence of change. This may seem obvious—we usually know the date of major events. But much of historical change happens gradually, or in fits and starts, or in the background, to be felt only at a later time. Part of what historical thinking allows us to do is to identify change (and its absence) whether or not the people involved felt it. When we work to identify points of disruption or continuity, we ask *when* changes occurred, but also who or what was affected by the change, when, and where. We identify patterns or seek larger meanings by comparing different periods, in order to judge the relative importance and influence of different historical factors over time.

For example, historians have asked not only what changed (in what ways, for whom) during the European Renaissance and Reformation, but also who missed out on those changes. These questions have helped us to see past the obvious—that European culture became more secular, that secularism, science, technological advances, and hence commercial advances led to larger numbers of white European men gaining wealth and authority—to also see that women and poor men tended to lose various means of security or influence that had been associated with the domination of the Catholic Church or with earlier forms of commercial activity. At the same time, Europeans of color and religious minorities such as Jews and Muslims were affected in totally different ways or "left out" of changes.

When historians debate the starting and stopping points, and ultimately the meaning and influence, of various periods of time, this can be called "periodization." For example, the historian Eric Hobsbawm suggested we should think of the "long nineteenth century" as the period from 1789 to 1914 and the "short twentieth century" as the period from 1914 to 1991. This may seem arbitrary (though no more arbitrary than dividing time by round numbers). But Hobsbawm used those terms and dates to encapsulate a broad interpretation of modern history. The long nineteenth century was, in his view, a period defined by industrialization, the consequent rise of the middle class in wealth and influence, and by European efforts to expand through imperialism. The short twentieth century was defined by three global wars (World War I, World War II, and the Cold War with its associated proxy wars), all of which Hobsbawm saw as a single battle over ideology. This battle was in some ways a result of issues raised in the long nineteenth century, because it was about how to organize mass political systems (made possible by the dominance of middle classes, but also critiqued by the still larger and still excluded working classes), was fought in new ways made possible by technological innovations (made possible by industrialization), and was fought on an unprecedentedly huge scale (made possible by imperialism). By dividing modern history into these two periods, Hobsbawm made an argument about which factors in the first caused effects we see in the second and also about how seemingly separate events like the two world wars were actually deeply interconnected.

3.1.3. What/How (Influence)

Much of the groundwork that allows us to consider what caused or resulted from a set of historical changes is about first establishing what happened and how processes operated. Asking *what* or *how* is about discovering what factors were at play in a given historical change and how they interacted with each other.

For example, in trying to explain a major shift in power in a representative democracy, historians need to understand how political parties and voters changed their positions by first asking who voted for whom and how the dynamics of the electoral process made a series of small shifts happen. Embedded in those questions are many smaller ones about what motivated individual voters or politicians.

3.1.4. Where (Context)

Asking *where* changes occurred means asking what surrounded the people or actions we're interested in. In other words, what was their context? The most obvious first place to look is geography. Where on the globe did events take place, and was this place small or big, thinly or densely populated, under what kind of political system? We can also think about place in other ways. Did events occur within an institution or involve people who were part of some larger organization? What kinds of physical spaces—rooms, buildings, landscape—surrounded the people we examine? And we can look beyond the physical at what kinds of ideas, expectations, or habits prevailed in this culture or society.

For example, in Mary Beth Norton's reinterpretation of the Salem witch trials, she found a new way of understanding the evidence from these already much-studied events by looking closely at where the participants lived and where they came from, finding a pattern that linked participants with the Indian wars that were taking place around the same time in New Hampshire and Maine and displaced refugees back to the villages around Salem, Massachusetts.

3.1.5. Who / For Whom (Identity and Categories of Analysis)

All of these questions relate in some way to how context influences behavior and when it doesn't. One of the most direct ways to look at how context influences behavior is to ask, "Who?" Which people acted in which ways, and how were those behaviors associated with different aspects of a person's life? Where did people work or live, how did they compare themselves to others, what ideas inspired them, whom did they identify with?

Therefore, underlying the big questions of cause and effect are questions about the role played in a given time and place, for given people, of historical categories such as class, gender, nation, ethnicity, culture, law, politics, religion, family, language, ideas, and education. These categories of analysis are areas of human activity and identity that can help us tease out the factors that motivate us to act.

A category is "historical," and therefore potentially useful as an object of historical study, if it changes over time and place. How categories like race or gender have been constructed and manipulated and the effects of this on human experience are all historical questions. Universal aspects of the human experience or unchanging facts of our environment do not lend themselves to historical inquiry, so historians do not ask "What is love?" or "What is the sun composed of?" or "What makes a plant green?" The biological differences (in both reproductive systems and hormones) that determine how our bodies develop do not change from one society to another or vary from one decade or century to the next, although our understanding of how those mechanisms work has grown over time. So there is a history of the study of sexual biology but no history to our bodies' various sexual characteristics. The differences in how we express or demonstrate our gender, in how roles are or are not assigned within a society based on gender, and in how status and power between men and women are perceived and negotiated are all historical concepts, because they change over time, place, and among individuals. "Gender" is therefore a category open to historical analysis, but biological "sex" is not. The fact that humans have sexual preferences is biological, not historical, but the ways various societies have encouraged, restricted, marginalized, celebrated, or adopted different ways of talking about (or not talking about) how people act on their sexual preferences is constructed or performed within each culture and changes over time, so it is historical.

Similarly, "race" and "ethnicity" are historical categories, not biological ones. We have no genes for "Italian" or "Asian," only tiny differences that vary across a continuous spectrum of the whole human population (there are only rough ranges of probability that some features tend to cluster in some population groups more than others, none of which can be distinctly delineated). But over time humans have defined and attached meaning to racial and ethnic categories and then acted on them. The latter is a process open to historical understanding.

Asking who does what and who is affected by historical change is partly about asking what cultural categories that were attached to a person had meaning in a certain time and place and therefore can shed light on that person's behavior. The most obvious of these categories are those most closely associated with personal identity: gender, race, class, occupation, religion, and ethnicity. But we also define ourselves by the institutions with which we associate, by our ideas, by other social categories such as generation or subculture, by what we care about or try to protect, and by our strategies for achieving our goals.

The rest of this section is a list of the most common categories of historical inquiry. These are avenues through which different contexts influence people's experiences and behavior. These are the places historians most often look for factors that create change, for the impacts of change on people's behavior, or for the moments when change does or doesn't occur. You might think of these as the common lenses we look through to help us understand people's sense of who they are (their identity) and the motivations behind their behavior.

- **Social identity.** How did people define themselves by gender, class, race, religion, rank, ethnicity, nationality, occupation, or other social categories or affiliations? Which categories meant more or were valued more highly than others? How were social categories defined and reflected legally, culturally, socially? How were social identities constructed and disseminated? How widely were they accepted or rejected? What categories were in flux or under challenge? What were the relationships between different groups? In what other ways did people identify themselves? In what ways did identities overlap? How did definitions differ from the ways we use them now?

- **Culture.** What were the ways that people expressed their mores, mentalities, traditions, feelings, or manners? Where were the divisions and alliances in a group of people? Who could "speak to each other" and who could not? What lines could be crossed and which couldn't? What options were open? Who had access to what? What was taboo? What was censured or punished? Who was protected by certain prohibitions, and who was disadvantaged? Where were the silences? How was status marked, and who had it? Who created culture, and how was it shared and taught?

- **Ideas/ideology.** What were people's religious, philosophical, or political beliefs? What terms were used for ideas and how did their meanings vary? What concepts or ideas were perceived as usually good or usually bad, strong or weak, and by whom? How were ideas disseminated or reinforced or undermined? How were people influenced by ideas? How did people use ideas to make sense of their world or impose meaning on it?

- **Education.** Who was taught? What was taught to them? How and where? Who made the decisions? Who were the teachers and what was their place in society? What were the goals of education? What status did it confer? How was it perceived and valued by those who had it and those who did not? How effective was it in achieving its goals?

- **Power.** Who had power and who did not? How was it distributed among different people? How was it displayed? Was it used to coerce, persuade, distract? In what ways? How was it perceived, used, or manipulated by those who had it and those who did not?

- **Politics.** National, international or local, official or unofficial, dominant or subversive—how were policies enacted and used, for what purposes, with what effects? How was power organized?

- **Law.** Whom did law privilege and whom did it punish? What principles did it value most and least? Where did those principles come from? How important was law, and to whom? How complicated was it? How was it enforced? To what degree was the letter of law reflected in practice?

- **Institutions.** What kinds of institutions were there? How were they run and who participated in them? How important were they? Were there many or few? Were they hierarchical? Centralized? Autonomous? Contained in specialized single-use building(s) or embedded in other parts of society?

- **Technology.** What could be done and what could not? What were technological priorities? Who had technological advantages? Who had access to how much and for what purposes? What uses was technology put to, with what intended and unintended consequences? How did technological changes lead to other changes? What drove technological change?

- **Economics and labor.** Who had prosperity, how much, and who paid for or produced it? How did people work, and where, under what conditions? Who worked and who did not? How big and how frequent were highs and lows and what drove those changes? What were people's perceptions of economic activity, success, failure, results? How were money or goods exchanged, under what terms or mechanisms? How were assets valued?
- **Property and material culture.** What did people own, buy, and sell? How did these transactions occur, and with what meanings attached to them? How did property and things drive or express human behavior? What did people desire, how did they use things, what did things represent to people? What did people keep and what did they get rid of? Why and how?
- **Demography.** What were the population, mobility rate, sex ratios, age ratios, languages, or religions of a given group, and how and why did they change over time? How diverse were they? What were the most significant differences or patterns of change, what caused them, and how did these patterns affect behaviors?
- **Geography, space, and environment.** How were people's experiences affected by climate, agriculture, natural resources, natural defenses, transportation and communication, cities, or landscape? How did people impose themselves on their environment? How did they use their environment and for what purposes, with what results?

3.2. How Historians Work

Historical knowledge develops out of the collective work of thousands of academic historians. Though one historian may find significance in a previously overlooked source or come up with a new angle on a big question, the importance of these singular discoveries comes from what they contribute to larger questions that many historians are working on. Because the past leaves us only fragments of contradictory clues, no single historical interpretation can ever be a definitive answer to a significant question of why or how. It is only when the weight of research by a number of people leans overwhelmingly in a certain direction that historians as a group accept it, and that consensus is always contingent on new evidence or perspectives that could adjust or undermine it. In some cases the weight of evidence becomes incontrovertible, leaving debate only about the details or peripheral questions. Many of the most important historical questions, however, are in a state of perpetual debate: individual historians work on various aspects and argue for or against various explanations, but there is little general agreement. All historical inquiry reflects the present-day concerns of historians and the societies we come from: whenever we look to the past, our attention is drawn toward aspects that compel us, which means we are selecting from the past to reflect ourselves rather than discovering a real past as it was once lived. This is not only unavoidable, it is what makes history continually relevant.

Today's academic historians are trained in doctoral graduate programs, in which they master the existing scholarship in several broad fields of history and write a book-length argument that establishes an original interpretation of primary source evidence in answer to some question of general historical interest. In other words, historians are trained to manage large amounts of information, to identify, evaluate, and interpret a variety of sources, and to synthesize broad ranges of evidence to support an argument. Doctoral study is more like an apprenticeship or medical residency than just additional years of coursework.

After earning the PhD, historians who become university professors usually combine research with teaching and professional service (such as advising, peer review, organizing conferences, sitting on committees that oversee admissions, fellowships, hiring and promotion, and so on). Some academic historians do research only, through government or private organizations, including think tanks, museums, libraries, archives, and corporations. Other academic historians hold teaching-only appointments, though some continue to research and publish on their own time and expense or as freelancers, if they can.

Historians conduct research primarily in libraries and archives. The nearest university library may have or be able to get millions of published works, but historians often need texts that were published a very long time ago in few copies or never published at all, so we travel to libraries or archives that hold rare or unique documents. Archives are repositories of unpublished texts, such as government documents, manuscripts, or letters and diaries by people both famous and obscure. Historians rarely browse document collections the way you might browse a well-stocked library, because original documents often get deposited in whichever archive is nearest or convenient for other reasons. Thus the relevant materials on any one topic can be scattered across many institutions and are not always well described in finding aids. Research can thus resemble hunting for needles in haystacks, and serendipity can play as big a role as strategy. Part of the creativity of historical research lies in finding ways to "read the silences": to use fragmentary or indirect evidence to get at questions that left no direct record.

Historical research is relatively inexpensive. It costs the scholar's time, travel expenses, and access to libraries and archives, but requires little or no special equipment and usually no support staff or research assistants (though when funding is available, scholars sometimes employ an assistant or two, allowing them to tackle larger-scale projects). Most historical research is funded either directly by the scholar's employer, the university, or by grants from independent organizations, some of them funded partly or wholly by a government. The major funding sources often seek to fund scholarship that is relevant to policy, but do not choose to fund research depending on its expected results. However, there are exceptions to this rule, which make it always worth examining the acknowledgments section of a book, where authors usually disclose the source of their funding.

The sequence of historical research is, not coincidentally, much like the sequence we ask students to follow in their coursework. Historians first master the basic facts, evidence, and existing interpretations of a question or problem by reading the available scholarly ("secondary") sources. In this process, we identify questions worth pursuing further. Next we seek evidence ("primary sources") that could help resolve those questions, using specialized databases and reference works to find out what is available and where it is located. Once we have located, accessed, read, and analyzed whatever evidence is available or feasible to acquire within the limits of a project, we write. We do not, however, simply write up results, because our reading of the messy, equivocal, contradictory, and fragmentary evidence that is left to us is never so clear. Therefore we brainstorm and draft as a means of making sense of what we see and of generating ideas about how evidence could be connected. We seek feedback from our colleagues at conferences and workshops, where we engage with each other's research-in-progress and shape the direction of future research. We revise our work, with the help of this feedback, until eventually we have something that makes convincing sense of the evidence and connects it meaningfully to significant questions.

Academic historians mostly write specialized works that are primarily intended to bring new evidence and interpretations to the historical community so that others can build on them. Though the insider nature of this work is often denigrated in the humanities, it is no different from specialized literature in medicine or law, where we take for granted that such work is necessary to the development of knowledge that will be applied later in other ways and contexts. Smaller and more specialized projects usually take the form of an article or essay that will be published alongside others on related subjects. Larger projects are published in book form, and while these may seem overly specialized or impenetrable when compared to popular history, most academic history books are less formal and less prone to jargon than other social science or humanities disciplines.

Historians also sometimes write synthetic overviews that bring together the specialized work of many historians into broad narratives suitable for any reader. For scholars' books to be credited toward the "research" portion of their job description, however, publications must have an original argument and usually original research. Writing by academic historians that exclusively repackages existing scholarship, as well as appearances in documentaries, on the Web, and in other public history venues, is most often considered "outreach" or "service" and is becoming more common, either on our own time or insofar as our employers value it. Scholars engage in public history more frequently in the United Kingdom, where there is a larger popular audience for history in TV, film, and synthetic books.

The most common way to structure a written scholarly argument is to make a series of claims and support each one with evidence and reasoning, more or less in that sequence. Historians do this often, especially in articles and essays. But because we are probably asking why an event occurred and with what consequences, our answer to a research question—especially in book form— may also be structured narratively, meaning we tell a story in chronological order. This is because understanding what caused X depends on an enormous amount of context: John did A because he knew K, wanted Q, and expected L, while Joe tried to prevent John from doing A because he knew B, wanted R, and didn't think L was important because he really wanted Y, based on his belief in G. Jane began on John's side but change her views or shifted allegiance to Joe because of N and M. X was an unexpected consequence of Jane's changed view because of the coincidence of L happening at the same time as N and M. In this example, the final sentence contains a claim supported by reasoning and evidence, but none of it would make any sense without the first two sentences of narrative.

Scholarly historical argument can therefore be easily confused with chronological narratives about the past in popular history or textbooks that lack argument. With practice, readers of scholarly history learn to focus on contingency in order to spot the thread of the argument woven through the tapestry of detail: Which factors depended on which other factors? Which factors were decisive? Chains of cause and effect take on significance as far as they offer convincing explanations of the biggest questions. We work to make the thread of argument clear in these kinds of narratives by explaining in our introduction what to look for and then emphasizing the decisive points throughout. If we were writing fiction, we could simply eliminate extraneous or overly complicated facts to ensure the thread was clear. However, as scholars we cannot mislead future researchers or distort the evidence through omission.

Similarly, we must pepper our narratives with the constant distraction of footnotes or endnotes so readers know where each piece of evidence comes from. This provides a path for future researchers and a means of vetting our work. Where a writer of historical fiction may take a fact from a diary and another from an advice book and not care about the difference because it doesn't matter in constructing a believable fictional world, the historian must recognize that advice books don't describe reality as it was, but as its authors wanted it to be (which implies people were not already behaving as prescribed). Knowing what kind of source the statement came from tells us how to read it, and disclosing that information allows our readers to judge our conclusions.

In short, many of the features of scholarly writing that readers find obstructive are essential to scholarly integrity and make it possible for others to build on our work. Where readers seek objective facts and a clear narrative arc, scholars are working on the boundaries of knowledge (empirical fact is not sufficient to answer our questions) with a high degree of uncertainty (our evidence is inherently unreliable). Since no human author can achieve objectivity, we aim instead for transparency. Composing any narrative involves choosing some facts and leaving out others, so we explain our choices at the risk of boring the reader. We include caveats, asides, and qualifications that bog down the narrative but keep us honest. We distinguish our claims from our facts ("I argue that . . ."), and we note where we found our evidence, to invite further questioning. Despite these safeguards, no one product of these rules can claim to "prove" a point, so we subject our work to constant re-examination.

Academic historians are often accused of harboring disdain for or jealousy of popular history. Academic history has different goals and methods, but there should be no hierarchy embedded in these differences: any example of popular history may or may not successfully meet its goals, just as any example of scholarly history may succeed or fail. Each should be judged according to its purpose, not compared to the other. However, since the goals and methods of academic history tend to be unfamiliar, many people do assume scholarly work should look like popular history and be judged as such. Some people accuse scholarly work of tedium or bad writing while missing its real purpose—to contribute new knowledge in ways that can be tested and built on by others. Any single example of that new knowledge may not in itself seem earth-shattering, but it does add to a collective effort to improve our understanding of the larger world. Scholarly frustration can also develop from popular history that relies on the hard-won, archival research of scholars yet sometimes misrepresents or abuses that research while profiting from it. Such works do not reflect the best of their genre.

Scholars usually publish through university-sponsored publishers who oversee the peer review and editing process as well as print and distribute our work. An author submits her manuscript (the unpublished working version of the text) to the publisher, and if the editor at a press or journal thinks the text is appropriate and interesting enough to publish, she sends it to two or three other scholars who work on similar topics. The author does not know the peer reviewers' identities, and the reviewers may not know who the author is until after publication. Reviewers are instructed to read and comment on the manuscript, judging whether it is original enough for publication, follows standards of citation and uses sources appropriately, accounts for other relevant research on the topic, and demonstrates sound reasoning. The peer reviewer should not need to be convinced: arguments are by definition contestable, meaning reasonable people will disagree with them. When reviewers recommend publication, they usually do so with suggestions for revision. The author then revises the manuscript, and it goes back for more review before a final decision is made to publish. If a manuscript is rejected, the author may try submitting to another press or journal to start the peer review process again. On average, it takes five to ten years to produce a scholarly book. An article or essay can take about a year to prepare and another year in the publishing process (when all goes well).

Scholarly authors rarely earn appreciable royalties from published research, and in many cases actually pay—either out of pocket or using funding from their university or an outside funding agency—to make publication possible. The high cost of scholarly books is due to the costs of the production process relative to the small number of buyers. The even higher cost of scholarly journals (containing articles written by scholars) reflects these constraints plus the additional costs and profits of the private companies that often control distribution of articles through databases. Open-access digital publishing is not yet a substantial part of historical academic publishing and does incur significant costs, though it is not nearly as expensive as that which goes through private companies.

Most of what historians do is invisible to students or the public. We work in our offices outside of teaching hours, at home, or in coffee shops, as well as in libraries and archives. Our work is rarely depicted in movies or television because the excitement of it exists almost entirely in text form and requires a great deal of background to appreciate. There is nothing magical about historical expertise, but it is also not a mere memorization of facts, let alone a passion or belief. Expertise is a matter of method: by what means do you discover, vet, and use knowledge? Historians train for many years to identify and use sources reliably, to balance huge amounts of information, and to construct rational arguments about what all that work adds up to. The average person may encounter our work only after it has been reprocessed into a popular book, textbook, encyclopedia, museum exhibit, or documentary, but we are the source that allows those popular forms of history to ground themselves in evidence.

Our other purpose, of course, is teaching. As active researchers, we bring to the university classroom the very latest findings of our fields and first-hand experience of how that knowledge is created. As active practitioners, we are uniquely suited to teach students how knowledge is constructed, how to question narratives, and how to evaluate evidence.

3.3. Why Everyone Should Take a History Class

As with any other discipline, exposure to history at the college level gives you the tools to become an educated consumer of history. Students are often required to take science in college because an "educated person" should know enough about the scientific method to read an article in the popular press about new health research and be able to see through journalistic hyperbole to notice whether the study showed causation or only correlation, or whether it was based on rigorous testing methods that suggest reliable results. In the same way, an educated person should be able to read a newspaper editorial that suggests a historical analogy and be able to poke holes in the reasoning if necessary. You should be able to read about a controversy over the content of high school history textbooks or Holocaust denial and know enough about how historical knowledge is constructed to form your own conclusions grounded in reality. You should have a basic sense of where your own culture comes from and what it shares and does not share with other cultures. When you read a work of popular history or visit a museum, you should have enough perspective and sense of context (and of the importance of context) to ask questions and make connections. This will increase your enjoyment of popular history and allow you to connect it more deeply with your own life and with issues of public interest.

Taking even one history class should also begin to teach you how to do the following:

- Recognize that most major changes and events have more than one cause
- Distinguish among multiple causal and contributing factors
- Separate causes from effects (symptoms from the disease)
- Be able to correct popular myths or conventional wisdom
- Avoid reducing people to hero or villain
- Identify gaps between rhetoric and reality
- Distinguish between expertise and second-hand knowledge or myth
- Distinguish between primary evidence and interpretation
- Practice new ways of finding patterns and connections
- Practice seeing the world from new perspectives
- Recognize the breadth of diversity in the human experience over time and space
- Distinguish universal phenomena from that which varies over time and space
- Distinguish systems from individual interactions
- Manage uncertainty and complexity
- Weigh and organize large amounts of information in various forms

- Become more informed about how politics, government, society, culture, and media work
- See current events as arising out of earlier events and intersecting with related systems
- See seemingly objective phenomena such as science and technology as affected by their social, cultural, ideological, political, and economic context

3.4. What Is the History Major?

Most undergraduate history programs in North America are not designed to produce future historians. They are intended to produce citizens with a broad range of skills that are useful in almost any environment. Programs vary, but most are intended to give students an introduction to the major geographical regions and time periods, with more intensive study of one area or time period of the student's choice. Usually a history program also exposes students gradually to higher-order skills as they move through the program. Sometimes introductory courses—which are often the same courses that non-majors take to fulfill general education requirements—can seem to be heavy on "names and dates" and may require memorization of factual details. This is groundwork for the sophisticated analysis that is expected, to increasing degrees, throughout the program.

Because it reflects the complexity of life seen through fragmentary and often unreliable evidence, there is always a tension in history education between learning factual material and learning methods, questions, concepts, and the competing arguments already made by historians. Successful critical interpretation of historical questions (using large amounts of specific evidence and framing interpretations in light of other arguments) cannot be accomplished without learning and managing factual information.

History is as much a reading- and writing-intensive field as literary studies, but this fact is not well recognized. For students this means that reading assignments in history classes may be more demanding even than in other reading-heavy fields. Textbooks and historical secondary sources, containing analysis and interpretation, account for most of the pages on your syllabus. Historical interpretations are not usually as dense or difficult as theoretical works in philosophy or sociology, however: they are written in comparatively plain language and organized at least partly in narrative form (like a story).

Historical documents can be more difficult to decode, but undergraduates are usually given only short excerpts of these to read closely. That should mean the reading is relatively manageable, but many students don't find it so because they are alarmed by the sheer amount of facts and unsure of what they need to remember. History readings are not like a biology textbook, where you may need to memorize each process and rule presented. History reading requires—and develops—the ability to sort through forests of details to identify key turning points and the most convincing points of evidence. This is a difficult but enormously useful skill that applies to many endeavors.

History programs today face a challenging landscape. Until the last few decades it was assumed that students entered college with a basic factual understanding of the "master narratives" of US and European history (that is, the people, events, and chronology of accepted political history) and sufficient literacy to approach long, detailed texts with sometimes archaic or specialized language and write coherent, structured essays in grammatically correct English. The purpose of college-level instruction carried out by active historical researchers was to ask students to unravel and disrupt the master narratives they already knew and to construct their own narratives based on evidence and in light of existing scholarship.

In the past few decades, several changes have challenged these expectations. Technology has pushed our society to read less overall and to read shorter pieces of text, often in an informal or simplified style. Both the "master narratives" of US and European political history and the assumed centrality of this "Western" civilization to what we should teach are now questioned, so that there is no single canon of established facts considered necessary for every graduating high school student. Globalization has moved students around the world, diversifying classrooms in enriching ways but also disrupting our assumptions about what students come in knowing. Depending on their background, today's students may have tremendous breadth of knowledge in one area, such as Chinese history, but not know who Thomas Jefferson is. And most American students coming to college today have had less practice writing formal academic prose than was previously common, both because more time in secondary schools is spent on preparing for standardized tests and because students come to college from more diverse backgrounds, sometimes having experience in other genres or cultures of writing but little familiarity with the expectations at American colleges.

At the same time, historical scholarship has developed enormously over the past few decades, so that we not only cover literally more history to encompass recent events, but also have a richer range of interpretation and conceptual complexity to convey to students in order to responsibly introduce them to history as it is understood and practiced today. This responsibility cannot be taken lightly: today's students face a more complex, globalized world where critical thinking about cause and effect, empathetic understanding of diversity, and the ability to process and analyze vast amounts of information coherently and via multiple media forms is critical to professional survival and democratic citizenship.

In short, we are experiencing a crisis of declining student preparedness and increasing learning expectations. History programs attempt to cope by being more explicit about expectations in introductory courses while offering a broader range of upper-level courses that examine cutting-edge ideas from around the world. For students, it can feel like a rude awakening, but the opportunities we offer are also exceptionally well suited to our rapidly changing world.

3.5. What Comes after the History Degree?

The skills history majors practice most are reading and writing critically; understanding, sorting, evaluating, and using large amounts of information; finding and making fine distinctions in meaning and evidence; identifying causes and effects of change; understanding diversity in all its forms and comparing perspectives; and reasoning by context, which involves identifying and distinguishing patterns of evidence, concepts, or behavior in individuals and their environments.

Most people realize that understanding the past helps us to know ourselves better. It also helps us to understand how societies behave and how the constraints of particular societies affect human behavior. This understanding is inevitably imperfect, but it is better than guessing or falling back on prejudices, propaganda, or myth. Understanding ourselves through our past is worthwhile in its own right and can help us to better understand our choices in the present.

In addition, any liberal arts education should provide a solid grounding in critical thinking, reading, and writing, which are crucial skills in all professional endeavors as well as the key to whatever future learning you may seek. Critical thinking is not seeing the world in a negative light, but rather using rational tools to see the world more clearly, beyond what we can personally experience (see section 2.8). We gather, interpret, and connect evidence, notice patterns and systems, and draw larger meanings from many small pieces of information.

Beyond these essential skills that are taught in various ways throughout the liberal arts curriculum, there are several specific attributes of a history degree that prepare students for whatever comes next. Studying change across time and place is like having the broadest imaginable bird's-eye view of the world. As the closest we'll ever get to a time machine, historical study exposes students to the incredible diversity of human experience and behavior, while they also learn to rationally analyze the connections between people's context, their actions, and their worldviews. Every individual sees the world as through a pinhole, with the vast majority invisible. History is about gathering these individual perspectives and analyzing how they interrelate, including weighing which perspectives provide the most convincing explanations of known facts.

This broad and rational view is essential to effective problem-solving. History majors learn to separate causal factors from effects. We learn to see the real experiences of individual bystanders or participants as evidence of a larger phenomenon or system. To understand the system—and if necessary to change it—you have to distinguish its causes and effects and how the parts make the whole. The small artifacts we use as evidence will not, in themselves, explain the whole. Historical training is a systematic and rational approach to putting the puzzle pieces together. This is training in investigation, especially in handling fragmentary or unreliable evidence, such as personal testimonials, without taking sides or falling into false equivalence.

Another way to look at how historical problem-solving fits into other ways of knowing is to think about how literature puts the reader in other people's shoes, teaching perspective and empathy. Sociology and political science and other social science fields offer evidence-based approaches to solving our current problems. History can be a bridge between the two approaches, connecting real, individual human experiences and perspectives with patterns and solutions, each embedded in a specific context that helps us to discern the patterns determining causes and effects.

Finally, and perhaps most centrally to what we do, historians learn which factors create change, how to find and explain those factors, how change happens—often with unexpected consequences—and how to recognize change even when the process may be happening too slowly for participants to notice. For example, after the fall of communism in Europe and the end of the Cold War in 1989–91, the political scientist Francis Fukuyama declared an "end of history," hoping that the series of global conflicts that had consumed the twentieth century had ended and would be followed by something less eventful. To many people it did feel like big changes were over and that the world's worst problems had been resolved. But as we now know, that period was quickly followed by new upheavals. Historians learn to see the world as constantly changing and are suspicious of the notion that anything lasts forever, is inevitable, or is either better or worse than an imagined past.

Ask a historian how to make a desirable change happen, and she will probably give you a few examples of how similar changes have occurred in the past, as well as times when such changes were inhibited by this or that factor. Trained historians will also take your flippant historical analogy (which major world event is "happening all over again" this week?), and break down which aspects of the comparison do or don't work, and therefore which parts of the analogy may actually be instructive and which probably are not. This specific form of reasoning through problems taught in history classrooms can be applied in almost any setting. In studying the effects of change, we also examine how innovation is recognized and responded to, how new evidence is accepted (or not). Noticing what has changed allows us to see when existing solutions may no longer work.

A history education thus offers a flexible set of core skills that can prepare a graduate for careers ranging from teaching, law, or government to information sciences, journalism, politics, law enforcement, business, marketing, public relations and communications, any form of research, management, or administration, or just about anything else. Even if your history instructors don't explain assignments in terms of "finding out what makes change happen," "applying ideas in a new context using evidence," "arguing persuasively in writing," "sorting and weighing large amounts of information," or "understanding diversity," you can notice that you are in fact doing these things and explain them that way to future employers. As just one example, consider Harry Hinsley, a history student at Cambridge University at the outbreak of World War II. He was recruited to work for the Government Code and Cipher School at Bletchley Park, where he pioneered "traffic analysis" by identifying patterns in the call signs, timing, and frequency of encoded German naval signals that allowed him to draw conclusions about how their navy was structured. He was using historical thinking to unravel a totally new problem in a seemingly unrelated realm.

More importantly than practical skills, a history education offers a rich perspective on our world and teaches meaningful tools for making sense of human existence that will serve you well in all aspects of your life, as we all move forward in an information age that makes sorting and judging information as crucial as food to our survival and enrichment.

4

The Short-Answer Identification Essay

Assignments described as "IDs," or "identification essays," appear most often on in-class exams, though they can also be done at home. These include any short, factual essays you may be asked to write in order to test your knowledge—that is, they don't ask you for an argument, response, comment, or opinion. They ask you only to identify, describe, define, or explain a historical idea, concept, person, event, or phenomenon.

On an in-class exam, your time and space are limited, depending on how many IDs and other questions you have to complete in the time allotted for the whole exam. The length requirement may not be formally set, but the usual expectation is that you fill about one blue-book page or equivalent, or about five to six sentences of handwriting. Some IDs give you a quote, and you need to identify who the author is as well as explain its context and significance. Others give you the name of a person, place, event, or idea to explain and define.

Preparing an ID answer requires several steps. Not all of these steps will be possible during an in-class exam; most should be done at home as preparation. Before taking your first exam, it would be wise to practice a few ID answers all the way to the point of proofreading. With experience you will be able to do more preparation as you take notes, and more revising as you write, and the whole process will not seem so elaborate. If you are given a short-answer ID essay to do at home, proceed through all the steps as laid out here.

4.1. What's Your Goal?

A short-answer, or "identification" (ID), question is usually intended to test three things:

- How many of the most significant facts you can recall
- Your understanding of the most important concepts
- Your ability to connect these concepts to course goals

For example, in a survey course on modern Europe, the term "Thermidor" could be on an exam as an ID. You are expected to state what that term represents (a specific period in the French Revolution), explain what it was about (what period, what happened, what changed, who did what to whom?), and why we should care (what impact did this event have on subsequent events? How did it change things?). An answer that meets all three goals to an exceptional degree—therefore earning full credit—should pack each sentence with several facts and ideas.

4.2. Studying from Textbooks and Taking Lecture Notes

The sheer number of names, dates, and other facts in history can be intimidating. But you are not expected to memorize every fact; instead, you're supposed to train yourself to judge which facts are most important because of the way they connect. Specifically, you're looking for which facts *cause* significant events. History textbooks and some kinds of lectures provide a factual overview of a whole period or series of events. These help you to connect other course materials into a broad whole and provide details that you will judiciously select as you compose your own arguments and interpretations. For short-answer identification essays, you are expected to pack your sentences with as much relevant information as possible. This does not mean recreating whole sections of a textbook or lecture. It means noticing which details are most relevant and bringing just those details together in a way that reflects course goals and priorities.

This is why you usually can't cram for a college history exam the night before: if you haven't been paying attention, last-minute scrambling will allow you only to throw facts on the page at random. If your exam takes place at home, or you are allowed to bring a cheat sheet to class, you still need to be able to find relevant details quickly and put them together in a sensible way, and you will know how to do that only by keeping up with class content and readings throughout the semester and taking good notes.

For most people, taking notes in longhand is more effective than typing because the physical act of forming letters helps you make memories better than hitting keys. However you take them, keep your notes for each course in one place, separate from notes for other subjects. Most of us start taking notes by writing down as much as we can, resulting in a chronological narrative of the contents or even a full transcription. These kinds of notes are hard to navigate later and don't help you understand the material as you write it down. Aim to work toward a more conceptual way of taking notes, where you sort the information as it comes in and record it in categories or hierarchies. Compare the two sets of lecture notes in figure 4.1.

The example on the left is a more or less complete account of the lecture; the student could go back to it later as if hearing it again. The example on the right

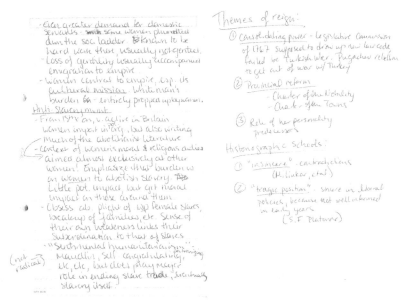

Figure 4.1 The example of notes on the left is in the "narrative" style that records almost everything as the lecturer said it. The example on the right is more conceptual; it organizes terms and ideas into logical groups.

is organized conceptually, showing that the student has already grasped which information is important and why. The student will remember more from this version, and when she refers to the notes to use details in an assignment, she can go straight to what she needs. It takes considerable practice to process the information as you write it down, but it's worth aiming for.

When taking notes on a lecture, start each day with the date, course name, and the day's topic. Make notes about administrative matters such as deadlines or assignment instructions differently from subject-matter notes (in a different color of ink, a different part of your notebook, or set off with markings of some kind). Divide your notes on the subject matter into at least two columns, one for topic headings and other keywords, the other for details. Work toward listening closely and then summarizing the key questions and answers, definitions, names, and dates, rather than transcribing every word.

Similarly, when you first open a textbook, start by "pre-reading" it: read any introductory material, then scan for and read bullet points, headings and subheadings, images and their captions, charts or graphics, maps, timelines, and discussion questions. This will help you understand what kind of information is available. Look back at your syllabus to find the subject matter or theme for the date this part of the textbook was assigned. Tell yourself in your own words what you're reading about and what you're supposed to get from it to use in class or in a writing assignment. Only *after* you have a clear idea of your purpose should you go back and read the main body of the text. Instead of trying to memorize facts, try to follow "who is doing what to whom, how, and why." Ask what problems or questions the text is raising or explaining. Stop after each major section and write down in your own words how the "who does what" explains "why" or how" major events or outcomes happened. It might be helpful to create a template for your textbook notes like this:

> WHO DID WHAT:
> => HOW?
> => WHY?

On the first line, distill the factors that were most decisive rather than rewriting the entire narrative. That process should help you figure out, or find stated in the text, the mechanisms ("how") and reasons ("why") behind important events and outcomes.

If you are not assigned a textbook but only secondary readings (books or articles written by historians to answer specific historical questions rather than overviews or summaries of whole time periods), see section 5.2. For primary source readings (such as documents, memoirs, or fiction produced at the time you are studying), see sections 9.2–9.5. You can still find the details you need to write an ID essay in secondary and primary sources, but they will not be as conveniently organized for this purpose as they often are in a textbook. Secondary historical sources are composed as arguments about cause and effect, though each source will usually have one argument of its own, in contrast to how a textbook might summarize several competing arguments. Primary sources are evidence: each provides documentation of things that happened and what people said, believed, or assumed. Those are all details that may help to explain a historical phenomenon you've been asked to define, but they will not be announced as "the three ways rural people were affected by Enclosure," as they might be in a lecture, or listed in one place in plain language, as in a textbook.

If you don't have a suitable textbook or other reference specific to your course (and you should feel free to ask instructors what reference text they would recommend if one isn't required) and you can't find where an ID term appeared in other kinds of course readings or your lecture notes, the next step might be to look up the term in an encyclopedia (dictionary definitions are too limited for this purpose). First make sure the term you find is the same one asked for in your course. There may be multiple people with the same name, multiple events known by the same names, or varying definitions of a concept.

The one you're looking for should fit the chronology and themes of the course you're taking. Once you have identified the correct term, do not use an encyclopedia entry to study from, because these entries are intended to define the term in any context, whereas on your exam you need to define the term as it is relevant to your course material. Use an encyclopedia entry only to help you identify dates, names, or associated terms, in order to locate it in your course readings or notes.

If you know that ID terms will appear on your exam, make it a habit to notice when a keyword is emphasized in either a lecture or a reading: any concept that is specifically defined, that receives special attention, that shows up as one of the main subjects of a unit, and so on. Mark these terms in some unique way in your notes and make sure you write down where to locate explanations from the readings as you encounter them. If your instructor does not provide the list of ID terms, make your own list.

Now you're ready to study, but this does not mean you simply memorize this information. You must not only define, but explain the significance of, your term for the course you're taking. The best way to think through your notes and arrange the information to best suit this goal is to brainstorm and draft actual ID answers, even if you will have to write them again for an in-class exam. Writing and revising them in longhand at home will help you to learn the material and to strategize how best to present it.

Skimming and scanning. To skim is to jump around in a text, reading only key passages such as the beginnings and ends of paragraphs. To scan is to run your eyes lightly over a text looking for keywords or typographical signals marking an important passage. Skimming or scanning mindfully—knowing what you're looking for and maintaining that focus—can help you orient yourself in a text and jump ahead to parts you most need. Use these techniques to find what you need, but then closely read the passages relevant to your goals.

4.3. Brainstorming Lists

Writing an identification short answer is a lot like converting a list into complete sentences, so it makes sense to brainstorm in list form. Start by listing every factor that defines the term: who, what, when, where? If your term is a person's name, you will of course spend more time on "who," but you will also explain where and when that person lived and what he or she did. If your term is a place, you will focus on what significant events or people are associated with it that are relevant to your course, which involves explaining who was there when, and what they did there. If your term is an event, you will also explain which individuals or groups were involved, and when and where it took place. If your term is a concept, you will focus on how it is defined, by whom, with what purpose, and come up with examples of its use. If you are identifying the author of a quotation, your focus is on both the author and the particular text given, but you will also explain why the author wrote that text, what it signifies, what it was meant to accomplish, with what consequences. In each case, be as specific as you can with the information you have.

- **Answering "when."** The more recent the term, the more exact your dates are likely to be. The Cuban Missile Crisis took place in October 1962, whereas Hitler rose to power in 1933, the French Revolution took place in the 1790s, and the Wars of the Roses took place in the fifteenth century. Some events took place on a single day and can be identified as such—the Archduke Franz Ferdinand was assassinated on June 28, 1914—but other historical events were processes that occurred over months, years, or even centuries. Western European industrialization, for instance, is usually described as getting underway from the middle of the eighteenth century to the late nineteenth, since it didn't happen overnight and began as an accumulation of inventions and changes. Think about how specific you need to be to capture the event's significance. For most purposes it doesn't matter that Franz Ferdinand was assassinated on June 28 rather than the twenty-seventh or twenty-ninth. It might be worth noting that the event took place in June, or summer, if you are focusing on the lead-up to World War I. But if your exam is covering a century or more of material, just the year 1914 is probably detailed enough.
- **Answering "who."** When identifying people, you need to include not only their name and what they did, but as much as possible about gender, ethnicity, nationality, social class, occupation, ideological position, or other identifying factors, depending on what is known and what is relevant for your course. There may be other appropriate identifying factors to list, such as what the person published if she was a writer, or his title or party affiliation if he was a government official. If the people involved in your ID term acted as a group, describe that group: was it a formal organization, a loose formation with something in common, a random set of people who happened to be present at an event, or a category that historians use to describe people who did not necessarily identify themselves as a group, such as "middle-class white voters"? List as many ways as you can think of to describe who was involved, and how to distinguish him/her/them from other people.
- **Answering "where."** The name of a place where an event occurred or a person lived was probably given to you when you read about your ID term, if the place is relevant enough to include. But the name means nothing

in itself—find out where it is on a map, whether it's a capital, a large or small city, a village or region, a mountain range or an empty field made famous only because a battle took place on it. Not everything about a place will be significant, though. You don't need to know its map coordinates or every event that ever took place there. Consider what about its location was significant enough to justify including it as an ID term. For example, if "Munich" appears on an exam in a survey course on European history after a unit focusing on the twentieth century, include that city's role in the rise of Nazism and the Munich Agreement (1938), not its Bavarian architecture or its importance as a capital city from the sixteenth to nineteenth centuries.

- **Answering "what."** Saying what happened is usually the easiest part, but it's easy to fall into error by describing the qualities and outcome of an event rather than the actions that took place. For example, "The New Deal was a successful policy that helped ease the Depression" describes only the outcome of the New Deal. "The New Deal was a series of policies establishing public works projects that provided jobs while improving infrastructure and making culture accessible to ordinary Americans" actually defines the term. At this brainstorming stage, write down everything you know about what happened. Notice when you are writing adjectives or adverbs like "successful," "ruthless," or "significantly" and try to add the concrete actions and results. This should require that you refer to class readings and notes.

- **Answering "how."** Explaining how something happened means you're describing a sequence of causes and effects—one thing led to another, which led to another thing. By now you should have a fairly long list of what was happening related to your term. A good way to brainstorm the causal connections is to draw some arrows on your list, wherever you see one item causing or resulting from another. Draw as many arrows as you can. Now try stringing together as many items from your list as possible into a sentence that describes these links. Often a good place to start is to use your sentence to answer the general question, "Who did what to whom, when, and with what results (or what for)?" For example, let's say your ID term is "German Unification." Your list so far might contain the following items you would be likely to find in your notes or textbook: 1871, Bismarck, German states, Prussia, Franco-Prussian War, nationalism. You could string this into a sentence like "Bismarck of Prussia unified the German states in 1871 following the Franco-Prussian War out of his desire to strengthen German nationalism." This sentence needs more detail and explanation, but it's a good start that puts the most crucial facts into an accurate, logical order.

4.4. Distilling: Choosing the Right Details

The next step in preparing your ID is to make thoughtful choices about what to exclude from the information you have brainstormed. The key to doing this well is to keep in mind the subject area of your course or the part of it that has been covered so far for the exam you're taking. Every detail in your ID answer should clarify and explain material directly relevant to the course theme(s) and chronology, and any details *not* relevant to the course should *not* appear in your answer.

One way to describe what you do when you *select* some details to include, leaving others behind, is to say you are "distilling." This is a metaphor, borrowed from the scientific process of manipulating a solution to make one component separate out. Contrast this to a basic summary, which usually means that we find the most important parts in a text to represent the whole. A distillation is slightly more specific. When we distill, we take out the parts we need for another purpose, even if they are not the central points of the source material, just as a scientist will distill a particulate needed for the next stage of the experiment, rather than looking for some representative or most important component of the original solution. In this case, you are looking for the details that fit your course and assignment, not details that fairly represent everything there is to know about the term.

Let's say your ID term is "Theodore Roosevelt." You don't have space to write an entire biography explaining his life and importance to history. You have about six sentences, so instead you need to cram in a selective, directed distillation of what he did and how he was important *for the purposes of your course.* Compare the following answers on a midterm exam for a US history course in which the class has reached only about 1910 (the end of Roosevelt's presidency) in lecture.

Teddy Roosevelt grew up a sickly child (asthma) but overcame this to eventually become a symbol of American adventurism. He was related to another president, Franklin Roosevelt, and besides being a president he was also a taxidermist and explorer of South America, which makes him one of the most fascinating Americans. He worked his way up from the New York Assembly to be police commissioner and governor of NY and was also an Assistant Secretary of the Navy and Vice-President before he was President. He was a Republican President from 1901 to 1909, having stepped in to save the day after the previous president, William McKinley, was assassinated by an anarchist. After that he started his own Progressive Party and ran for president again, becoming the most popular third party candidate ever even though he didn't win. He was still very important for leading the progressive movement, which helped to regulate food and get rid of corruption. Ironically he was also almost assassinated, but he survived and later died of natural causes.

Teddy Roosevelt was a US president 1901–1909 important for his "square deal" policies including "trust-busting" (where he broke up corporate monopolies), introducing regulation for food and drug safety, negotiating a labor strike, and conserving land by creating the National Parks system. He's maybe most significant for the Roosevelt Corollary to the Monroe Doctrine, part of his "big stick" diplomacy that justified American intervention in the western hemisphere, which happened in the Dominican Republic, Cuba, and Nicaragua and had big longer-term impacts in building the US's international profile, along with Roosevelt's building of the Panama Canal and his Nobel Peace Prize for negotiating the treaty that ended the Russo-Japanese War. Before he was president Roosevelt expanded the navy and its role in asserting American interests abroad and provoked the Spanish-American War, in which he fought heroically with his own "Rough Riders" regiment. Roosevelt also previously served as NYC police commissioner and NY governor, where he was known for fighting corruption.

Both answers are accurate, specific, and appropriate in length. But only the second is an effective distillation of the material for this course. The first answer chooses seemingly random details and gives roughly equal weight across Roosevelt's whole lifetime, with the most specific details on what he did after 1910 (starting the Progressive Party). It could be called a "summary" and it would acquaint a general reader with who Roosevelt was (if that were the goal), but it is not a distillation, and it does not serve the primary function of the exam question: to demonstrate the writer's understanding of course concepts and historical argument. It therefore would not receive full credit on this exam. The second answer focuses on the period of Roosevelt's life covered in the course and on Roosevelt's most important domestic and foreign policies, which demonstrates that the writer understands historical significance. Every fact in it can therefore count toward that student's score, making it by far the more successful answer of the two.

Look at your brainstorming lists again, and ask of each item whether it illuminates the main theme(s) of your course and falls within the chronological range covered by the exam. Cross out anything that doesn't fit those parameters.

4.5. Explaining Significance

An identification essay is more than a list of relevant facts. The other, equally important, part of your answer must be an explanation of how or why your term is historically significant. Historical significance is one of the most difficult and most important concepts you'll face in history classes. In its most basic sense, historical significance refers to how something influences our understanding of the past. How does it influence the causes or effects of major events or changes?

Significance versus interest. One of the biggest differences between scholarly history and most people's everyday experience of history is the difference between what is merely interesting and what has analytical "significance," by which we mean something that changes or adds to scholarly interpretations. It is interesting that Teddy Roosevelt enjoyed taxidermy, but for the purposes of understanding US history it is not among the most important things he did.

As another example, if you have visited historical museums or watched historical documentaries you may think of the incredible amount of painstaking research put into something like replicating the exact dress worn by people in the past. Getting those facts of historical dress right is important to a museum or film dedicated to bringing history alive and can be inherently interesting, but it doesn't usually have interpretive significance. Scholarly historians do pay attention to things like dress, just in a different way. It does not generally affect our interpretations to know that sleeve lengths were just so in a given year, but knowing that pink was considered a masculine color in eighteenth-century France does help us show how gender norms change over time and place. Similarly, whether a certain garment was made of wool or linen may be significant mainly for a museum curator, but whether the community it came from was dependent on sheep husbandry or flax production can have much significance to a historian assessing that community's economy and divisions of labor.

Answering, "Why do we care?" To explain historical significance is to show why we should care about the term, how it changed things, explains things, or is evidence of something. The explanation should be a result of your own thinking, though your readings should point you in the right directions. Your job is to consider, and discover, ways your term might be important or to explain its importance in your own words. To do this, start a second list, looking at your first list of facts and now brainstorming reasons your ID term has played a role in big changes discussed in class, as either a cause or effect.

Looking at this second list, decide whether your term is significant in one really big way that requires explanation in itself, or is significant in several ways. If your term is important primarily for one big impact (such as "the Munich Agreement"), you will make a list of the reasons why that one big impact matters (list its many effects on various people or groups) and how the term made such a difference (why was this term the cause? what about the term had these effects?). If your term had a variety of impacts in several areas (such as "Theodore

Roosevelt"), you will list the ways that your term changed or influenced events, ideas, and people, and then add how the term made that specific impact in each case.

Use the following questions to help you brainstorm the specific ways your ID term made changes occur, reflects the effects of changes, or otherwise influenced the historical context you're studying.

Significance of persons, groups, or organizations

- Did they influence others to do something? How?
- Did they write or say something that changed the way people thought? Why was it so powerful?
- Did their actions alter the course of events? In what ways?
- What makes them different from others?
- Did they affect the way other people lived? In what ways?
- Are they representative of something bigger?

Significance of a place

- What major event(s) took place there?
- What about its geographical position or other qualities influenced events? In what ways?
- How did its culture or the experience of being there influence people's actions or ideas? What were the connections between the place and what happened?
- What about its culture or setting affected the lives of people there?

Significance of an event

- Does it mark a major break or disruption from what came before? How?
- Did it influence people to take some action or embrace some idea? How?
- Did it show the effects of some change on people's behavior or experiences? In what ways?
- Did it affect the ways people lived? In what ways?

Significance of an idea, text, or concept

- Did it cause people to do something or think differently? Why was it so inspiring?
- Does it explain or describe people's behavior? What does that behavior consist of, and what difference did it make? Is a text or idea representative of some movement or shift?
- Does it explain or describe some phenomenon or development over time? What changes were involved, and why do they matter?

Significance of a system, law, document, process, or phenomenon
- Did it change something? In what ways and for whom?
- Did it affect the experiences of large numbers of people? In what ways?
- Was it seen as a reaction or solution to some problem or difficulty? How?
- Was it the result of some change or experience, reflecting how people were affected?
- Is it evidence of some behaviors, ideas, or reactions? What does it show?

As you did with your first list, concentrate on your term's significance *for this course* and for the material you have covered so far if your exam is taking place before the end of the semester. Eliminate explanations that go beyond the framing of your course and expand the ones that remain to make sure they address important topics or themes the course has focused on (such as the topics that appear on the syllabus and define the focus for each class day).

4.6. Revising: Packing Your Sentences

Now that you have at least two lists for your term that answer the questions who, what, when, where, how, and why do we care, you are ready to write your ID answer. Fill every sentence with as many factual details, explanations, and examples as possible. Pack your sentences as if you were packing a suitcase for a long trip. If your first draft refers to "ordinary people," expand that to "most middle-class German voters, especially men and people in cities." Wherever possible, add examples and explanations, in parentheses if necessary to keep your sentences from getting too complicated or taking up too much space. In the following examples, the first sentence is from a draft, and the second has been expanded in revision.

> Aryanization is about the integration of Aryan and non-Aryan people through epic oral literature.

> Aryanization describes the political, economic and social integration of Aryan (Sanskrit-speaking) peoples and non-Aryan (Mleccha or originally non-Sanskrit-speaking) peoples from approximately 1200 BCE to 600 BCE. This process was facilitated by the popular epic oral literatures that allow for many groups to develop a shared regional story/culture as diverse groups add their own narrative into the larger epic's story. A powerful example is how a local cattle-herding caste wrote (orally) their local god Krishna into the popular Mahabharata epic in its most famous segment, the Bhagavad Gita.

4.7. Revising: Cutting the Crap

For your second round of revision, look for words that do not add relevant facts or connections between facts. These are taking up space without serving your goal. Look especially for common fillers like these:

- **Verbal tics.** Words like "uh" or "you know" in our speech sometimes have written equivalents. Since they don't add meaning, we want to delete them from drafts. If you're not sure whether you have words functioning in this way, try taking them out and seeing if the sentence still makes sense. As you become more aware of your personal tics, editing them out becomes second nature.
- **Emphasis tics:** very, much, literally, actually, truly, really, etc.
- **Commentary tics:** (un)fortunately, obviously, clearly, strangely, etc.
- **Hedges:** maybe, perhaps, often, sometimes, apparently, etc.
- **Descriptions:** ruthless, heroic, impressive, cruel, etc.

Summing up. Explaining well is about choosing good details, not avoiding details. Compare the following examples, where the first sums up the gist of the term, but the second distills key details that explain it, as asked for in the assignment:

Aryanization was important in political and religious and also social ways, having a notable impact on things like caste.

In addition to the political and explicitly religious effects of Aryanization like intermarriage and reorganized pantheon relations, Aryanization also meant the spread and recognition of Brahmins, their monopoly authority on the Vedas, and their language (Sanskrit, an Indo-Aryan language). By accepting and intermarrying between "non-Aryan" and "Aryan," the non-Aryan group then adopted caste identities, such as Brahmin, Kshatriyas, Vaishyas, or Shudras. With their adoption of the caste structure (not system), there was eventually the development of a Varna structure (the precursor to caste).

Vagueness and generalizations. The same word may be the closest description possible in one context, but hopelessly vague in another. For example, in a course on the Civil War where the ID term is "the Confederacy," your first attempt to define it might be "the Southern side in the US Civil War." It would be better to revise this to "an independent government declared by eleven slave states when they seceded from the Union" followed by further detail about how the Confederacy was formed and organized, and its fate. But if the course was on US history as a whole and the ID term was "the Civil War," then specifying the

Confederacy as "the Southern side" might be as much detail as you have room for, since the rest of your ID needs to describe the origins and course of the war. The following kinds of terms are always worth checking to see if they can be narrowed down. Also look for placeholder words like "something" and "this" to replace with more specific terms (see section 5.10).

- **Generalized terms for people:** people, Italians, peasants, women, etc.
- **Broad or badly defined regions:** the West, Africa, the Orient, etc.
- **Broad categories:** governmental, societal, popular, tyranny, etc.

Introductions and conclusions. An ID is usually a single paragraph with no need for an introduction or conclusion. Every word should help explain the meaning of the term or its significance, once. Anything else should be deleted.

What did you miss? Having taken out what wasn't adding value to your answer, you may now have extra space to fill with more examples, explanations, and more specific language. Check whether you may have overlooked anything major. For example, any ID that attempts to define the American Revolution would have to mention French involvement, since it was one of the key factors in the American victory. But when we're focusing on defining the two main sides, their reasons for fighting, the key turning points in the war, and other factors in American victory and British defeat, we can run out of space and leave out something slightly indirect like an ally. Similarly, use your common sense to notice inconsistencies that may reveal you've confused something, such as defining South Slavs as "people living the eastern part of Russia."

4.8. Revising: Grading Yourself

One last check to do for any assignment is to look it over as if you were grading it, as your professor will do. In most cases your grader will assign points, usually something like three or five maximum points per ID. Most instructors do not have three or five specific things they're looking for, but will give credit for any factual details that are correct and relevant to the term as it is used in the course. At the same time, most instructors will not give full credit to an answer that does not address the significance of the term or that misses facts so vital to the definition of the term that it doesn't make sense without those details. Any parts of the answer that do not add specific, accurate, relevant, and significant explanation of the term are disregarded.

Follow these guidelines to give your draft points (out of five), as in the following examples of IDs for the term "Underground Railroad" for a survey course on US history to 1865. (Answers that receive zero points are usually those that confused the ID term with something else, for example an essay describing the Underground Railroad as a real train or dating it after the Civil War.)

Answers earning one or two points. The term is recognizable, but the explanation is vague or incorrect, such as by repeating conventional myths or off-topic tangents rather than reflecting the factual material provided in the course:

> The Underground Railroad from the South to the North led slaves to freedom. Slaves were running away from terrible conditions where they were treated like property. Some of them ran away because they just couldn't take it anymore. This is important because people shouldn't treat other people that way. It's good that other people were willing to help them out and that so many people reached safety. America had a Civil War because of stuff like this.

> The Underground Railroad was a path to safety for escaping slaves from the American South before the Civil War. People like Harriet Tubman used quilts that had codes sewn into them to escape on the railroad run by Northern Whites, who hated slavery and tried to help. Slaves faced terrible, frightening deprivations running through woods and fields to safety, and when they stopped on the Underground Railroad they were hidden in people's cellars and closets, which were built specially to be kept secret. Today in old houses sometimes you'll find hidden rooms that used to be used as stops on the Underground Railroad.

Answers earning three or four points. The term is accurately but not fully explained, or the answer is detailed but not entirely accurate:

> The Underground Railroad helped slaves to escape from the South to the North in nineteenth-century America. Anti-slavery activists helped people to escape and gave them places to stay. This was very brave because it was a risky thing to do at the time. Not that many people were involved, maybe a few thousand. The Underground Railroad is important because it is part of what led to the Civil War, because Southern states saw it as illegal.

> The Underground Railroad helped slaves to escape from the South to Canada in the decades leading up to the Civil War. White abolitionists organized secret networks of routes and safe houses for fugitives to use, and helped thousands reach safety. The Fugitive Slave Act was part of it and was one of the events that caused the Civil War because it seemed unfair to the South, which is why it's important.

Answers earning five points. The term and its significance are fully explained, with abundant, accurate details:

> The Underground Railroad was a loose network of abolitionists in the US North who helped fugitive slaves escape from the American South into the North or Canada in the first half of the nineteenth century. The network was developed by free blacks like Harriet Tubman with help from white abolitionists like John Brown and operated in secret without formal organization so they couldn't identify each other, especially after the 1850 Fugitive Slave Act required people in free states to cooperate to return fugitives to the South. "Agents" helped groups of fugitives, usually young men, to travel and sometimes provided safe hiding places ("stations") along the way. The numbers of people who helped and escaped were small, but the existence of the "railroad" became a prominent political issue and was a significant factor in the secession of the Southern states, leading to the Civil War.

4.9. Proofreading: Handwriting, Spelling, and Grammar

Since most ID answers are written in class during timed exams, you may not have time for proofreading. However, keep in mind that instructors can give you credit only for what they can read. Check the following:

Handwriting. Try printing instead of cursive or even writing key words in all-caps. If you have time after finishing your exam, go back and clarify your handwriting.

Spelling. If you're not sure of the spelling of the key words in your answer, spell them phonetically rather than leaving them out. But you may also need to focus some of your study time on learning the spelling as well as the meaning of these important terms, since bad misspellings may make a word so unrecognizable that you can't get credit for it.

Grammar. Ideally, your answer will be written out in clear, correct, full sentences. But if you run out of time or have difficulties with grammar, it is still better that you put important details on the page than to leave them out. If you're becoming tangled in grammar, write down what you know in list form. Since the connections between concepts (what caused or resulted from what, what was done by whom, etc.) are essential to showing your understanding, this may not be enough for full credit, but it is still better than nothing.

4.10. In-Class Exams: Strategizing

Even the best-prepared student should think through how to work efficiently. Students who are not completely prepared need to make the most of what they do know. If your exam is taken in class under timed conditions with no cheat sheet, you will need to prepare your answers (at least to the point of having revised lists that define and explain the significance of each term) and memorize enough to recreate your answers in class. Focus on knowing the facts, their connections, and their significance, not on being able to recreate exact sentences from your draft. If you have worked thoughtfully and thoroughly, you may find you can already do this, but reading over your draft answers before the exam is still advisable. If you are allowed some form of cheat sheet, your revised lists should serve the purpose.

Assuming you can get partial credit, it is worth your time to write as much as possible, even when you don't fully know the answer. These kinds of answers show your instructor what you do know and that you are making an effort. Small amounts of credit can sometimes make the difference between passing and failing.

You don't know the date. If you don't know the exact date, give the closest range that you are sure is accurate. For example, if you can't remember when the stock market crash that brought on the Great Depression took place, you could write "the late 1920s or early '30s." If you don't have any idea of the date, you may still be able to place it relative to other events, such as "Archduke Franz Ferdinand's assassination was part of the lead-up to World War I."

You don't remember names. If you have trouble recalling exact names but have a general idea of what people were doing and why, try to explain it in your own words. For example, while section 4.8 shows an answer that will earn full credit, writing something like "the Underground Railroad was a way that people who were against slavery helped slaves to escape to the North," shows your instructor that you at least understand the concept.

You don't remember other details. If you don't remember specifics about a term but you do know why that concept matters in the course, spend more of your answer explaining its significance, which is the most important part anyway. For example, if you can't remember most of the main characteristics of fascism but can write that it was Germany's side in World War II and was in opposition to communism and the Allies, that might be enough to earn you a point or two.

5

The Response Paper

A "response paper" is a short at-home assignment that requires you to comment on but not analyze a text. If you are asked to make an argument of your own, refer to chapter 6 instead. An assignment described as a "position paper" could refer either to what is called here a response paper or to an analytical essay, depending on how much of the essay is expected to be commentary and how much should summarize the reading.

In most cases, the text you will respond to is a secondary source (a text written by a historian that makes an argument or offers an interpretation about the past). If your assignment involves summarizing a textbook (a straight chronological account of what happened, with little or no argument or interpretation), that is more like preparing for a short-answer exam question (chapter 4). If your assignment involves responding to a primary source (a document, film, or object written or published at the time you are studying) read both this chapter and chapter 9, skipping the parts of each that don't apply.

5.1. What's Your Goal?

The main purpose of a response paper is to demonstrate that you did the reading. So your first goal should be to *select* the most important details from the reading in order to demonstrate that you understood it. This requires thinking and judgment. The other reason it's worth summarizing a reading in your own words is that the process itself helps you to grasp difficult concepts. If it feels hard to convey your understanding without relying on quotations, that's a sign you are working at the right task.

Usually your instructor also wants you to go further than selecting the important details and putting the main ideas into your own words. Implied in the word "response" is that you also comment on what you read. This does not mean whether you liked or didn't like the reading, or agreed or disagreed with it, or found it readable. Instead your instructor wants you to show how you think through the text to explore its possible *implications* and *applications*:

- **Implications:** If claims made in this text are true, what else might be true? Does this text contradict other evidence or claims you've discussed in class? What does it add to what you have already learned?
- **Applications:** How could the ideas from this text be applied in other ways? Could the questions, methods, assumptions, or conclusions from this text shed light on other questions your class is discussing?

5.2. Reading Academic History: Secondary Sources

If you've tried reading a scholarly book or article the same way you would approach a terrific new novel of your favorite genre, you've already noticed that the scholarly work doesn't flow in the same way. You may have difficulty focusing, retaining what you read, or getting to the end. Because scholarly works have different purposes than fiction, they should be read differently. Reading these kinds of texts is an active process in which you search, sort, and apply facts and ideas rather than lose yourself in a world. At different points you will browse, skim, or read carefully depending on your needs. As you read you should also be marking up the text itself or making a note of important passages as you encounter them. For any text you will use in an essay, you should also write up separate notes after you finish reading, in what are here called "afternotes."

5.2.1. Find out why you're reading this text

Look at where you are on the syllabus and ask yourself how the assigned text fits into the goals of the course and the topic for this date. Think about the ideas covered recently in class. How does this text connect to those ideas and move them a step forward? In what direction does it take the discussion? To what degree will you need to answer questions about this text, discuss it in class, or use it in assignments? Look it over to get a sense of its length. Is it part of something larger (such as a chapter from a book-length work)? Or does it stand alone (it's an article)?

5.2.2. Look for the main idea

Next, identify the main idea of the text, because everything else about it should be understood in light of that main idea. The main idea in a scholarly work is the question or problem that motivates it and the author's answer or contribution that resolves this question (this is also known as the main claim or thesis statement).

In a scholarly book, you'll usually find the main claim in the introduction or preface. Each chapter may also have an argument of its own—these together add up to the overall main claim of the whole book. In a scholarly article, the main idea will be expressed in the introduction, which can be anything from the first paragraph to the first few paragraphs to the first few pages, but is usually in proportion to the whole article (so a longer article will have a longer introduction). Sometimes the introduction is labeled with a subheading, sometimes it is separated from the body by a blank line, and sometimes the best way to know that the introduction is ending is that you hit a paragraph that begins with some form of the words "I argue that . . ."

In most books and articles, a more fully articulated version of the main argument is also presented in the conclusion. Sometimes this last version of the argument is the most detailed and therefore clearest. In other cases this final articulation of the argument uses terms and evidence that were defined in the body, so it might not be clear to you yet. Take a quick look, therefore, at both the introduction and the conclusion to determine which gives you the clearest sense of the purpose and contribution of this text.

When you find the main thesis stated, don't just double-underline it; think about it. Write it out in your own words—this is the best way to be sure you really understand it. You might have to refer again to the text a few times before being able to restate the thesis accurately, and you might revise it again later when you've read more. Also jot down any questions or doubts that occur to you about whether the claim(s) made here could be true. Then ask yourself in what ways the argument helps to serve the purpose that you identified for the course or your own research project. Jot down a few notes about that, as well.

5.2.3. Look at scope and organization

For a book, look at the table of contents and the beginning and ends of each chapter. For articles and essays, page through for subheadings, blank lines, or asterisks separating sections, and then skim the first sentence of each paragraph to get a sense of what topics are being discussed in each section.

Ask: how did the author limit the material being covered? There is usually a limit to the time period and geographical region involved, often stated right in the title. Did the author provide an outline of what would be covered and where and why (probably in the introduction)? Such outlines are usually easy to spot while skimming because the author may number sections or refer to chapter titles or section headings. This examination should tell you, first, how much of the work is directly relevant to your project or goal; second, whether the author's own goals make sense (did he exclude something that seems relevant? Can you find out why?); and third, how to prioritize what you read next. Jot down some questions, such as "Why didn't the author cover X?" "What is so important about the limiting dates/location?"

5.2.4. Find out what the argument is based on

Now find out what evidence the claims are based on. Skim through the preface, introduction, conclusion, bibliography, and footnotes or endnotes (at the back of the book) to find what kind of sources the author used. Are they documents from archives? Published memoirs, diaries, letters? Is it a new interpretation (new reasoning) using the same evidence as other historians have used? Are the sources in the language of the place being studied, or are they all in English? How many different kinds of sources are there? In many scholarly books, there will be a direct discussion (in the introduction or preface, or at the beginning of the bibliography) of what kinds of sources were used and why.

Ask yourself whether the sources used seem adequate, but also consider (and find in the text, if it's provided) what sources were possible. When dealing with long-past periods, the sources we would want to consult have often been destroyed or were never written in the first place. Historians must work with what has survived. See sections 3.2, 10.4, and 10.7–10.8 on how secondary sources are published and vetted and how to judge their quality and relevance. Take some notes on what you find in this process, and jot down a few more guiding sentences, such as "Something about X sounds confusing so far." "Does X explain the thing we discussed in class yesterday?"

5.2.5. Take a breath and read

Thinking about what you've discovered so far and how it relates to what is going on in class should tell you what parts of the rest of the text you should read first (there's no obligation to read in order even now, though that often will be a sensible route). Most importantly, knowing your goal will tell you what you're looking for as you read.

The most difficult thing about reading history is the sheer volume of details and how to decide which ones are the most important. The process of active reading and note-taking will teach you—with practice—to figure out which details are critical and which simply fill out a story that needs to be read but not studied. The questions and notes you've written so far are your guide. Anything you read that answers a question is worth writing down (ideally, write it out in your own words in answer to the question you already composed, but at a minimum, annotate it on the main text). Now that you understand your goals for your course and the author's goals for this text, you should recognize the most important passages when you see them. You can also rely on the typographical signs and cue words and phrases listed in section 5.3.

As a rule of thumb, the argument always provides the backbone to any scholarly text, informing how it is organized and what is included. To understand the argument fully, you need to know the reasoning and evidence it's based on. To judge those fairly, look for qualifications or counterarguments and pay attention to how key terms are defined. What remains after you have identified all these key components of the text is probably background information or description that is not as important to recall later. Depending on how closely you need to use the text, these passages may be skimmed.

5.3. Reading: Annotating Your Text

Annotating a text means marking it up as you read. Annotating helps you to read more actively and to engage more parts of your brain for better recall. The marks you leave can help you navigate back to important passages when you study or write about the text later.

Annotations are personal; develop a system that feels natural to you and that you can remember easily. Annotations work best when done on a physical book, not electronically, but annotating on a device is better than nothing. Never put permanent marks on a library book. Instead use sticky notes to mark passages and remove them when you return the book. If you take notes on separate paper while reading, be sure to indicate for each note what text you're working on and what passage you're referring to (with a paragraph number as well as the page). Leave extra space to add more notes later.

Don't just underline or highlight "whatever seems important." This can lead to wasting time deciding what's important enough to mark or underlining so much that the result isn't useful for navigating later. The following list gives categories of passages worth annotating. Each category should get marked differently. These suggestions are for marking with pencil, but you could instead use a different ink or highlighter color or type of flag for each category, or make equivalent marks on sticky notes instead of on the page.

As you read, look for linguistic or typographical cues to help you identify passages that should be marked up, such as a phrase like "I argue that . . ."

indicating that the author's main contribution is being stated, or a numbered list that clarifies the structure of an argument or definition. Examples of these cues are provided.

Thesis statement and other claims. Wherever the author makes a statement that a reasonable person could disagree with, he is making a claim. These are the author's original contributions and are the most important key to understanding the text. The main, or most important, claim is also called the thesis statement. **Mark: double underline. Cues:**

I argue that	I suggest
This research shows	It would be fair to conclude that
My aim is	In my view
Therefore we can conclude	The most important factor is
In sum	Yet/however/rather
In conclusion	On the contrary

Points of evidence and reasoning. Often the evidence and reasoning that support a claim are discussed throughout a paragraph or even over several pages. **Mark: put a dot in the margin at the beginning of each new point of evidence or explanation of a claim. Cues:**

This is illustrated by	X shows
We know this because	X explains

Statements flagged as important. When an author uses phrases such as "most importantly," those are obviously passages worthy of special attention. **Mark: underline. Cues:**

Significantly	One of the most important reasons
It bears emphasizing that	Most of all

Definitions of key terms. When authors provide their own or another scholar's definition of a term, that term is probably crucial to understanding the argument. **Mark: circle the term, underline the definition. Cues:**

For the purpose of this study, I define X as	As [author] defines it, X refers to
X is understood here to include	Following [author], X includes

Numbered lists. Sometimes an author will use numerals or spelled-out numbers ("first, . . . second, . . .") to clarify and separate a list of several points. Points emphasized in this way are usually crucial. **Mark:** put numerals in the margin alongside the author's list, to make the list more visible. **Cues:**

The first reason . . . the second . . .   (1) . . . (2) . . . (3) . . .

Qualifications and hedges. When authors limit how broadly their claims apply or qualify them as true in certain circumstances but not others, this information is essential for you to evaluate how convincing the argument is. **Mark:** put large parentheses around a phrase or in the margins on either side of a relevant passage. **Cues:**

Of course, in some cases   However, sometimes
Usually . . . but . . .   Exceptions include

Other people's arguments. When authors summarize another scholar's work, they are showing what makes their own argument important (how it answers questions other people care about) and what makes it distinct (how it contradicts or adds to what others have claimed). These other arguments provide context and contrasting points of view that help you put the text in perspective and consider its merits relative to other work. **Mark:** circle the name or title of the work being discussed and put quotes around the passage, in the margin on either side. **Cues:**

As X writes/claims/argues   Compared to X, where
According to X   Contra X's evidence of

Points you find convincing. When you read a passage that makes you think, "Ah! that makes sense" or "Good point!" mark it. These passages represent a list of the points that make the author's case for you and that can be very useful to review later. **Mark:** put a check mark in the margin.

Points you find questionable or confusing. When you read a passage that you can't follow, that isn't plausible, or that just doesn't seem quite right, even if you can't say why, mark it. These marks show where the author's argument may not be solid or not clearly conveyed. These are passages you may go back to later to try to understand better, or to help you explain why you find an argument unconvincing. **Mark:** put a squiggly line under phrases or alongside longer passages vertically in the margin.

Connections between points. Sometimes a question comes to mind that the author answers later on, or you understand a connection between points only after a discussion is complete. Mark these so that you can see at a glance later how points from different parts of the text are connected to each other. **Mark:**

draw arrows if they're on the same page, or write in a page reference in both places, such as "See p. 63" at the first point and "See p. 41" at the second point.

An idea you want to follow up on. When you come across an idea—it may be a passing mention or something more prominent—that you might like to ask about or use as a topic for your own writing assignment, that might be useful as an example or a piece of evidence in an essay you're working on, or that might be important for some other purpose, give it its own mark, even if you also mark it as a claim or other kind of important point. **Mark:** a star in the margin, or your initials.

Questions. Sometimes you come across a question you need to follow up on by asking your instructor about it or looking it up in another text, or a question the author poses that you might want to think about further, especially if it seems likely to end up being asked in class or on an assignment. **Mark:** a question mark or letter "Q" in the margin.

Other reactions. It can also be helpful to mark your reactions to a text with emoticons, exclamation points, or any other marks that seem apt. These help you to engage with the text, and when you read over it later, they provide a record of how the text struck you that can trigger your memory of other details.

5.4. Afternotes for a Secondary Source

After you finish reading a scholarly text that you intend to use in your writing, pull together the most important information from it into one organized place. This may mean going through your annotations and paraphrasing the key points on a separate sheet, or pasting quotes into a computer file, or some combination (paraphrasing is better for your comprehension and memory). You may also do some of it as you read, rather than afterward. If you do this for each reading—or at least each reading that you will write about for an assignment—by the end of the course you should have an excellent set of notes that will prove useful for a final exam or research paper. For this reason, if you're keeping these notes by hand, put them in a binder or notebook so nothing gets lost. If you're doing it electronically, name the file accurately and back it up.

If you keep these kinds of notes systematically for even one course, you will begin to see scholarly readings in a new way. The structure will start to leap out at you, and you will find and understand key passages more quickly. This skill alone may be one of the most practically useful things you can get from your college experience—remember that many careers requiring a bachelor's or higher degree involve reading large amounts of boring and dense information, often texts that are much worse than you will see in your classes!

Type or write the following prompts into a file or notebook where you will record your afternotes. As you work with the text, insert your notes after each prompt and add page numbers as necessary. Refer to the instructions for each prompt as needed. This is not a worksheet to turn in; it is a tool to help you learn how to navigate and understand complex texts. It's useful only to the degree that you fill it in accurately. Some prompts may not apply with a particular text—in such cases enter "n/a" (for "not applicable") in that space.

- **Citation.** Enter or copy the full bibliographic and note/parenthetical citations in the citation style you are required to use for your course (Chicago/Turabian style is standard in history). You can later copy these into an essay as needed, but it also tells you all the key information about the form of publication you're looking at, so you know what your notes refer to and can consider relevant details like the form or date of publication (see section 5.10.1).
- **Topic.** What is the text about, and how does it relate to the course, the current topics under discussion, and other readings? Why was this reading assigned on this day? How does it add something useful to class discussions? What main question(s) or problem(s) is it trying to resolve?
- **Main claim.** What is the author's contribution? What does this text add, argue, claim, or try to convince the reader of? How does this author interpret evidence differently than other scholars?
- **Evidence.** What kind of evidence are the author's claims based on? Did the author do original research, or is he reinterpreting evidence others have also commented on? What kind of sources are used, how diverse are they, how appropriate are they to the claims being made?
- **Reasoning.** How does the author explain why and how her evidence supports her claims? Include any subclaims here (these are smaller claims that the main claim depends on).
- **Hedges/qualifiers.** In what ways does the author qualify or explain limits to the accuracy or usefulness of the claims made?
- **Counterarguments.** Does the author address any counterarguments by other historians or those the reader might raise? How does the author refute them?
- **Definitions.** Does the author use any specialized terms with definitions, or quote specialized definitions by others? Put those terms and definitions here.
- **Organization.** Note any lists, headings, or signposting or describe the overall organization, such as "three parts: [part 1 topic/claim], [part 2 topic/claim], [part 3 topic/claim]."

- **Other points.** Are there any smaller points, subclaims, or asides that you found interesting or particularly useful to class discussions or your own work, even if they were not necessarily most important for this author?
- **Author.** Is there any notable information about the author that may affect how you understand the text? What discipline and specialization is the author writing in? Is the author associated with any particular school of thought or position, from the information you have?
- **Doubts.** What questions or doubts do you have about what you read? Do you fully follow the argument and are you convinced by it? If not, note any terms, claims, omissions, or reasoning that bothered you.

5.5. Distilling an Argument

As with the short-answer exam question, part of what you need to do in a response paper is to distill, or selectively summarize. In this case, you need to distill the main ideas—usually the argument—from the assigned text. You do not want to simplify or generalize, but rather *select* the right details. The details you need may not be the most important points from the perspective of the text's author. You need whatever points are most relevant to your own purpose as a writer of your essay. Focus on what is most important *for the course you're taking* and for the particular assignment or unit you're working on. A typical distillation of an academic text answers the following questions:

- What is the topic of the text—what is it about?
- What problems or questions does it raise?
- What is the author's solutions or answers to those questions?
- What evidence or reasoning does the author use to support this argument?
- How are the author's claims a response or addition to other people's answers to the same questions?

If you have taken good notes as described in section 5.4, you already have your first draft of a distillation of the text.

What to include, "opinion" or "facts"? The best answer to this question is "neither." You are looking for an argument, which is a serious of claims supported by evidence and reasoning. Evidence may include facts, but not primarily in the everyday sense of facts as names, dates, and events. You will include specifics like that but only as needed to convey the argument.

Similarly, in ordinary speech we think of claims and reasoning as a kind of opinion, but it is more useful here to distinguish between claims that obey the laws of logic and are based on evidence versus personal "opinions" or judgments, such as "I like this" or "This seems important to me." Personal opinions do not belong in any formal academic writing. There is nothing wrong with a personal view; it just can't serve the purposes of scholarship, since it can't answer questions of general interest (that is, your friends and family care about whether you enjoyed a reading, but your enjoyment makes no difference in whether the evidence in the reading supports its claims and therefore reliably answers a question about cause and effect).

Simplifying and generalizing. Part of what you need to accomplish in your response paper is to prove you did the reading, so you don't want to be so vague that it looks like you're guessing at what the text was about. More significantly, academic writing is about conveying complex ideas so they can be fully understood and built on by others; if you simplify or generalize those ideas, you are likely to misrepresent or misunderstand the argument.

The following example shows both simplifying and generalizing:

> Hitler did a lot of terrible things to millions of people, with the support of all Germans.

"A lot of terrible things" is a simple, but also vague, way of describing Hitler's crimes. What kind of crimes were they? All crimes could be described as "terrible" in some sense, so this phrase doesn't allow us to distinguish between Hitler's crimes and, say, those of a professor who is merely arbitrary in the classroom. "All Germans" is so general it's not accurate. Not every single German was actually involved. This writer seems to be trying to use as few words as possible—a worthy goal—but when we simplify we can end up just repeating the same vague and inaccurate statements, compounding the error:

> Hitler did a lot of terrible things to millions of people, with the support of all Germans. It's unprecedented to do these kinds of things to people. So many were affected, some of them Jews and some of them other people, and these were civilians. A lot of other people supported Hitler, for various reasons and it's unclear how many but probably a lot.

Compare this to the following example, which still simplifies what happened, but is at least accurate because it does not generalize about who supported the crimes:

> Hitler murdered 12 million civilians, with the help of the government, police, and military that involved many German citizens, so that to some degree most Germans participated in the murders.

That's better than the first two examples, but it still hides much of the significance of what happened by describing the crimes in vague terms. Contrast it to this example, which is specific, including details that fully explain what happened, how, and by whom:

Hitler's "Final Solution" to the so-called Jewish Problem was to exterminate Jews. He attempted this genocide through a network of death camps that Jews were deported to from 1933 to 1945. The question of how many German citizens participated in, accepted, or supported the Holocaust is difficult to answer, because there were different degrees of participation, and because perpetrators or even just bystanders were likely to deny their connection to these events. But if we include all the people who actively supported the Nazi Party, manned the Gestapo and SS, helped operate the camps, ghettos, and railroad networks, and participated in the propaganda machine that tried to justify the mass murder of Jews to the German population and the world, that is already millions of people.

Notice that when you name specific people, places, and actions and give examples, you have no trouble making the required word count without repetition.

5.6. Responding to a Reading

When you have drafted a full distillation of the most important points in your text, you are still only halfway to a response paper, even if you are approaching your page limit. The most difficult part of a response paper takes less space than your distillation but is critical to the effectiveness of your essay. This part is your "response," your comment on what you read.

For this kind of assignment, you are not expected to explain and support a fully-fledged argument of your own, but you are expected to show that you have thought about what the text says and what it means. To brainstorm a thoughtful response, ask yourself questions about the text as outlined in the bulleted list that follows, while being careful not to confuse superficial or personal reactions with critical questions about the implications and applications of the text, as defined in section 5.1.

A superficial reaction is the first thing that pops into your head—therefore it is by definition not reasoned or supported. There are times when you may be asked for your first reaction in an academic setting—for example, in class discussions, when the professor might ask what people think about an issue in order to contrast these first reactions to what the research shows. Similarly, an opinion poll can tell us how many students found a certain text challenging or readable or painful, which can help instructors think about whether to use it again. Sometimes instructors ask for your reaction just to get you talking, to warm up for more difficult questions to come. These kinds of first reactions don't belong in an essay, though. Saying whether you liked or disliked a text is like announcing that your favorite color is blue.

By "respond" we mean instead to begin the process of thinking critically about the text. This is a first step toward the deeper thinking and analysis you will be asked to do in an exam essay, primary source analysis, or research paper. Thinking critically about a text does not mean finding flaws or being negative. It means asking whether an argument is valid and convincing. An argument can be valid whether you agree with it or not, whether you like it or not, and whether or not it fits what you already believe. The sole criterion for whether an argument is valid is whether its evidence and reasoning are rigorous. If a valid argument also makes you agree with it, then the argument is also convincing.

In addition, we think critically about a text by asking what the implications of the text are and how it might apply in other contexts:

- What is the author's goal, and does the author achieve it?
- Is the goal a reasonable and appropriate one?
- Could the author have been more or less ambitious (taking practical restraints into account)? Would that have brought more useful results?
- Does the author make the best use of existing evidence?
- Does the argument answer important questions?
- What related important questions are not asked or answered?
- If counterarguments were raised in the text, did the author respond to them fully?
- How did the author choose evidence? What other kinds of evidence might have been used?
- Does the evidence used show what it's supposed to show?
- Does the author fully explain the connections between evidence and claims?
- Do those explanations make sense and account for all the information we have?
- Can you think of exceptions where the author's claims wouldn't hold? Does the author consider such exceptions?
- If this argument holds, what else would be true?
- If this argument holds, how would it alter or add to what we knew before?

If these questions don't lead you toward any particular observations or doubts, try the following exercises, which help you amplify your first reactions into fuller and more critical responses.

Exercise 1. Write a sentence that describes your reaction to the whole text or to a particular passage, using the most closely matching template from the left column. Then revise that sentence to fill in the blanks in the sentence from the same line in the right column.

I liked / didn't like X	X seems (un)convincing because Y
X makes sense	X reminds me of Y, which suggests Z
X is interesting	X is interesting because Y
I (dis)agree with X	X doesn't make sense because Y
I'm confused by X	If we compare/contrast X with Y, we see Z

Exercise 2. Another way to move from a simplistic reaction to deeper thinking is to identify a passage that you can tell is important but don't know what to make of. You can write, "This passage is . . ." followed by one of the words from the list that follows, choosing the one that fits best. Then add "because . . ." and brainstorm what should follow. Search the text for clues about how the author gave you this impression: from the use of particular words or examples to the way the text was organized or what was left out. Explaining how the author's choices made you see the text in this way is how you explain and support your critical response.

convincing	thorough	strange
unconvincing	unsatisfactory	paradoxical
balanced	satisfying	contradictory
one-sided	provocative	interesting
incomplete	suggestive	surprising

5.7. Revising: Structure and Weight

Consider how much of your essay should be distillation of the text and how much should be focused on your response. Your professor may provide specific instructions, but if not, be guided by your assignment goals: in most response papers, the first goal is to show that you thoroughly understood the reading, so that will take the most weight, and therefore space, in your essay. Often a proportion of roughly two-thirds to three-quarters of the essay should be distillation, depending on how complicated the original text is, with the remainder taken up by your response.

Next consider whether you will include your response to the text as a separate section, or weave it in by explaining a point the author makes and then adding a comment of your own, point by point throughout. Unless you are told otherwise, this decision is usually up to you. Which structure works better depends on the nature of your response: do you have many small observations, or one big comment or criticism?

5.7.1. Introductions

Response papers are not a good place to apply the five-paragraph model of essay structure that you may have learned in high school, since it is not an argument-driven essay. Your first goal is to distill a text, so lead with what the text is about. A response paper is short, so that also tells you that your introduction should be short, proportionately less than the one-fifth of the total length assumed in the five-paragraph essay model. Ideally, aim for an introduction of only one or two sentences, maximizing space for the substance that counts toward your grade.

A short introduction of this kind should state, as specifically as possible, the who, what, where, when that your essay is about. This allows you to get straight into explaining how the author accomplishes her goals (your distillation) by the second or third sentence. The introduction of any essay makes a first impression on the reader, and the first impression you want to make on an academic reader is that you are knowledgeable and in control of your essay: you have something valuable and interesting to say, and you will not waste your reader's time with anything else. Avoid the labored attempt at a "hook" that is supposed to connect to broader issues but really just makes generalizations or unsupported claims:

> Throughout history, there have been oppressed people, a lot of them women.
>
> Inevitably, even bad governments are supported by some people.
>
> People are very flawed, and sometimes they support even policies that later become seen as evil, like slavery.
>
> Mao's regime was one of the most ruthless regimes there ever was.
>
> When it comes to the topic of Progressivism, we can all agree that in the US it ran from about 1890 to 1920.

Compare these more effective examples of first sentences:

> In *Medical Bondage*, Deirdre Cooper-Owens argues that . . .
>
> Sarah Covington's account of religious dissidents suggests . . .
>
> As historian Amy Chazkel demonstrates, Brazil's underground lottery is a surprising way to understand how . . .

These sentences are accurate and specific and provide the information the reader needs. In your draft introduction, hunt down and eliminate adjectives and adverbs, universal statements like "throughout history," "always," or "inevitably," and generalizations where you refer to large groups of people as if they are all the same.

Conclusions provide a "takeaway" thought that summarizes broader implications and connects the text to new questions and future research. For that reason, the conclusion is often a good position for your response, where you explain the implications and applications of your text. This may consist of the bulk of the response portion of the essay, or it may pull together the commentary that you spread throughout the paper as you distilled the text. Often an effective conclusion for an essay of this kind will consist of at least one dense paragraph. Don't then repeat and generalize that information in another paragraph in imitation of the five-paragraph model—your specific discussion of implications and applications already fulfills the purpose of a conclusion.

5.8. Revising: Showing, Not Telling

The best way to make sure your essay demonstrates your thoughtful and thorough reading of the source text is to point back to its details frequently. Another way to describe this is to say your essay (like all good writing) should do more "showing" than "telling": instead of telling your readers what to think about the text, you show them what's there with examples.

Compare this general summary of what an author does

> Historian Satadru Sen explains the many ways criminals responded to their punishments

to this revision where each action and actor is named and examples are provided:

> Historian Satadru Sen explains that Indian criminals of the Andaman Islands penal colony responded to punishments imposed by the colonial state in several ways, such as X, Y, and Z.

If necessary, you might put some examples in parentheses, to make sure you are including all relevant details without derailing your main point, as in this example:

> While Sen describes many responses (such as X and Y), one of his examples is particularly revealing: Z.

5.9. Revising: Handling Quotes and Paraphrases

"Pointing frequently to the text" does not mean that you fill your essay with quotes linked only by a thin string of connecting words of your own. Your essay needs to demonstrate your own thinking, but closely tied to the source text. How? By paraphrasing key passages (always with a citation to the page where the original appears). Putting the author's ideas into your own words shows your comprehension because you can't paraphrase accurately unless you understand the ideas.

The only time you should need to quote directly is when the author uses a word or phrase in an unusual or particularly expressive way to make an important point. In that case, quote only the keywords and explain why the passage is important or how it fits into the larger point in your own words. For example:

> Paulicelli argues that popular film images of strong female bodies suggested "a dynamic vision of women" (81) that was important because this marks the first time Italian women were publicly encouraged to be active in a sphere beyond the kitchen and childcare.

Contrast that example with the next, where the author added a full quote that merely repeats what is already paraphrased:

> So football was more of a leisure sport for which the masses had little time. As stated in Martin, "Among the working and peasant classes there was simply not the time, money or will to consider the pursuit of any sporting activity, as the majority concentrated their energy on merely staying alive" (24).

In the next example quotes are strung together so excessively that the reader can't know whether the author understood the content:

> A "return to parliamentary democracy was for most people almost unthinkable. Liberalism was regarded as weakness," in other words as "having failed in Italy and to go back to it would mean reverting to a political system that is . . . historically and culturally unsuited to the needs to the country" (xviii).

These passages could be paraphrased instead, with perhaps a word or two quoted to show how emphatic the language was in the original:

> Most Italians saw parliamentary democracy as having failed so completely that it became "unthinkable" and was even seen as inherently weak and "unsuited" to Italy's needs (xviii).

Citing and attributing quotes and paraphrases. Whether you are quoting or paraphrasing, whenever you refer to a source, you must both cite it and attribute it to its author. Citing tells the reader what kind of source you have and where it can be found; attributing the source tells the reader who contributed the thought you're sharing and sometimes other explanations of why it is relevant to your essay.

In a response paper based on one text, provide a full citation the first time you refer to the source. Subsequent citations can just be to the appropriate page numbers. Leaving out a citation, even unintentionally, is plagiarism. While Chicago-style citations (footnotes) are customary in history, MLA-style in-text citations (in parentheses) may be preferable for a short essay that refers to only one or two sources. Consult with your instructor and see section 10.10.

In addition to citing every source so readers know where it came from, within the main text of the essay you also need to tell readers what they're looking at so they can understand how it fits into your essay. This is an attribution. The most common kind of attribution is the simple "Historian Grace Davie argues . . ." Consider the following examples where an attribution was omitted:

> Abigail Adams is an example of the rule, "Well-behaved women seldom make history."[1]
>
> "Peasant culture is generally misunderstood."[1] In this paper I will argue that the diary of a French peasant can show . . .

We don't know who wrote the quoted statements. We could refer to the notes to find out, but this makes for an awkward reading experience. See how much smoother it is to read the following revisions, which not only attribute the quotes to their authors, but give us some context to explain why the quotes are meaningful, relevant, or interesting:

> Abigail Adams is arguably an exception to the rule expressed by historian Laurel Thatcher Ulrich that "well-behaved women seldom make history."
>
> "Peasant culture is generally misunderstood," wrote the author of *The Peasants of Europe*. In this paper I will argue that the diary of a French peasant can show . . .

A common problem when quoting the same author throughout an essay, as we do in a response paper, is to use vague or unclear attributions:

> Also it says, "Both speakers also made significant contributions to . . ."
>
> They say that "history doesn't repeat itself, but sometimes it rhymes."

If you have to refer to the same author and text frequently, you can vary the way you attribute these references while still being specific:

> In Translating America ...
> Conolly-Smith's argument ...
> The author ...
> Conolly-Smith ...
> The book ...

When you refer to a title in your essay you must format it in italics for books, in quotation marks for articles, chapters, and essays, and in title case either way (see appendix 1, section A1.6). This keeps your title from getting confused with the rest of your sentence and tells your reader whether you're discussing a long or short work. Compare the following examples, where only the second sentence makes clear that a book is being discussed:

> In this noble house the importance of lineage was that ...
>
> In *This Noble House* the importance of lineage was that ...

5.10. Revising: Word Choice

Students are often concerned that their essays will sound too simple, but efforts to avoid this problem can lead to more serious errors, such as misused words and unnecessarily complicated sentences. Since the ideas we discuss in academic writing are by definition new and abstract, we need our words to be as plain as possible. At the same time, making meaningful distinctions between new and abstract ideas requires that we use words so specific that they may seem "formal" or "fancy" compared to the way we talk. Use the most accurate and specific words that convey your ideas rather than aiming to sound plain or fancy or formal or academic. For example, the following passage may seem too simple:

> Theodore Roosevelt was an important American president who introduced many new policies. These policies were in different areas, like domestic and foreign. Most of his policies had a bigger impact on other things.

But the real problem is not that the words are plain and the sentences short. It's that it's vague: what "new policies"? Which were domestic policies, which were foreign? What was their impact on what? The most important information has been left out. The next example could also be described as "too simple," but in a different way from the first:

Theodore Roosevelt was a US president. He was known for "square deal" policies. Some examples of square deal policies are trust-busting, regulation of food, and support for labor. The Roosevelt Corollary encouraged intervention abroad.

This example is more useful than the first because it conveys specific details, yet it still feels "simple" because the sentences are so short. When every sentence is this short, the author is missing an opportunity to explain how some ideas are linked to others. Now look at an example that could be described as too fancy:

Theodore Roosevelt's eminent contributions to American presidential legend, perhaps best encapsulated by his innovation of the concept "square deal" as applied to domestic policy, are widely recognized as inclusive of trust-busting, the regulation of safety in food and drug production, negotiation of labor conditions largely in favor of workers without simultaneously alienating the ownership or bourgeois class, as well as his conservation of federal lands through establishment of the so-called "national parks" system. Roosevelt can also be creditably noted for his Roosevelt Corollary to the Monroe Doctrine justifying interventionism of American interests into matters foreign, such as his "big stick" diplomatic adventures in South America. Other sources of Roosevelt's justified place in the pantheon of American presidents include his Nobel Peace Prize, development of the Panama Canal, heroism in the Spanish-American War and anti-corruption crusadership in New York.

This passage contains more information than the first example, and unlike the second it does mostly explain how the details are connected to each other. In this case the words are all used correctly and grammatical rules are followed. But the text is still hard to follow because the words and sentence structures are more complicated than they need to be. Compare it to the second example in section 4.4, which contains most of the same content but is much easier to follow. Finally, consider this example, which is neither too simple nor too complicated, but is still unsatisfactory for the reader:

Interestingly, Theodore Roosevelt was best known for his admirably fair-minded "square deal" policies, which of course included trust-busting, food regulation, labor negotiation and land conservation. Roosevelt was more ruthless when it came to foreign policy, where he's justly rather infamous for adventurism abroad. Obviously this has an impact on his legacy, though it did help to establish America's reputation as a great power.

The words used here are plain but specific, and the sentences are not needlessly complex. However, it still feels fuzzy because it contains a lot of commentary ("interestingly," "admirably," "of course," "ruthless," "justly," "obviously"). The author is adding filler that attempts to lead the reader to a particular way of interpreting the facts. Some writers do this because it's how they talk, or because they are trying to sound relatable or forceful, but since this kind of commentary undermines the goals of academic writing (by telling the reader what to think), it can be distracting or annoying for the reader.

With your goal in mind of choosing the simplest words and sentence structures that still accurately convey the complexity of your ideas—and deleting anything else—your first tool should be a dictionary. A thesaurus may help you to find a more accurate word than the first that comes to mind, but never use a thesaurus just to add variety. And do not rely on the dictionary and thesaurus built into your word processor—these are simplified. You will get better information by consulting a separate dictionary, whether online or in hard copy. The *Oxford English Dictionary* will give you the most information of all.

Dictionaries and thesauruses can only help you with standard definitions, not the specialized definitions often used in academic writing to capture new ideas or nuances of meaning that are specific to a particular area of study. Some of the most common specialized terms used in history are defined later in this chapter or elsewhere in this book (see section 8.5 and consult the index). You should also notice such terms in your readings and lectures and take notes on their meaning(s). When in doubt about how a word is being used in a specialized way, ask your instructor.

The following sections define words that are most commonly misused by students as well as words that are often used by historians and academics. These small distinctions of meaning are important; when you use the words inaccurately your text becomes harder to understand. When you use words precisely your text becomes powerful. Being able to describe what you are reading, distinguish between related concepts, and articulate the nuances of an argument in precise and accurate language is essential to distilling well.

5.10.1. Types of Publications

What kind of source are you distilling? An academic **journal** (with a title in italics) like the *Journal of Modern History* is equivalent to a popular magazine or newspaper like *Teen Vogue* or the *Washington Post*. Each of these is a **periodical**: a publication that comes out with new issues on a regular ("periodic") basis. Within each issue of each journal there are several **articles** (with titles in quotation marks), each by a different author. So it's not accurate to write, "In Joan Scott's journal 'Gender: A Useful Category of Analysis'" because that's an article she wrote that was published alongside several other articles within the fifth issue of the journal titled *American Historical Review*. This information is provided, if you know how to look, in the full citation for any source (see section 10.10 for more on citations):

> Scott, Joan W. "Gender: A Useful Category of Historical Analysis." *American Historical Review* 91, no. 5 (December 1986): 1053–1075.

The citation tells us that we are looking at an article because it has a title in quotation marks, and we know that the larger publication it is part of is a periodical because there is an issue number and a month as well as a year (book citations have only the year of publication).

Another confusing case is when we read an **essay** that was published alongside other essays in a book, called an **essay collection**. Essays are often similar to articles in length but are published in a book, not in a periodical, and the book has an editor (or several) who selects and edits the essays to be included. See the difference in this citation:

> Engel, Barbara Alpern. "Marital Choice and Marital Crisis in Late Imperial Russia." In *Domestic Tensions, National Anxieties: Global Perspectives on Marriage, Crisis, and Nation*, edited by Kristin Celello and Hanan Kholoussy, 16–36. New York: Oxford University Press, 2016.

Still another case is when we cite just one **chapter** from a book that was written entirely by one author. In such cases there is only one author for both the chapter and the book, but we cite the chapter title in quotation marks and the book title in italics. Contrast the following citation to the one above:

> Richardson, Kristina. "Literary Networks in Mamluk Cairo." In *Difference and Disability in the Medieval Islamic World: Blighted Bodies*, 36–71. Edinburgh: Edinburgh University Press, 2012.

The only case where you will see both italics and quotation marks in a title is when there is a quote embedded in the title, as in the following book:

> Carlson, Maria. *"No Religion Higher Than Truth": A History of the Theosophical Movement in Russia, 1875–1922*. Princeton, NJ: Princeton University Press, 1993.

A citation to a whole book does not have page numbers, since it's referring to a whole publication, not a section within it, and there is a colon, not a comma, separating the main title from the subtitle.

Use the clues given to you in a citation as well as other identifying information on the text itself or in library database records to tell you whether you are referring to an "article," an "essay," a "chapter," or a "book." A less commonly used term, **volume**, refers to a single physical book, usually from a series or multi-volume title, each numbered as "volume 1, "volume 2," etc. "Volume" can also sometimes refer to units of periodicals, often with each physical publication called an "issue" and all the issues for one calendar year numbered as a "volume." See also section 10.3 on how to navigate a physical source to find crucial identifying information.

You can also refer to any written work as a **text**. Any text based on research can also be called a **study**, while texts that only explain or assess other people's research can be referred to as a **review**. Confusingly, the term "review" is also used for publications in a second sense, as in an overview of a field rather than an assessment of one or a few works. We see this in common journal titles like the *American Review of China Studies*.

You can refer to a text that is part of some larger publication as a **piece** and a brief part of a text (a few sentences or paragraphs) is a **passage**, while a **section** is a separate portion of text smaller than a chapter (such as the introduction). **Excerpt** usually refers to a portion longer than a passage but not a separate section.

A "**monograph**" is a book-length study written by one person (as opposed to a collection of essays). Monographs and essay collections can also be referred to simply as a "book." But a **novel** is a book-length work of fiction and can *never* be accurately used to describe a work of scholarship. **Literature** usually refers to artistic fiction, but in a scholarly context the same word is used to refer to all existing scholarship on some topic, as in "the literature on Alexander Hamilton is well developed."

Image is a general term for any pictorial representation, parallel to "text." There are many kinds of images, with different names based on the technology that produced them, including **photographs** (invented only in the early nineteenth century), **daguerreotypes** (the technology that came just before photography), **engravings** (made by carving a picture into a block and then using the block to print many copies, as was common in books and newspapers before photography), **drawings, paintings, murals, mosaics,** and others. When you encounter an image among your sources, its type should be named somewhere in the accompanying information. Refer to it by its specific type or as an "image," but be careful not to call an image created with pencils in 1700 a "photograph" or a pen-and-ink drawing a "painting."

5.10.2. Government Terms

Distilling a historical argument often involves government terms with precise technical meanings that differ from common usage. A modern **country** has its own independent government, defined by borders, and the term includes both the government and the people living there. In ordinary speech we use this word interchangeably with **nation**, but technically "nation" refers to a self-identified ethnic group that may or may not be the same as the borders of a country (for example, the "German nation" has been used to include German-speakers in various countries). **State** technically refers only to the government and is therefore a narrower term than "country." A **nation-state** is a country where the government (state) and nation (a more or less closely defined ethnic identity) are the same, as in France. It is in opposition to a **multi-ethnic state** (such as the United States). **Government** and "state" are terms that include the leaders, offices, institutions, and bureaucrats who make and enforce policies and laws. Policies that affect matters within a country are **domestic**, but matters between countries are **foreign policy**, and relationships between countries are **international relations**. There are many layers of government:

- **Head of state.** The figurehead who represents a country, whether a monarch (king, queen, emperor, tsar, etc.) or president. Some systems separate the figurehead, for example, a constitutional monarch, from a "head of government" like a prime minister. Each country has its own name for the most responsible single person in a government, and how powerful that person is also varies (in some countries dominated by one political party, the head of that party may be more powerful than the nominal head of state).
- **Executive bodies.** The most central and powerful body of government, usually subdivided, as into ministries or a cabinet, each with a different area of responsibility.
- **Legislative, representative, or advisory bodies.** The US Congress, the British Parliament, the Russian Duma, the Norwegian Storting, or similar bodies in other countries that debate and sometimes propose laws. Use the name specific to the country you're discussing.
- **Law enforcement bodies.** Judicial entities like courts and judges that decide matters of criminal guilt, issue sentences, and adjudicate civil disputes; and police, who investigate crimes and enforce laws.
- **Military.** An army, navy, air force (since the twentieth century), and a few other smaller branches that together make up a country's military force. Military decisions are made by officers, described collectively as an "officer corps," with the top officers called generals and (in the navy) admirals; the best-trained officers belong to a "general staff" or equivalent. "Rank and

file" soldiers are not officers; sergeants, corporals, and others are in an in-between category usually known as "non-commissioned officers," or NCOs. "Conscripts" are soldiers who were required to join or coerced into entering the military, usually temporarily. "Mercenaries" are soldiers motivated by monetary compensation rather than political or ideological loyalties. The area where battles take place during a war is a "front," while decisions are made at "headquarters." Decisions are divided by level: the smallest scale, on-the-ground decisions are "tactical," while larger-scale planning to win a war is "strategy." Similarly, military units are arranged in a hierarchy, varying by country but usually roughly descending from armies and army groups to corps, divisions, brigades, regiments and battalions, and then platoons and companies. The overall military policy of a state is known as "grand strategy." Unofficial or ad hoc military bodies can be called "militia" or "paramilitary" organizations.

In addition to these basic government bodies, laws and policies are usually carried out by some form of bureaucratic apparatus, which can be made up of many subdivided institutions, offices, or departments with names specific to each country. Outside of official government bodies there are other political entities like parties, factions, activist groups, lobbyists, donor groups, and non-governmental organizations that often work with a government or attempt to influence policy but are not formally part of the government.

Forms of government are ways that power can be distributed through a society, such as the following:

- **Autocracy, authoritarian regime, dictatorship.** Most of the power is in the hands of one person.
- **Oligarchy.** Power is shared by a small group of people who run the government cooperatively or in competition with each other.
- **Republic, democracy, representative government.** The population, or some part of the population, elects officials to represent them or votes directly on policies.

Similar-sounding terms are used to describe the way a government functions but do not define its form. Several of these could apply to a democracy, oligarchy, or a dictatorship depending on how it operates:

- **Autarky.** The government is self-sufficient, not needing to trade internationally to meet basic needs.
- **Kleptocracy.** The government is so corrupt that it serves more to siphon money to its leaders than to keep order.

- **Theocracy.** Power is held by a religious organization, or laws and policy are religious in nature and goals (religious bodies hold formal power or dominate those who do).
- **Military dictatorship ("junta").** Power is held by military officers, who operate the country with military hierarchy and discipline (this is not the same as a head of state who happens to have a high military rank but governs according to civilian standards).
- **Plutocracy.** Power is held by a small group of the most wealthy (whether they inherited it, seized it, or merely dominate electoral results).
- **Kakistocracy.** The least able and least qualified get the most power (this describes government dysfunction rather than a way of functioning).
- **Tyranny.** Though often used as a synonym for dictatorship, this term describes a government in which the power, concentrated in one person's hands, is exercised in unjust or cruel ways.
- **Monarchy.** The ruler usually inherits that position and holds it for life, passing it on to heirs.
- **Feudalism.** The legal and military system is organized by an exchange of landholding for service obligations (no longer accepted as an accurate description of medieval Europe).
- **Political spectrum ("right and left").** This term comes from the French Revolution, and traditionally describes how European politics developed from 1789 to the present, though it is adapted for other contexts. In the wake of the overthrow of the French monarchy, those sitting on the left in the National Assembly pushed for more change, while those sitting on the right held back changes.
- **Reaction ("far right").** Reactionaries were nineteenth-century Europeans who opposed the French Revolution and wanted to restore or defend the old order of authoritarian monarchies and aristocratic privilege. The word is sometimes used to refer to any backward-looking or extremely conservative political position.
- **Fascism ("far right").** In twentieth-century Europe, the farthest "right" position viewed the nation as more important than individual rights, and their own nation as superior to all others. Fascist regimes were characterized by xenophobia, violence, militarism, and political repression.
- **Conservatism ("right").** As a general term, it refers to a political position that is skeptical of change, especially expanding individual liberties.
- **Liberalism ("center" or near "left").** This position favors individual political rights and liberties, aiming primarily to defend existing rights (center) or to expand them (left).
- **Socialism ("far left").** Socialists favor expanding economic rights more than political rights, aiming for economic equality.

- **Communism ("far left").** Some socialist countries have chosen this label based on their stated goal of achieving a Marxist, utopian communism of perfect economic equality that makes government unnecessary. It is also used to describe the realities of those countries, which often contrasted markedly with the stated goal.
- **Anarchism ("far left").** A political position that opposes government, preferring voluntary, local self-organization without hierarchy. It varies between individualist and collectivist persuasions.
- **Totalitarianism.** Used to compare communist regimes to fascism in the wake of World War II and during the Cold War, this term posits a modern, industrialized authoritarianism that has or attempts to have "total" control over a country's population through propaganda, surveillance, terror, and secret police coercion. The idea of "total" control, however, tends to obscure popular participation that was present in both kinds of regimes, as well as the extreme ideological differences between them. Propaganda and surveillance are broader phenomena common to most modern industrialized states.
- **Empire.** A government that encompasses several smaller entities with some degree of independent administration. There is often a "center," referring to either a capital city or dominant territory that holds power over "peripheries," a name for the other component parts of the empire that do not control the overall administration. Territories that are entirely subordinated to the central power are "colonies." "Colonialism" and "imperialism" refer to the practice of European powers subordinating other territories and extracting resources, settling their own citizens, and imposing their own political administrations. Empires are often distinguished as either "contiguous" or "land" empires, where center and periphery are geographically neighboring, and "overseas" empires, in which a central authority asserts control over a distant territory.

The various terms related to monarchies and nobility can be particularly confusing since they are often misused in popular culture:

- **Royalty:** people who rule by right of heredity. Usually all members of a ruling family, even if they do not personally rule, are considered "royal." The title of a ruler varies from one state to another, including not just kings and emperors but also in some cases princes or dukes (or princesses or duchesses) if they hold independent power over a region (they are "regnant"). To add to the confusion, in some cases monarchs are appointed or elected (especially when no direct heir survives) but still rule for life, and it is expected that their heirs will succeed them. **Succession** refers to the line of rulers, usually passed from father to son. **Accession** refers to the moment a new monarch succeeds to the throne. A **coronation** is the ceremony that marks this accession and usually confers a religious blessing.

- **Aristocracy/nobles:** people who hold hereditary privileges, often including titles and inherited land, but who do not rule (this makes them different from royalty). Aristocratic titles vary by country. Noble privileges often include exemptions from taxes as well as rights to revenue from land, but nobles are often also required to serve their rulers in some ways, usually in government or military leadership roles.
- **Gentry:** sometimes used interchangeably with "nobles" in English, in more precise usage "gentry" are lesser nobility who live off of revenue from large landholdings and may serve the government in local offices but who do not have significant roles in the national government or military. They are less influential and usually less wealthy than aristocrats. "Nobles" can refer to both aristocrats and gentry together.
- **Court and courtiers:** when used in reference to monarchies rather than a justice system, "court" refers to the nobles who personally serve monarchs at their residence and are themselves called "courtiers" (distinguishing them from other nobles who are not "at court"). These people tend to have both governmental power and great social influence. A royal "court" is not specific to a building or location, but instead refers to wherever the monarch is living at a given time.
- **Rank/title:** rank is a person's place in a formal hierarchy. In some times and places the highest ranks in a hierarchy came with titles, which are used socially to identify people in parallel with their names. Royal titles (**king/ queen, emperor/empress**, etc.) are a marker of independent power, but most titles are merely social markers of noble status and privilege. British titles (in order from highest to lowest) are **duke/duchess, marquess** or **marquis/marchioness, earl/countess, viscount/viscountess, baron/baroness, baronet/baronetess, knight/dame**. The rules of title usage and address, as well as the considerable difference in usage between countries, should be looked up in a suitable reference work if needed.

When we refer to the way someone held power over a certain period, we can talk about the time "under" that leader, but this form isn't used to describe democracies or republics. The period during which a person or set of people are in power has a different name depending on the kind of office involved:

- **Monarchs** have **reigns** and **rule over** a certain people or time. Long periods marked by the influence of a particular ruler are often named after them, as in "Victorian England" or "Petrine Russia."

- **Dictators** have a **regime** and their time as head of state will often be named after them, as it is closely associated with their personality, such as "Maoism" or "Franco's Spain."
- **Presidents, prime ministers,** and other elected heads of state have a **presidency** or **administration,** or we can refer to their **term** or time **in office.**

Still other terms describe the condition or tendencies of a given country at a given time, such as the following:

- **Hegemony/hegemonic.** To have hegemony is to dominate over another country. A hegemonic power is a country that dominates its region or the world. **Great powers** traditionally refers to a group of the most dominant powers in Europe during the modern period.
- **Revolution.** A change in the form of government, not just a shift in which people or parties hold power or what policies are formed. When a country shifts from democracy to dictatorship or from a monarchy to a representative government, it undergoes a revolution. We also speak of "revolutionary" changes as fundamental changes in how power is distributed. In a **coup d'état** or **putsch** the head of state is overthrown and replaced by someone else, but this does not necessarily mean the form of government is changed.
- **Radical.** Striving for extreme changes
- **Reform.** Changes within a consistent form of government
- **Irredentist.** A country that aims to restore previous borders or reclaim territory that was previously lost or ceded
- **Imperialist/expansionist.** A country that has ambitions to take other territories under its own control
- **Militarist.** A political system that is dominated by its military leadership or military goals

The following terms describe ways a government acts on people (see also section 5.10.7 for a list of verbs that are frequently used to describe government actions):

- **Repression/oppression/suppression.** Literally to hold someone back from something (to repress), to burden someone with something (to oppress), or to put down or prevent something from appearing (to suppress). When used in a political context, these terms describe extreme situations where people are prevented by their government from carrying out an ordinary life, as when they are prevented from earning a living or subjected to arrest, interrogation, or imprisonment for "political crimes," meaning disagreeing with their government.

- **Liberation.** To give rights, powers, or opportunities to people
- **Representation.** To give people a say in how government is run and what policies or laws are adopted

5.10.3. Social Categories

The following terms are associated with people and groups and how they relate to each other or express themselves. It's important not only to use these words correctly in your essays, but also to think about the substantive differences in meaning between them when you consider the impact of causes and effects over time: a change in rhetoric might be more or less significant than a change in policy, but they are very different things.

- **Ideas.** Can be traced back to original thinkers, may or may not be acted on
- **Policy.** What was actually proposed or done by a government
- **Rhetoric.** The ways ideas are described or what people say (in contrast to what they do)
- **Reception.** How audiences understand or interpret what they hear/read
- **Analysis:** How scholars describe and differentiate actions in order to understand or explain them

Distinguish between the following areas of collective activity:

- **Political.** How power is distributed in a government
- **Economic.** How money is distributed in a society
- **Social.** How people relate to each other
- **Ideological.** A society's ideas about what is most important
- **Cultural.** Traditions, habits, assumptions, and values that are held in common by a group
- **Institutional.** Organizations such as schools, community groups, clubs, churches, and so on

Use the following terms to indicate on what scale a phenomenon affects people:

- **Local.** Affecting only a small geographical area
- **Regional.** Affecting a large geographical region, but not a whole country
- **National.** Affecting a whole country
- **International.** Affecting more than one country
- **Transnational.** Involving movement or interactions across national borders

- **Universal.** Applying to the whole world, and usually throughout time
- **Global.** Involving the whole world, but usually specific to a time period
- **Top-down.** Action that is initiated by leaders (such as laws, edicts, military actions, propaganda, etc.)
- **Bottom-up.** Action that is initiated by ordinary people (such as protests, strikes, mass political movements, cultural movements, etc.)
- **Relative.** Changes or effects that have greater or lesser influence compared to something else
- **Absolute.** A quality that exists independently of other factors, such as something that is entirely new or newly absent, rather than growing or shrinking

Historians distinguish social groups by different categories in different times and places depending on how people described themselves, or using terms developed by a previous analyst because they prove useful. Some of the categories that follow overlap or are only used for particular periods, areas of the world, or types of societies.

- **Slaves.** People who were owned by others, legally treated as property
- **Peasants.** People who worked in agriculture and usually owed some allegiance or dues to others. **Serfs** were peasants who were legally bound to the land they worked, which was owned by others. **Tenant farmers** paid rent to landowners for the right to work land. **Farmers** usually refers to people who work their own land.
- **Laborers/workers/proletariat.** Used from the period of industrialization (mid-eighteenth century) to the present for those doing factory or other manual labor that is not agricultural. Sometimes defined as wage-earners as opposed to salary-earners. **Blue collar** is a parallel term used from the twentieth century. "Proletariat" is a noun; the adjective is "proletarian."
- **Lumpenproletariat/underclass.** A term from Karl Marx, it refers to criminals, homeless or vagabonds, and prostitutes, who were not considered workers in the Marxist sense. Adjectival forms include "classless" and "déclassé."
- **Petit bourgeoisie / lower middle class.** People who may work in shops or offices or in lower management roles who have greater independence than workers but less than upper management or property owners
- **Subalterns.** Collective term for categories of people who do not have decision-making power or control within their society
- **Bourgeoisie / middle class / upper middle class.** People who own property and usually also earn income from that property (the difference between middle class and upper middle class is usually the degree of wealth or ownership)

- **Professionals.** People with specialized skills, such as doctors, lawyers, or educators—generally considered part of the middle class or upper middle class in economic and social terms, but they earn their living at least partly from their skills and knowledge rather than property ownership, on a salary rather than an hourly wage
- **White-collar workers.** People who work in specialized office jobs, part of the middle class, sometimes also identified as professionals. The term usually implies management staff or people with specialized skill of a less advanced degree than doctors, lawyers, or professors, and often specific to commerce, such as accountants, bankers, and financial advisers.
- **Bureaucracy / civil service.** People who work in government, usually not elected, appointed, or hereditary leaders but those who enact, carry out, or enforce policy
- **Intellectuals.** People whose influence or self-identity is based in knowledge and ideas, such as writers, philosophers, critics, scholars, and sometimes artists
- **The avant-garde.** Used starting in the twentieth century, it refers to people who set new directions in art and culture
- **Vanguard.** The advance guard in a military formation, but in Vladimir Lenin's usage, a "revolutionary vanguard" is the most revolutionary portion of the proletariat that works to convince the rest of the working class to support revolution.
- **Elites.** People who enjoy special privileges, such as wealth, power, or influence
- **Minorities / marginalized people.** A minority group, defined as making up a smaller portion of population identified by some "majority" characteristic(s), may be "marginalized," or pushed to the margins, if it is excluded from rights or opportunities enjoyed by the majority.
- **Rulers / leadership.** Collective term for those who hold political power, which can refer very narrowly to heads of state or to all the people who make up a government

Distinguish different kinds of involvement in an event or series of events:

- **Witnesses.** People who were present and aware of what occurred, but not involved
- **Bystanders.** People who "stood by," with the implication that they could and perhaps should have done something, but did not (it is usually worth asking whether these people **condoned** the actions or feared **reprisal** if they had intervened to stop it)

- **Participants.** People who were involved in events, though usually by "going along" rather than determining the direction of events
- **Perpetrators.** People who personally committed some act(s), such as crimes or acts of violence
- **Ringleaders/instigators.** People who inspire, direct, order, or otherwise incite others to commit some action
- **Victims.** People who suffered from violence, persecution, or oppression
- **Opposition.** People who hold a position opposite to the one in power
- **Resisters.** People who actively work to stop actions they oppose
- **Protestors.** People who participate in public demonstrations expressing opposition to some policy, action, or leaders
- **Supporters.** People who actively work to support actions from afar
- **Fifth columnists.** A term derived from the Spanish Civil War, it can be used to describe any people who undermine a group from within.

In discussions about who **committed** certain destructive or harmful acts, we also sometimes consider who was **complicit**, meaning people who played some role in allowing the acts to occur without initiating them, and who was **co-opted**, meaning people who were brought into some behavior through **persuasion** (being talked into it or offered a reward in exchange for participation) or **coercion** (being forced or threatened).

Religions are a kind of social group that comes with elaborate specialized vocabulary. The major world religions include **Christianity** (adherents are divided into Catholics, Eastern Orthodox, Uniates, and Protestants, with many subdivisions within Protestantism), **Islam** (adherents are Muslims, in several subgroups, including Sunni and Shia), **Hinduism** (adherents are Hindus), **Judaism** (adherents are Jews, a term also used for people of Jewish heritage even if they are not religious, divided into two ethnic groups, Ashkenazim and Sephardim), and **Buddhism** (Buddhists, including Theravada and Mahayana branches). More specialized vocabulary should be explained in your readings; if not, look up terms in an encyclopedia of religion.

5.10.4. Time

Not surprisingly, historians use words that define time more precisely than in ordinary speech. Confusion over these terms may introduce embarrassing errors or even render your essay incoherent. Remember that the "first century" must refer to the years from 1 to 99, so that the "eighteenth century," for example, refers to the years from 1700 to 1799. While you may be familiar with the Latin abbreviations **BC** and **AD**, referring to dates before and after the birth of Christ (defined in Christian cultures as the year 1), these are being replaced by the neutral English-language abbreviations BCE for "before Christian era" and CE for "Christian era." Avoid relative terms for time periods such as "traditional"; instead, name a specific period.

- **Period/time/stage.** The most general terms, can refer to any length of time
- **Moment/phase.** A brief period, especially in comparison to longer-term trends
- **Era/epoch/age.** A long period that marks a notable transformation or development, such as "the civil rights era," "the epoch of Viking expansion," or "the industrial age." Do not use these words for short periods, like "the era between Watergate and Nixon's pardon" or for periods that are not characterized by any particular development or interpretation, such as "the epoch of the fifteenth century."
- **Prehistory/prehistorical.** Refers to any time before the introduction of writing or survival of texts (when traditional historical methods do not apply; studied primarily by archaeologists).
- **Ancient.** The period from the beginning of written documentation (about 3000 BCE) to the fall of Rome. More specifically we speak of **classical antiquity** as the period of the Roman Empire and ancient Greece.
- **Medieval.** Between the fall of Rome and the Renaissance, this period was marked in Europe by, generally, greater religious power than secular power, while political power was generally distributed among many shifting territories and small-holding rulers. Historians do not use the term "Dark Ages," since it is inaccurate as well as judgmental.
- **Early modern.** The period of Renaissance and Reformation in Europe, circa 1500 to circa 1750, a time of growing secularism, religious turmoil, and the earliest developments toward the amalgamation of small principalities into what would become large nation-states during the modern period
- **Modern / modern period.** The period between about 1750 and 1960 or (by some accounts) 1980, otherwise known as the **industrial age**. It is marked by the development of powerful, mostly secular centralized nation-states and a long series of conflicts over ideologies and political systems.
- **Postmodern.** Usually refers to the period from the 1960s (or sometimes 1980s) to the present, and can also refer to a particular way of looking at the world or scholarly interpretation based on "deconstruction," multiculturalism, and multiple perspectives. Historically it can be used in a restricted sense to refer to current and recent events, which are increasingly also being referred to as the **digital age** or **age of information**.
- **Contemporary.** "The same time as." In reference to a historical person or event, it means the time during that event or person's life. In reference to

yourself and your readers, it means the current time. Thus, "Franklin was mindful of contemporary events on the continent" means that Franklin was aware of what was happening elsewhere in Europe during his own time, but "looking at the term 'empire' through our contemporary lens" refers to our current understanding in contrast to a time in the past.

- **Fin de siècle.** French for "turn of the century," usually used to describe the period around 1900. It overlaps with the broader, retrospective term **belle époque,** for the period from 1871 to 1914 and the flowering of European culture of that time; the English "turn of the century" can be used for any period surrounding the end of one and beginning of another century.
- **Long nineteenth century.** Now in common scholarly usage, this term was originated by historian Eric Hobsbawm to refer to the time from the French Revolution (1789) to the beginning of World War I (1914), which coincides with the most significant phase of the Industrial Revolution and the expansion of middle classes in Europe.
- **Short twentieth century.** Used in combination with "long nineteenth century," the short twentieth century is dated from 1914 to 1991 and emphasizes World War I, World War II, and the Cold War as a single, long development and a continuous clash over political ideologies.

These chronological boundaries are based largely on developments in Europe or, for the ancient period, the "Near East," which Europe saw as its predecessor civilization, because of the dominance of Western history over the modern historical profession. These Western terms are often used analogously for other parts of the world with slight adjustments in dates to make them work, but more specific terms and periodizations are preferable, such as the Middle Empire in China (581 CE to about 979 CE), the "early," "middle," and "late" Byzantine periods, or the Islamic caliphates. These terms vary from place to place, so you will most likely find them defined within your course and readings.

5.10.5. Geography

We refer to places by their names as you would see on a map, but remember to use the names in use during the time you're discussing. For example, "Germany" did not exist before 1871 and what is now "the United States" should be referred to as "the American colonies" before 1776 and distinguished as either "the Union / North" or "the Confederacy / South" during the Civil War from 1861 to 1865. It used to be conventional to refer to a country as "she" (as in "Italy's industrial capacity was insufficient to meet her military needs"), but the neutral "it" is now preferred.

Every country has its own administrative divisions within it, so find the appropriate terms for the country you are studying in your readings. However, keep in mind the following levels of distinction that can play an important role in assigning responsibility to historical actors:

- **Federation/federal.** A federal system is one where several mostly independent entities band together to agree on policy in particular areas, like trade or defense. The United States and the European Union are both examples of federations, though the United States is a much closer one with far more "federal" policy (policies and laws that apply to all the included territories) than the EU.
- **State/province.** While "state" is usually equivalent to "government," it can also be used in a different sense as the official designation for a region within a country, as in the United States. It is not a coincidence that the founders chose a term that normally refers to an independent, sovereign government—it was meant to emphasize the independence of the states (which has waned since the Civil War). Many countries have administrative divisions of relative size and importance similar to American "states" that are often designated or translated as "provinces."
- **District/county.** Used to describe smaller areas, usually an official administrative region that includes more than one town but is still smaller than and within a province
- **Municipality.** A general term to describe a town or city of any size. A city is the largest kind of municipality, followed by **town**, **village**, and **hamlet**.
- **Area/region/territory.** These terms are usually the least specifically defined, and can be used to describe geographical areas of unknown or mixed official designations, but in some places (like Australia) one of these terms can be used in a specific and official way, as in "the Northern Territories." You can tell when a geographical term is an official designation because it will be capitalized in published works.

Other than map names, there are a few general geographical terms you should be able to use correctly:

- **Western / the West.** Though Americans may first associate the word "western" with cowboys, it is also used as shorthand for "western civilization" or the much newer concept of "the West" (note the capital "W") specific to the second half of the 20th century. The "West" in this sense is understood in opposition to a non-western Soviet Union or Soviet bloc. But we also speak broadly of "Western civilization" as a master narrative of historical development beginning in the "classical" world of ancient

Greece and Rome, continuing with medieval and early modern Europe, and expanding to include North America in the modern period. This concept was constructed (invented) to serve political purposes. Americans are not any more, or less, inheritors of the culture of ancient Athens than anyone else. "Western civilization" has actually been so diverse across time and space that nothing can be accurately said about it as a whole. That which we have defined as "Western" has also always interacted constantly with that which we define as "non-Western." And we have defined what counts as "Western" in different ways when it suits us—an example is how Russia is sometimes part of the "West" and, especially during the Cold War, not at all "Western." Capitalize "West" or "Western" when those words are describing the constructed concept, but do not capitalize them when they are used only geographically.

- **First/Second/Third World.** Also originating in the Cold War, when "Western" liberal democracies defined themselves as "first" in industrial development and economic success, leaving the rival Soviet bloc as "second" (because, though industrialized, it was not as prosperous), and the Third World as those countries without appreciable industrial development. We now use the more accurate terms **industrialized states** and **developing states.**

5.10.6. Historic/Historical

The terms "historic" and "historical" are often used interchangeably in normal speech, but can have a useful distinction in formal contexts. Anything that changes over time can be studied by historians and is "historical." Gender and race are historical, photosynthesis and genetics are not. By "historic" we mean "something so big it'll be remembered a long time." We can talk about "a historic election" when really unusual things happened and everyone will remember it. Society decides what is "historic" by remembering some events more than others. Historians may later explain a "historic" event, but we do not make it "historic" or decide on what should be "historic." (See section 8.5.3 for still other terms based on the same root to make sure you deploy them correctly in your essays.)

5.10.7. Verbs

Most students are aware of the common writing advice to use strong action verbs but justifiably wonder how that can apply to an essay where the only thing anyone is doing is "writing" or "saying," as when you distill a source text. It can be tempting to throw in a variety of other verbs to spice things up. But the result is perplexing when your synonyms for "say" don't really match what's happening. We need to accurately distinguish between closely related meanings (which often depends on having a clearer understanding of the source text as well as a good vocabulary). We should also not fear repetition of this kind quite so much. We do want to avoid repeating the same idea, but the use of a single word several times is not necessarily a problem if it is accurate and precise.

Verbs to avoid. Unfortunately, many of the verbs we turn to first because they are familiar are the least accurate or effective. For example: "Historian Francesca Bregoli proves that . . ." Academic history is not primarily about establishing facts, as journalists or lawyers might do. When historians establish facts, it is only in service of an argument, where we deal in claims and interpretations that can be convincingly supported with evidence but not proven.

At the same time, scholarly arguments are not a matter of faith. They are a matter of evidence and logical reasoning, so the verb "to believe" can be ambiguous, and we should usually avoid statements like "Historian Peter Vellon believes that . . ." We can talk about what historical actors (people in the past) seem to have believed, based on what they said or did, but we do not report that historians "believe" when they really "argue" or "claim." Historians can "speculate" based on evidence or "extrapolate from" evidence, but faith is for religious or philosophical debate, not modern academic history.

Similarly, scholars rarely "praise" someone except in reviews of other people's work. Instead they usually "agree with" someone's argument or "explain" what a historical figure is saying or doing. Scholars also almost never "declare" anything—a declaration is a major announcement. A king can "declare" that his courtiers must wear silk, but scholars merely "suggest," "defend," "explain," "assert," "state," "ask," or "argue."

Some verbs commonly misused as synonyms for "say" mean something else entirely. For example: "Historian Bob Wintermute exemplifies a story about World War I veterans." This actually means that Wintermute is an example of the story, not that he uses this story as an example. It should be revised to say one of the following:

Historian Bob Wintermute relates/recounts/tells a story about World War I veterans.

Historian Bob Wintermute uses a story about World War I as an example of . . .

Another verb often misused in the same way is "exhibit," which means to put something on display. Similarly, the verbs "portray" or "display" are often used to mean "show," "demonstrate," or "explain," as in "Joel Allen portrays the importance of hostages in the Roman Empire." To "portray" is to draw a picture of a person or to play a role, as an actor does. You could say a biographer metaphorically "portrays" the subject of the biography, but otherwise the word rarely makes sense in a historical context. To "show" or "demonstrate" will work better: "Joel Allen demonstrates the importance of hostages in the Roman Empire." To "demonstrate" is to walk through how something works, which is an appropriate way to describe how a historian explains cause and effect. To "show" can be simpler or briefer, as in "Bemporad shows several ways that Jewish identities were expressed." We can also say that a historian is "revealing" information that was not previously known, or "illuminating" something that was known but not clearly understood. To display something means to set it up for viewing, as in "The library's special manuscripts were put on display." Historians rarely "display" anything, unless they are working with a museum to set up an exhibit.

Another common mistake is to use "mention" as a synonym for "say" or "claim," as in "Julia Sneeringer mentions that the political use of women's issues had only limited success." To "mention" is to say something briefly and in passing. Major claims are never just mentioned. This sentence should be revised to reflect the importance of the statement: "Julia Sneeringer argues that the political use of women's issues had only limited success." Note that Sneeringer is still not "declaring" anything, unless she gets up on a podium and announces that everyone must believe her argument or else!

Although we often use "say" both for literal speech and for something someone wrote, be careful of synonyms for "say" that are used only for live speech, like "talk about," as in "In her new book, Frangakis-Syrett talks about . . ." It is usually safer to use "write," "claim," "describe," "explain," and so on.

Finally, be sure the connotations of the verb you use are appropriate to the subject you're discussing. It would be inappropriate to write that the Nazi Party "frowned upon" Jews when in fact they murdered millions of them, since "frown upon" means "disapprove of." At the same time, it's inappropriate to write of the Tories "oppressing" or "suppressing" the Whigs when they simply disagreed and competed with each other.

Verbs for what people say. There are many ways to describe how an author "says" something in historical writing. Some are interchangeable, some are not. Consider the following possibilities:

- **State/write** (neutral)
- **Articulate** (when an author puts into words something that is usually hard to describe or define)
- **Point out** (when an author raises an unexpected point)

- Imply (when the author does not make the statement directly, but it seems clear between the lines)
- Suggest/offer (when the author offers up an idea or proposal, not a certain fact or definite claim)
- Hint (when the author suggests something indirectly as a possibility)
- Note/mention (for minor statements made in passing)

Arguing verbs (making a contestable claim and supporting it with evidence and reasoning):

- Claim/contend/assert/submit/suggest/offer/propose/posit/contribute/add
- Support (a claim)
- Assume (a point that is not made explicit)
- Defend (when an author argues why her own claims are more convincing than others)
- Employ/deploy/use (for how the author uses evidence)
- Declare (when the statement is made very strongly or dramatically)
- Insist (when an author reasserts the truth of her claim despite a counterargument)
- Insinuate (when an author suggests something underhanded or critical in an indirect way)
- Qualify (when explaining the limits of one's claims)
- Admit (when acknowledging something that weakens the main argument)
- Refer to / point to (when an author brings in some outside author or fact)
- Mention (when an author brings something up very briefly, only in passing, not as a major point)
- Agree/disagree (when an author relates how his own argument does or doesn't align with someone else's)
- Speculate/explore (when the author suggests what might be, rather than showing what is based on evidence)

Discussing verbs (considering a subject at some length):

- Examine/explore/explain/describe/consider/study
- Define (to explain how one set of circumstances should be distinguished from others)
- Expose (to explain how something has been overlooked and why it matters)
- Highlight/emphasize (to draw attention toward something)

Criticizing verbs:

- **Discredit** (when an author completely topples someone else's claim)
- **Undermine** (when an author shows someone else's argument to be weaker than it seemed)
- **Challenge** (when an author poses questions or concerns to be addressed in future)
- **Question / Call into question** (when an author raises questions or presents evidence or reasoning to show some other claim to be weak or false)

Asking verbs:

- **Ask/question/inquire/query**
- **Wonder** (when a question is asked speculatively, with no expectation that an answer is possible)
- **Ponder** (to explore possibilities without expectation of resolution)

Verbs for what people do. While authors are usually doing only some form of "saying," the historical figures they analyze are often doing much more interesting things, even in a text that is primarily about abstract concepts rather than concrete actions. The following verbs capture actions related to people and ideas. Look them up in a good dictionary to consider the subtle differences between them. Try using each one in a sentence. Notice these words when you read. Try them out in your own writing, but only when they accurately capture your meaning.

abolish	deplore	limit
accept	develop	manipulate
act	disapprove (of)	objectify
adapt	discourage	operate
adopt	downplay	perceive
apply	drive	prioritize
assume	encourage	reflect
believe	expect	represent
celebrate	favor	resist
censure	fear	support
coerce	frown upon	sympathize (with)
convince	hope for	trust
cooperate	imagine	understand
co-opt	initiate	value
deny	invent	validate

Verbs for how historical events or phenomena operate:

affect / have an effect on	change/alter/modify/transform
effect / bring about / cause / instigate	reform/revolutionize
enact / be enacted / come into effect	develop/evolve
result in / eventuate	revolve around
begin/start	operate
occur/happen	animate
end/cease	inhibit / hinder / hold back
increase/decrease	disturb/disrupt

Verbs for what governments say and do. A fairly narrow set of verbs describe how governments behave. Government bodies that have the power to make a law or policy simply by declaring it (such as absolute monarchies), can **decree** something, but a representative government can only **legislate.** Laws and policies can **require** that we do certain things and **prohibit** other actions. Politicians can **declare, support, defend,** or **criticize** a position or platform (a set of positions) as well as laws and policies. Governments **enforce** laws that are intended to **punish, incentivize, encourage** or **discourage,** or **allow** certain behaviors. Governments can **persecute** some groups by unfairly punishing them or excluding them from rights or services based on who they are rather than things they do or say that violate laws. People can be **coerced** or **forced** by governments to do things they would not otherwise do, or people can be **co-opted** or brought into agreement with a policy when the government offers them something else that they want. Courts **decide** questions, **uphold** previous decisions, or **overturn** them. (See also section 5.10.2 for other words specific to describing governments.)

Verbs for how time moves. When we describe changes across time, we use verbs like **drift** for slow, undirected movement, **evolve** or **progress** for gradual change, and **shift, turn,** or **pivot** for quick changes.

5.10.8. Hedges and Qualifiers

Authors frequently qualify or hedge their claims by explaining the cases when their claim does not apply or works differently. It's important to describe these accurately when you distill someone else's argument, because otherwise you might misrepresent the claims as more extreme than they are. This is often done as simply as writing, "The author qualifies this claim by saying . . ." or "The author admits, however, that in some cases . . ." But in other cases hedges are built into a claim with words like "usually" or "most." We use hedges to express the fact that evidence is incomplete, ambiguous, or only applies in certain cases.

However, be careful of using typical hedge words like "sometimes," "usually," "mostly," or "often" purely out of habit (a kind of verbal tic; see section 4.7) or as an unconscious expression of your uncertainty about your paper. When you see these words in your drafts, check each case to see whether it accurately limits the author's claim or is unnecessary by taking it out to see if the sentence is still accurate.

5.10.9. Banned Words

No words should be literally banned from academic writing. However, the following words, phrases, or specific usages should almost always be avoided in any history paper for the reasons given. Don't worry about them when freewriting a first draft. But when you revise, you should notice and delete linguistic cop-outs like the following:

- **Inevitable.** Since the discipline of history is about understanding the contingencies of cause and effect, nothing we study is "inevitable." When you tell yourself a given event was inevitable, you are avoiding the task of identifying its specific set of causes.
- **Strong/ruthless.** It is tempting to describe powerful people with these words, but this is really another way of avoiding explaining the ways in which they were powerful, how they used their power, and with what effects.
- **Throughout history / always / from the beginning of time.** By definition, history is the study of change over time, so if something has "always" been true, "throughout history," and "from the beginning of time," it is not historical and doesn't belong in your essay. Some things change rarely or slowly, but they still change.
- **Nowadays / olden days / ancient times.** These terms have no specific meaning (see section 5.10.4 for accurate terms for various historical periods).
- **People/humanity.** We sometimes try to make a statement stronger by saying it affects everyone or nearly everyone. It actually weakens the statement because it's obviously untrue.
- **All/very/quite.** These emphasis words are overused, add little to the reader's understanding, and often fill our drafts as verbal tics, the equivalent of "um"

or "you know" in our speech. Instead of saying "very important" try "vital," instead of "quite difficult" try "arduous," and so on.

- **Literally/ironically/unique** (for emphasis). Each of these words has a specific meaning, yet they are often misused as generalized emphasis words. "Literally" is the opposite of metaphorically. My daughter is metaphorically a wild animal. Literally, she is a little girl. A situation is "ironic" if the actual result is the inverse of what was expected—for example, if you are making fun of someone for being a klutz just as you trip and fall. "Unique" means "the only one." A custom-made car is unique. A limited-edition classic car of which only a few thousand were made may be special, but it is not unique. It is not possible to be "very unique."
- **Has to do with / relates to.** These phrases associate two ideas while avoiding explaining the nature of the relationship.

5.11. Revising: Cutting More Crap

In addition to the usual filler and vagueness we all find in our drafts (see section 4.7), there are four additional common problems to look for in this round of revision. Becoming aware of these problems is part of how we learn to think more clearly and critically.

Falling back on the familiar. When we encounter a lot of new, abstract information at once, our brains find it difficult to process. We may understand a statement as we read it, but even a few minutes later it slips out of our grasp. When this happens while we continue to add still more new information—which is exactly what college students are doing most of the time—sometimes we retreat mentally to whatever we knew when we started. This is why we may seem to misunderstand a text even after reading it carefully, and can even come away thinking the main argument is the opposite of what it actually is. The only way to combat this tendency is to constantly check your understanding against the words of the text itself. This is why you are encouraged to frequently paraphrase what the author is saying while you are working your way through a text and to take several layers of notes.

Check each statement you make in your distillation against the author's own claims and make sure you haven't misrepresented it by missing a crucial "not" or "only" or otherwise letting your summary slip away from the original. Make a particular effort to think about what you knew or believed before reading this text, and make sure that isn't coloring your distillation of what the author actually says.

Confusing the author's views with others'. A second common mistake when reading a dense scholarly text—especially when scanning for linguistic cues like "however" or "thus"—is to confuse the author's claims with others that are mentioned in the text but are actually separate from or contradictory to the author's argument. For example, historians will often describe at length the ideas of a historical person. Do not confuse them with what the historian thinks those ideas mean or why they're important. The historian may think the person who lived in the past said important or influential things without agreeing with them at all—in fact, whether historians personally agree with any views they explain is not relevant to their goal of explaining cause and effect over time. Historians also describe what other historians have already established as part of setting apart their own views, explaining why they're important, and clarifying what is already known. The only way to find and correct these errors is to go back to the original text and look at what came before and after the passage we quote or paraphrase, and make sure that we have attributed the claim correctly.

Repeating yourself. Each point you add to your essay should be a new fact, claim, or reason. But as you are learning the nature of argument, it can be difficult to distinguish between explaining the author's reasoning and restating the author's claim in several ways. Repetition can also result from the ordinary struggle to articulate an idea in a draft that just needs to be edited out in revision. Some writing cultures value formal repetition because getting to the point quickly is considered rude, but this is not true of North American academic writing (see section 2.3).

The following sentence uses more words than it needs to:

During his life as a writer, Jorge Luis Borges wrote many short stories during his time when he was alive.

It could be revised to say:

Short-story writer Jorge Luis Borges . . .

Having removed the repetition, we see that very little has actually been said, and what's left is just a phrase that needs an action or result added to complete the thought.

The following example suggests the author was struggling to express a thought and, instead of deleting the practice attempts, left them in the final version of the essay. The result is a passage that not only is repetitive but contains transition words that don't make sense (see section 6.13 for more on transitions):

Here Mohl implicitly refers to the nurture aspect as only so large a factor until genetics takes a bigger stage in your life. However, he does acknowledge that nurture becomes a factor in development. Yet, nature will always be the more dominant factor for Mohl.

Compare to this revision, which contains the same content:

Mohl argues that nature is more important than nurture.

In the next example, the author repeats a historian's claim instead of explaining the reasoning behind it (with a bit of extra information the second time):

One of the main opposing arguments Duggan counters is that many Italians wrote and spoke highly of the fascist regime simply because they were fearful of the consequences if they acted differently. In other words, Duggan mentions that some historians believe their lives were on the line and because many believed such actions would lead to some form of material benefit.

Compare this to the following revision:

Duggan opposed the argument that many Italians praised the fascist regime out of fear or hope of reward.

Having revised to eliminate repetition, you now have room to explain the reasoning by adding examples:

By looking at different kinds of sources or looking at them in different ways, Duggan shows how some Italians genuinely admired Mussolini because they saw him as a symbol of Italian strength and virility, while some even admired Mussolini's violence and suppression of dissent because they felt that Italy's political and economic problems had been caused by the weakness of liberal democracy or would be made even worse in the hands of socialists.

Revising to eliminate repetition not only clears space for you to add the content that you need in a successful essay, it clarifies your thinking.

"Redundancy" means using several words when one will do, such as the phrase "time of day" when we could just say "time." We are deliberately redundant in speech to make it easier for people to follow us when they can't refer back to what we said earlier. Redundancy can sneak into our essays when we write the way we talk. But redundancy in writing is less powerful and harder to follow.

For example, when you write, "Girganov came up with three questions. The three questions are . . ." you give an impression that you don't have enough to say. Revise to "Girganov's first question was X, to which he answered Y, which suggests Z. His second question . . ." This revised phrasing gives an impression that you understand and have thought about each of the questions raised. Compare the following examples of redundant phrases with the edited version that follows:

> the country of Mexico
> Mexico
> In his article Ort says that he argues that . . .
> Ort argues . . .
> When it comes to the topic of Populism and the Populist Party . . .
> Populism . . .
> One of the main opposing ideas Schlichting counters is . . .
> Schlichting counters the idea that . . .
> The consequences that would result from . . .
> The consequences of . . .

Belaboring the obvious. This refers to putting on paper what is already so clear that it doesn't need to be described, as in this sentence:

> It can be argued that it was not very fun to have been interrogated by the Inquisition.

The phrase "it can be argued" doesn't fit with something as inarguable as the fact that being tortured was "not very fun" (and the phrase "not very fun" is an extreme understatement to describe torture). It's easy to belabor the obvious when we are new to a subject and find it difficult to judge what needs to be stated and what doesn't. This tends to come up especially in introductions, where we need to orient a general reader. You may be well aware that "Shakespeare was a writer who wrote many plays," but you might put that sentence at the start of your essay anyway to make sure you covered your bases or for lack of a better way to start. One way to notice that you may be belaboring the obvious is to look for redundancy (the phrase "writer who wrote" should raise a warning flag), and to check that the tone is consistent (light phrases like "not very fun" don't belong with a subject like torture). There are also some tests to help you see problems that aren't clear at first glance.

5.12. Revising: Testing Your Draft

In addition to the common problems described in section 5.11, we often fill our drafts with vagueness as we struggle to describe our thoughts (see also section 4.7). Even once we become aware of these problems, they can be difficult to catch when we are writing on subjects that are new to us, since what makes a word or phrase "obvious" or "vague" is relative to how much we, and our reader, already know. The following exercises are meant to help you look at your draft with fresh eyes and to consider it from the point of view of the "educated reader" we are aiming for.

The **twelve-year-old test.** Picture someone you know who is about twelve years old. If you don't know anyone that age, try to remember yourself at that stage. Read through the draft and ask yourself about each sentence or phrase in it, "Does my twelve-year-old already know this?" If the answer is yes, then the statement is probably too obvious for a college-level essay. We are most likely to find these kinds of statements at the beginnings or ends of drafts. Such sentences are often absurdly broad:

Since the beginning of time, people have thought about money.

People often divide themselves into categories, such as men and women, black and white.

As everybody knows, Thomas Jefferson is one of the greatest Americans.

These statements should simply be deleted: what comes next is almost always the right place to start. For example:

As everybody knows, Thomas Jefferson is one of the greatest Americans. Annette Gordon-Reed's *Thomas Jefferson & Sally Hemings: An American Controversy* challenges Jefferson's legacy by suggesting that historians have ignored evidence of his affair with a slave.

If we delete the first sentence, what remains is an excellent beginning.

The **"replacing keywords" test.** Try replacing keywords such as names of people, groups, or countries with an alternative. If the statement is still true, then it is too generalized to be useful. For example:

Germany was devastated after the end of World War I.

This statement is equally true if we switch "Germany" with almost any other country involved: even most of the countries on the winning side were left with economic and demographic crises. Revise the sentence until it can apply *only* to Germany, like this:

> While Germany suffered from World War I in all the same ways other participating countries did, the terms of the Versailles Treaty imposed even greater devastation through the indemnity payments Germany was asked to pay to the victors, and the loss of some of its most valuable industrial territories.

Similarly, the sentence "Hitler was a strong leader who accomplished a lot" would be equally true if you replaced "Hitler" with "Stalin," "Churchill," or "Franklin Roosevelt." If you replace the vague description "strong leader" and the summary "accomplished a lot" with a list of what specific actions the person took, you will have added real value to your essay by demonstrating that you know the material. Using these more specific terms also gives you more evidence to reason from as you draw your own conclusions, which is likely to help you think of more substantive, nuanced, and interesting things to say.

Question words test. Go through your draft line by line and make a note at each place where a specific fact can be added. To help you think through what kinds of facts may be inserted, go through this checklist for every sentence in your draft:

Who?	What?	Why?
To whom?	Where?	How?
For whom?	When?	Example?

In other words, read each sentence, and ask if there is any person or group of people missing: *Who* did what? *Whom* did they do it to? *Who* was affected? *What* is it that was being done? (can you add more specifics?) *Where* was it done, and *when*? Always provide specific dates or, if a date is not known, get as close as possible (for example, "late forties," "early nineteenth century," or "medieval period"). Have you stated not just who was doing what to whom, when, and where, but also *why* and *how* they did it? And when you explain why and how, do you give *examples* to show what you mean?

Not every detail will be significant enough to include, but for this kind of assignment, err on the side of making your sentences as detailed and dense with facts as possible. Once you have noted all the places where details could be added, go back to your text to find the details and examples you need.

5.13. Proofreading: Grammar and Usage Errors

When we read a familiar text, especially one we have worked with for a long time, our brains automatically correct errors so that we don't even see them.

Proofreading requires that we somehow circumvent this tendency. There are a variety of ways to do this, and you should try them all to see which works best for you:

- Get someone else to check your text (especially if you know there are areas of grammar or spelling that you have not yet mastered).
- Print out the text to edit it with a pen or change the font and size.
- Read it from end to beginning, one sentence at a time (this keeps you from being distracted by the content).
- Read it out loud.
- Use Google Translate to have your paper read out loud for you.

Refer to appendix 1 to find and correct the most common errors.

6

The Short Analytical Essay

An essay assignment that does not require you to find your own sources but does want you to "form a thesis," "take a side," "explain your motivation," or "construct an argument" is an analytical essay. They are usually less than ten pages in length. You are usually given a question or "prompt" to respond to. (If you are instructed to formulate your own question or find your own sources, see chapters 10 and 11.)

This kind of short analytical essay is often assigned as part of an exam, whether in class or at home, and may also be referred to as a "position paper," where you are asked to take a position on some question or argue for or against a position expressed in one of your assigned readings. A traditional essay prompt is a few lines or a paragraph of text that sets up a problem, asks a question, or describes two sides to an argument and asks you to choose one.

If your essay must be written in class, you will not be able to revise and proof-read as fully as you would at home, but if you are given prompts in advance, it's a good idea to draft and revise an essay as preparation. If you are not given prompts in advance of an exam, use any available scrap paper to brainstorm, outline, and revise as extensively as your exam time allows. On in-class exam essays the mechanics of quoting and citation cannot be followed, and minor style and structure problems can be forgiven. But expectations for analysis, logic, and "showing your work" are just as high as for an essay you write at home, and you should still name the authors behind ideas you mention in your essay.

6.1. What's Your Goal?

Exam-style analytical essay questions ask you to think through some of the biggest, most important questions or problems of the subject covered by your course. These questions are by definition not fully answerable. Your goal therefore is not to come up with a definitive, final, correct answer. Instead your goal has these parts:

- Demonstrate that you understand the problem/question fully, including why it's important and why it's difficult to resolve

- Demonstrate that you can sort through the available evidence and organize it according to its various implications
- Come to some conclusion(s) of your own about what you think is the most useful way to weigh the available evidence.

One of the most important steps in answering an analytical essay question well is to think in terms of finding the *most useful* answer rather than the *right* answer. It does not actually matter (either to your instructor or to the world) what answer you settle on. Your classmates will settle on a variety of answers. What will distinguish the most effective essays from the less effective ones will be these features:

- How specifically and logically you use relevant evidence and how accurately you present it
- How thoroughly you account for *all* the available evidence, including that which may contradict the case you're making
- How thoroughly you explain your reasons for choosing one answer or another

It is almost always acceptable not to choose a "side" in your answer, but rather to explain why the most accurate interpretation lies somewhere in between or incorporates multiple possibilities. To be effective, your answer needs to account for the evidence, and since the evidence is usually incomplete, open to multiple interpretations, even contradictory, the best answers may be conditional, to accurately reflect the ambiguity and contingency inherent in the evidence.

6.2. Understanding the Prompt

The moment when you first receive the questions is crucial. First, think about the purpose of the question and whatever deeper themes it might be getting at. Be careful of the elementary-school advice about "turning around the language of the question" to begin an answer. This kind of question is meant to prompt you to think independently and critically about a historical question in light of the evidence. Recall the kinds of questions historians ask (section 3.1) and consider what form of cause and effect over time your prompt is getting at. Is the question asking you to decide what were the most important causes of an event? Or to decide when the most important changes occurred and whom they affected? Or to evaluate two or more competing interpretations by others?

For example, consider the following exam essay prompt:

Was the second phase of the French Revolution (the Terror) a logical outgrowth of the first, idealistic, Republican phase?

Taking it too literally, it's easy to be confused about what is even being asked— of course the second phase was a logical outgrowth of the first, you might say, because it is what happened next, after all! Being accustomed to busywork or simplistic worksheet-style questions, or just from lacking an alternative, students can find themselves falling back on answers like this.

If you think about the question in light of the goals of history, however, you can see that it's trying to prompt you to think about what events or characteristics of the first phase (which was idealistic and emphasized people's rights— "Republican") could have *caused* a second phase that was so different (a "Terror" in which people were killed for their political affiliations).

Since the goal of any exam-style analytical essay is to prompt you to show how you weigh historical evidence, look for at least two (and often more) sides to the question among the facts, events, documents, and statements by historical actors that you have encountered in your course materials. There will be factors related to the first phase that may be causes of the second. But there are also other causal factors unrelated to the first phase (affecting France from beyond its borders or sudden changes occurring at the period of transition from the first to the second phase).

Once you see the prompt in this light, what details you need to answer it suddenly become clearer. Your answer will need to include all of the following:

- What characterized the first phase
- What characterized the second phase
- What are the similarities and differences between the two phases
- What factors present in the first phase *caused* effects we see in the second phase
- What factors characterizing the second phase stem from some other, outside causes or were new to that second time period
- An argument either that the seeds of the second phase were planted in mistakes or problems created as part of the first phase *or* that the second phase happened primarily because of unrelated, outside, or sudden changes *or* that both sets of causal factors were necessary and sufficient to the outcome
- An explanation of why the weight of evidence pushes you to this conclusion *despite* your acknowledgment that there are other ways to look at it

The question can be answered thoroughly and accurately from several perspectives. What matters is that you understand what the question is getting at, gather and organize relevant evidence, and make a logical case for the overall weight of the evidence leaning one way or another. Consider another example prompt:

What is the relationship between the New Deal, Fair Deal, and Great Society and the emergence of the Silent Majority?

Your first temptation may be to think simply that these are all American political policies and that the Silent Majority was the result of them. But that is not the kind of answer you are being asked for on an exam. Instead, you need to show the following:

- The specific characteristics of each policy (not adjectives, but concrete goals, terms, and results), noting what they had in common and the ways they varied
- An assessment of how the social group, ethnic, white, working-class Americans, that became known as the Silent Majority was affected by and reacted to each of these policies over time, including how other factors affected their understanding of and opinions about these policies
- Your own conclusions about which specific goals, terms, or results of which policies led directly to which specific effects on this social group, and which effects, as well as which external circumstances, led to which reactions or opinions from them

In other words, you need to find a lot of detailed information (evidence), sort that information into categories, and then weigh the relative importance of some categories over others as having *causal* or *explanatory* power (in other words, which grouping of the evidence convincingly explains how something happened).

6.3. Studying for Analytical Essays

Besides annotating your readings and taking good notes so that you understand course material more accurately and fully, you can prepare for analytical essays by looking for and annotating a few specific kinds of information. Since analytical essays often ask you to sort and weigh causes and effects, look for reasons or results. Often in lectures your instructor might frame material explicitly in this way: "There are five reasons why..." or "four causes of..." or "three explanations of how..." Those phrases flag factors you might use in an analytical essay. Notice also when your professor describes major changes or points of disruption: these are the kinds of moments that have complicated causes requiring an essay-length explanation, and so are likely to turn up in essay prompts.

Your readings, whether textbook chapters or the analyses of historians (secondary works), may not identify the factors causing or resulting from an event or phenomenon quite so obviously. Textbooks, especially, are likely to explain causes and effects in story form, telling a chronological narrative of "first this," "then that." Your task is not to memorize the story, but to absorb the general trend of it and then think back and find details that had the biggest impact on the outcome or that mark the most significant results. Pay close attention when you see language that indicates a causal connection, such as the following phrases:

led to	because of
influenced	without X, then
was a factor in	based on
tipped the balance	since X, then

Analyses written by historians, as opposed to relatively neutral textbook summaries, are already presenting arguments about cause and effect or how and when changes occurred. In an analytical essay, you are being asked to demonstrate your own thinking, not to memorize and then recreate someone else's. So how do you use historians' analyses in your essay? Secondary sources offer you existing perspectives, lay out their evidence and reasoning, and describe existing counterarguments. They are full of lists of reasons for why things happened and claims about which of those reasons is more important than others. You might identify some of the same reasons but weigh them in your own way, and you might contrast one historian's interpretation with another's in order to come to your own conclusion, which may be some combination of what you read.

6.4. Brainstorming: Evidence

Since an analytical essay is about weighing causes, effects, or influences, the best way to start is to gather as much of these as possible. Go through your readings and notes (see sections 4.2, 5.2–5.4, 9.6–9.7) and make lists. You could start with one long list of all the facts or statements from the readings that you think are relevant, but as soon you can, divide this mass of facts into several lists, according to what you need to answer your question. These might include the following:

- A list of causes, a list of effects
- A list of causes of X, a list of causes of Y
- A list of A-type reasons, a list of B-type reasons, a list of C-type reasons

- A list of similarities, a list of differences
- A list of influences, a list of consequences
- A list of the influences of X on A, a list of the influences of X on B

When you have everything you can find divided into lists, go over your readings and notes once more to make sure you haven't left anything out, especially anything that might be contradictory, difficult to explain, or different from what you expected. Those kinds of facts must be accounted for as much as any others and are often the key to the most useful and nuanced explanation.

Next read over your lists and think about other ways you could group the same information. Would it make more sense in a different kind of list? Do you need another list or set of lists, such as how your causes and effects each apply to another part of the question? Can you draw connections between items on your lists (literally drawing arrows) or group them in new ways? Are some of the items more important than others? Circle the items that have greater influence than others. Group linked items, perhaps by highlighting them by color.

You can't decide where you stand on a question until you've fully understood the evidence and played with it a bit, by trying to make connections and questioning how the weight of all the facts might lean more one way or another, depending on how you look at it. What assumptions did you have to make in order to decide what list to put a particular fact on? Consider how those assumptions inform the way you understand how one cause leads to another.

6.5. Brainstorming: Claims

One of the most common mistakes students make in analytical essays is to avoid taking a stand. This may come from modesty, a sense of not being able to stand behind a particular position on a subject that is so new, especially in light of statements by professional historians. But no one's life is at stake in your answer, and in fact no one really cares what side you choose. What your professor wants to see is that you are thinking and how critically (how accurately and specifically you discuss evidence, how logically you reason your way through it, and how rigorously you question all possibilities posed by the problem).

If you're having trouble coming to any sort of conclusion about where the evidence points, try talking it through with someone—a friend, roommate, parent, even a pet. Often the exercise of putting the evidence into words for someone who has not read what you have can force you to group factors into logical categories more easily than you can do on your own. The exercise is even more useful if you are talking with someone who will ask questions and push back on your statements, forcing you to articulate your reasons and consider other points of view.

Summary versus analysis. When you begin drafting, the most common temptation is to fill your space with a summary of what happened. This is essentially a recording of what you learned from course materials, but that's not what is asked for in an analytical essay. But if you have started with brainstorming lists and decided what stand you will take based on those lists, then you can write your essay as analysis rather than summary.

The first difference between the two forms is that an analytical organization is not chronological and does not give equal weight to each fact or event described. Instead of starting with what happened first, you begin with what conclusion you are going to demonstrate, and then explain each point of evidence that supports it, as well as the evidence pointing other directions, with an explanation of why you find that evidence less convincing or important. Most importantly, analysis adds the writer's own reasoning, observations, and connections to the already-known facts. Consider the following contrast:

Summary: In the 1950s, following World War II, returning American veterans tended to start families and move out of cities, seeking new homes in a process called suburbanization. They longed for a sense of community, privacy, and comfort. Suburbs were close enough to cities for men to commute to work, but far enough away for there to be space for yards for children to play in. William Levitt, a developer, started the first suburbs on Long Island, quickly building huge numbers of houses on concrete slabs without basements, using cheaper composition board and non-union labor. As people moved in, they needed to buy furniture, appliances, and other goods, and the whole process led to a nation-wide increase in consumption that made the economy boom. At the same time, African Americans who migrated North in search of affordable housing were pushed out of the new suburban developments by white owners who feared the influence of "urban" migrants. This pushed the non-white poor into concentrated parts of cities where neglect led to a downward spiral in conditions. Suburbs also isolated women, restricting them to the home and away from adult company, while increasing social pressure to live up to the ideal of the perfect home.

Analysis: The migration of many American families out of cities and into new housing developments, known as suburbanization, brought both positive and negative effects. People were motivated by a search for community, comfort, and privacy following World War II, and the postwar baby boom led to a desire for yards and good schools for children. In some ways this dream was fulfilled for the white middle class. The construction of new homes drove consumerism, leading to a booming economy. On the other hand, developers like William

Levitt used shoddy materials and exploitative non-union labor to build quickly and cheaply, so the suburbs have not aged well. In addition, African American migrants who came North at this time in search of affordable housing were pushed out by white suburbanites, so that they ended up isolated in neglected parts of cities, leading to a downward spiral in conditions. Suburbs also isolated women, restricting them to the home and away from adult company, while increasing social pressure to live up to the ideal of the perfect home. Overall, suburbanization was a major factor in economic growth but came with numerous unintended negative side effects that had a huge social cost.

The summary provides only facts, of approximately equal weight, and the author does not attempt to interpret what those facts might mean or connect them to anything else. The analysis includes the same facts, but they are brought in as needed to support claims. The claims make suggestions about what larger lessons or conclusions these facts may signify, by sorting and weighing them.

From responding to analyzing. If you have written a response paper, you already know how to comment on a text beyond relating a personal reaction such as whether you agreed with it. To expand from that to an argument, you need to push that response still further. Compare the following:

Response: Christopher Duggan's *Fascist Voices* is very convincing when he explains how and why ordinary Italians enthusiastically supported fascism. However, he rarely addresses what women were saying or doing, other than a chapter focusing mainly on Mussolini's mistresses and women who wanted to be his mistress. We can't know how women's experiences may alter his overall argument.

Argument: Paulicelli's work on women's participation in fascism through fashion culture and parades, and the way they adapted fascist notions to reflect their diverse personal sense of "national" identity rather than accepting the single image offered by the regime, shows that while Duggan is correct about the often sincere popularity of fascism among ordinary Italians, he may not emphasize enough how fascism was re-made or changed by ordinary people.

In the response, the writer noticed an omission in this text and explained why it was important, but did not attempt to fill the gap herself. In the argument example, the writer has looked into other sources and used them to fill the gap identified in Duggan's work. Making the connection between the two sources is this writer's argument, or contribution, to the debate about popular participation in fascist regimes.

Expanding your response into an argument does not necessarily require bringing in new sources that contradict each other: there are infinite ways to frame your argument. So how do you develop your own argument if right now you have only a tentative response to the evidence you've gathered? Try these exercises:

Get more specific. Start drafting with whatever you can say at this point, even if it's vague or just a personal reaction. Then follow up on that first tentative feeling by rewriting your statement to make it more specific. Adding "because" and then forcing yourself to follow it with an explanation is often a useful way to move forward. Don't do it just once, but several times, each time adding new observations, explanations, or explorations. The following example is in response to a prompt asking how and why US immigration policy changed between the big pre–World War I wave of immigration and a second that began in the 1980s.

> The two waves of immigration were both similar and different.

> The two waves of immigration were similar because there were quotas limiting immigration from certain areas at both times, because Americans feared competition for low-paying jobs. They were different because the second wave had a different policy toward refugees.

Go back to the sources. Look again at your brainstorming lists or your readings and notes and add specific facts, quotes, or examples wherever you can. The result might resemble this:

> The two waves of immigration were similar because fears of job competition, foreign diseases, and worries over foreign influences on white Christian culture brought about restrictions on immigration both times, such as the 1921 Emergency Quota Act and the 1924 Johnson-Reed Act, which limited immigration from southern and eastern Europe, and the 1986 Immigration Act that restricted immigration from Mexico while encouraging it from northern and western Europe. The main thing that's different between the two periods is the introduction of the 1980 Refugee Act, which recognized asylum and created a path to citizenship for refugees.

Ask questions. To push yourself to delve still deeper, try these questions (which may require going back to the sources still more to pursue whether an answer is available, what it is, and what it might mean):

What's different about . . . ?	Why? How?
What are the results?	What does it all add up to?
What was intended and what was unexpected?	How do you make sense of this?

Answering these questions could result in something like this:

What made the difference come about? The 1980 Refugee Act added to and completed the 1965 Hart-Celler Act, which brought refugees under existing immigration legislation and lifted the quotas of the 1920s.

What was it intended to do? The assumption in the 1960s was that immigrants would mostly come from northern and western Europe, but also this was the era of civil rights and increasing pressure to acknowledge the rights and contributions of minorities.

What were the results? The unintended consequence was a rise in immigration from Asia, including numbers of people fleeing communist Vietnam.

Why? The 1980 act was passed partly out of guilt because of America's earlier failure to allow in Jewish refugees during World War II and the Cold War (because they feared they would bring political radicalism).

6.6. Brainstorming: Multiple Causes

As you draft your argument, you will likely run into the problem of articulating a clear position of your own while also taking into account many contradictory causal factors. There are several logical structures historians use to convey how multiple causes (or effects) can be weighed in order to sort the most important from the less important or to convey how some causes reinforce or set off others.

- **Tipping-point causes.** When one fairly small factor, though not decisive in itself, makes the difference in an outcome by adding its weight to other causes. This can also be referred to as a "trigger event."
- **"Perfect storm" causes.** When the combined weight of many factors, none sufficient in themselves, make a difference because they happen all at the same or near the same time.
- **Necessary and sufficient causes.** A "necessary" cause is one that is decisive: the outcome would not have happened without this cause. A "sufficient" cause is enough to bring about the outcome all by itself, even if all other factors were neutral. If you can claim that a single cause is "necessary and sufficient," while others do not meet those criteria, you can show that the "necessary and sufficient" cause outweighs others.
- **Contingency and preconditions.** Most causes can't be weighed separately from their context. They have power to influence events because of when, where, and how they happen and how they relate to and interact with other causes. In other words, one cause is contingent on, or depends on, another.

Most causes are contingent on others, and how they interrelate is what we need to explain. It can help to identify a chain of contingent causes, expressed as "If X, then Y." Since historians are explaining contingencies that happened in the past, we often write this in the past tense as "Once X had happened, then Y happened," or "because X, then Y, which in turn caused Z." Sometimes we isolate "preconditions," or factors that, while not causes in themselves, were necessary to set in motion the more decisive factors.

- **Deus ex machina.** This Latin phrase for "God from the machine" is used to refer to some element that seems to come out of nowhere to change the course of events. In reality every cause is embedded in a context, but this phrase (which technically refers to a plot device in fiction) can help to convey how one important factor—often one unexpected by participants—can suddenly alter what otherwise seemed like the most likely chain of events, or how a single, unexpected change can introduce new problems that alter people's decisions or behavior.

- **Accidental causes / unintended consequences.** One of the most fascinating and often entertaining drivers of change is simply random accidents, mistakes, or surprises. Although a "deus ex machina" refers to some major force that shifts whole situations, the role of unexpected or accidental influences can cause change in any number of ways, big or small.

- **Neglected / misunderstood causes.** Sometimes we make an argument to explain a causal factor that is not necessarily the most decisive, but that has been previously misunderstood or overlooked. We don't have to care only about those causes that made the biggest difference: our goal is a full understanding of change over time, so it is worthwhile to examine even small influences and the roles they played in the larger picture.

- **Competing influences (top-down / bottom-up, push / pull, long term / short term).** In the real world, there are many causal forces pushing in different directions, and outcomes are often some kind of compromise or unintended consequence of actions by various parties. One way historians sort through these competing influences is to identify some influences as "top-down," meaning decisions are made by people who hold power, affecting others who do not have as much control over events. By contrast, "bottom-up" influences are pressures put on people with power by those who don't have it. Neither is necessarily more influential or decisive than the other, but the distinction can help us untangle a complicated web of causes.

Another way we can map out interactions between causes is to point to those that "push" in a certain direction, such as disasters that push people to emigrate from their country, and "pull" factors, which are enticements that pull people to go to some specific other place, such as high wages.

We can also distinguish between long-term, or slowly developing factors that tend in a certain direction, and short-term causes, or alternately distinguish between long-term effects (which are felt for a long time after the change occurs) and short-term effects (which have some immediate impact but do not remain in place for long).

6.7. Brainstorming: Addressing Counterarguments

An important way academic writers address the limits inherent in their evidence is to consider counterarguments. Some scholars do this by naming other authors who have different interpretations, but often we raise and respond to objections that we think a reader might make, whether anyone actually is making that other argument or not. This is a way of strengthening our own argument by making it more accurate. Compare the following statements:

History is the most important discipline ever.

Although every discipline offers a valuable approach to critical thinking, if your goal is to understand change over time, history is probably the most useful.

The first sentence has more forceful language and assumes that no one could disagree. But most people won't find it convincing. The second sentence contains a verbal hedge ("probably"), takes other perspectives into account ("every discipline offers a valuable approach"), limits the claim ("if your goal is"), and therefore is more convincing. That's because it accurately reflects reality. If you imagine a reader who is skeptical that history has any value, the first sentence is unlikely to have an impact on her view, but the second sentence could change her mind.

There are many ways to take counterarguments into account. As in the preceding example, it could be implicit, where you simply note that other views exist. Or you could explicitly put the imaginary reader into the "conversation" of your essay, as in these examples:

One might counter this claim by asking whether X. However, as we see in Y...

If we argued X, it's possible that Y. But at the same time, it is equally true that Z.

A reader could question X on the grounds that Y. While this is true, it is equally important that Z.

6.8. Drafting: Argument-Based Outlining

When you have worked out what you want to claim and mapped how your evidence supports it, as well as how you account for other evidence as less influential or "necessary" to the outcome, you are ready to begin a full-sentence draft of your essay. To avoid excessive summary and to keep your evidence prominent, try organizing your material with an argument-based outline rather than the traditional numbered outline. Remember that "claims" are arguable statements—something that you assert is true, but that not everyone would necessarily agree with. "Evidence" means facts or documents that exist independently of whether your claim is true. "Reasoning" is your logical explanation of why the known evidence leads you to your claim.

An argument-based outline looks like this:

- **Claim:** The sky is blue.
- **Evidence:** I observe the sky, and it appears to be blue.
- **Reasoning:** If the sky looks blue, it must be blue.
- **Counterargument:** The sky appears to be blue only from our perspective on earth and only on clear days.
- **Response to counterargument:** We're all on earth, so for our purposes, that's all that matters, and at the moment we're looking, it is blue.
- **Qualified claim:** Viewing the sky from earth today, it is blue.

The number of claims, subclaims, qualifications, and counterarguments you make will depend on the material you have. Consider a more complicated historical example that includes subclaims (these are the parts of your claim that have to be demonstrated in order to show that your overall claim is defensible):

- **Main claim:** The most important change in modern US immigration policy, the 1980 Immigration Act that codified increased openness to refugees, was a product of the Cold War.
- **Subclaim 1:** The 1980 act changed the direction of twentieth-century immigration policy,
- **Evidence for subclaim 1:** The 1980 act recognized asylum as a legitimate reason to allow entrance and created a path to citizenship for refugees. Previous legislation, in contrast, was largely aimed at limiting immigration and refugee status didn't help, as in exclusion of Jewish refugees during and after World War II.

- **Reasoning for subclaim 1:** Thus the 1980 act represents a turn away from traditional quotas and toward increased openness under certain conditions.
- **Subclaim2:** The 1980 act was passed because people realized that excluding Jewish refugees during and after World War II had been a mistake and because the unintentional influx of Asian refugees fleeing communism since the 1965 Hart-Celler Act had strengthened the US position in the Cold War rather than weakening it.
- **Evidence for subclaim2:** Restrictive policies of the 1930s resulted in Jews being returned to concentration camps, where most of them died. The unexpected Asian immigrants of the later period were mostly fleeing communist countries.
- **Reasoning for subclaim 2:** By welcoming people who fled communism, the United States made itself look open and fair (restoring the reputation tarnished by turning away Jewish refugees) while bringing attention to the high numbers of people motivated to flee communist countries, making those countries look bad.
- **Reasoning that links subclaims to main claim:** The biggest thing that changed in the background of the 1980 policy change was the Cold War and the US need to assert the superiority of its values over those of the communist world.
- **Counterarguments:**
  - Why didn't the same logic apply during World War II to motivate the United States to take in refugees from the main enemy of that time, Nazi Germany?
  - Wasn't the civil rights movement also significant?
- **Response to counterargument:** Although it's true the Soviet Union was a US ally against Nazi Germany during World War II, it was a tense relationship. Fear of communism predated it and continued immediately after. US resistance to Jewish refugees was based on the fact that the United States associated Jews with communism in that period and thought immigrants would be political radicals. So there's a consistent theme in both cases of basing immigration policy on fear of communism.
- **Qualified main claim:** The most important change in modern US immigration policy, the 1980 Immigration Act that codified increased openness to refugees, was a product of both Cold War and civil rights-era pressures to live up to democratic values and of US worries about communism.

6.9. Revising: Logic

Your first task as you turn to revising your outline should be to examine the logic of your claims. The following are common logical errors:

- **Not making a logical claim.** A claim must be contestable; that is, a reasonable person could disagree with it. It must also be substantive, meaning something is at stake in whether it's true or not. And it must be specific. This example is not contestable: "Women instigated the Russian Revolution with bread riots." If your statement is about what happened and those events are well documented, then there's nothing to contest about it. It's a fact, not a claim.

    An example of a contestable claim that is not substantive is "Peter the Great was the tallest European monarch of his generation." We may not be absolutely sure this was the case, but nothing much rides on whether it's true or not, so it is not a worthwhile claim to pursue.

    Now consider an example that is both contestable and substantive, but not specific enough to work with: "Americans are exceptional." In order to support or refute that claim, we'd have to show whether Americans (all Americans? the American government? the population during a particular time? some part of the population?) are unique in some way. There's no way to do this without knowing what the criteria are or who we should be comparing.

- **Circular reasoning.** We reason in a circle when we use the basis of our question to provide the answer. For example, if we ask why the Chilean military dictator Augusto Pinochet murdered so many people, our answer cannot be "because he was cruel," because "cruel" is just a description of someone who would do something like commit murder. Instead we need to look for what Pinochet hoped to accomplish from these murders, the mechanisms that made them happen, and any characteristics specific to Pinochet, such as his need to disrupt existing democratic institutions that threatened his control.

- **Generalization.** When we take the characteristics or actions of an individual or small group and apply them to a larger group, we are generalizing. For example, when we say, "The Soviets believed Reagan might start a nuclear war," are we referring to all Soviet citizens? That can't be accurate. It would be more accurate to revise your claim to "The Soviet leadership believed Reagan might start a nuclear war." Lumping large groups of people together is the most common form of generalization. People don't think in groups ("peasants" don't all agree on every issue), and even people who are part of a group organized for some purpose, such as the International Revolutionary Brotherhood, do not all act the same way, and may each be part of the group for different reasons.

In some cases we do lump disparate cases together in order to make a bigger contrast—for example, we could refer to the entire antebellum American South as if it were one entity in order to contrast it to Russian serf-owning culture, even though doing so involves generalizing about both societies. If our focus is on one thing the cultures had in common (dependence on unfree labor), so that we can draw connections to how it affected the status of women, for example, then the many variations within each culture might be less important. But as soon as we want to explain anything more detailed about that comparison, we would have to consider the wide variations in income and land management patterns among Russian serf-owners, on one hand, and the regional differences in the economics of US slavery, on the other. In every case, we need to be as specific as we can while still including all the categories relevant to our question.

- **Appeal to authority fallacy.** When we attempt to support our claims by quoting a historian who says the same thing, we are essentially saying, "Believe me because someone important says it, too." That gives us no basis on which to accept the claim, as in this example: "The cotton industry was built on violence, because, as Sven Beckert argues in his important new book, 'war capitalism' was essential to its development." Appeals to authority should be revised to include the evidence and reasoning for the claim, so the reader has a basis on which to decide whether to agree with it. A revision might look like: "The cotton industry developed because of the availability of cheap raw materials, which was made possible through slavery and colonial conquest," with a footnote to Beckert's book.

- **Weak analogy.** It is usually best to avoid analogies in academic historical writing, because they are so difficult to do well. A good analogy depends on comparing apples to apples: the two sides of your analogy should be similar enough in several major ways that one could expect them to also be similar in the quality you want to expose with your analogy. Most analogies compare apples to oranges, by comparing the past to the present (this is an example of anachronism), or by comparing historical phenomena of very different scale or context. For example, consider this common but erroneous analogy: "We shouldn't be surprised that Soviet communism collapsed, because after all, if people don't own their own houses, why would they take care of them?" We can't compare a government economy to a household economy, because households do not have the power to levy taxes or issue currency, and governments do not earn salaries or feed their people (at least not directly). The best analogies are limited in scope and compare scenarios that are closely related, for example two government economies in the same region and time period.

- **False cause fallacy and confusing cause with effect.** The false cause fallacy occurs when we confuse the order of events with the reason one event led to another. For example: "The Terror came about because the French Revolution destabilized French society." Although the Terror followed closely upon the French Revolution, that does not mean it was a direct result. The following would be more accurate (it is still arguable, but not a logical leap from chronology to causation): "During the period of social instability caused by the French Revolution and the wars it set off, Robespierre took advantage of the chaos to eliminate rival factions in what was known as the Terror." In this example, the French Revolution caused instability and set off war, which created an environment in which someone could introduce a new element, the Terror. One way to help you sort out these sequences of cause and effect is to write them out in very simple sentences with the simplest words possible, to check that you're saying what you mean to say. You then add clauses, examples, or explanations as needed to restore the detail you left out.

  A closely related problem occurs when we confuse a cause with an effect or vice versa, as in this example: "The Black Death devastated Europe because it killed so many people that few were left to make society function." The part of this sentence after the word "because" should be an explanation of the first part of the sentence, but it is actually explaining the *effects* of the plague or elaborating on what devastation looked like. To really explain the cause is to look at what came before this event and brought about its effects, like this: "The cause of the Black Death is still debated, but was likely a bacterium that spread repeatedly through shipping and then overland trade routes."

- **The historian's fallacy and presentism.** The historian's fallacy is when we describe a historical actor's decisions based on our own information and perspective rather than what was known or contemplated at the time. For example, if we want to understand the motivations of the scientists who worked on the Manhattan Project (developing the first atom bomb), we need to remember that they could not have known about the later destruction of Hiroshima and Nagasaki and that many observers at the time believed the creation of the ultimate weapon would save lives by ending World War II and even prevent future wars by making war too destructive to contemplate.

  A related error, known as presentism, is the same problem in the other direction: when we project our ideas and standards onto the past and judge historical people accordingly. For example, a modern American looking at the reign of almost any hereditary ruler is likely to see that ruler as arbitrary and tyrannical, because the citizens of most Western cultures since

World War II expect rights and see hereditary absolute rule as unfair and exploitative. However, that notion was almost unknown to humankind before the mid-eighteenth century. This mistake causes us to paint all earlier rulers with the same brush, when by the standards of their times (different standards at different times and places) they varied dramatically from each other, and any given ruler's individual actions varied from moment to moment. We should instead consider how each ruler was viewed by contemporaries and examine the priorities that a particular society valued for what constituted successful or just leadership.

Another way these problems are sometimes described is "anachronism," or something that is out of its rightful chronological place. Using a twentieth-century term such as "schizophrenia" to describe the behavior of a person in the eighteenth century is anachronistic.

These problems stemming from conflicting perspectives or frames of reference are why historians, as a rule of thumb, try to "forget what we know" and immerse ourselves in the context of the time, stick as closely to primary evidence as possible, and avoid judgment. This does not mean scholarly historians do not see the past as relevant to the present. It's hard to imagine why we would bother with our work if that were true. But we see our job as understanding the past as accurately as possible, in order to make it possible for the reader, and for society, to draw what lessons they will from an accurate picture of the past. Historians will sometimes offer their own thoughts on the present-day or future significance of their scholarship in op-eds, interviews, or other occasions, but this is not the primary aim or substance of our written scholarship.

- **Determinism.** Because we know how events turned out, it is easy to assume they had to end up that way, or that certain outcomes were inevitable. Even if we recognize that current events are contingent (dependent) on our individual choices and on accidents, we can unconsciously assume that the past had to happen the way it did simply because that's the story we know. We must continually remind ourselves that past events were also contingent— they could have gone in other directions. If we misread the past as determined, we lose the opportunity to understand the many ramifications of cause and effect and the ability to apply that perspective to our own uncertain present. If X was a necessary cause of Y, explain why it was "necessary." In other words, what was the mechanism that transformed X into Y? Considering what alternatives there might have been can help you to identify the causes.
- **Counterfactual reasoning.** One way to trick our brains out of the trap of determinism is to ask, What if things had gone some other way? This is also known as a counterfactual question. For example, we know that in colonial

Massachusetts in 1775 Paul Revere and William Dawes traveled from Boston to Lexington to warn patriots that the British army was heading their way. What if Revere had been captured before leaving Boston and Dawes's horse had thrown a shoe and gone lame on the road? Lexington would have been caught unawares, and the war might have started out differently. Would there have been any long-term change resulting from that slightly different start to the war? We don't know, but the exercise of asking the question can help us think about events not as set in stone, but as they were: a set of contingent events that could have gone other ways.

Be careful with counterfactuals. A common problem with them is positing one historical change but assuming everything else would stay the same, or positing a change that is not really plausible in the circumstances. It is plausible that Revere would be caught or Dawes suffer an accident on the road, and even that both could happen (though that's less likely). But you'd have to work rather hard to find a plausible scenario for something as complex as the South winning the American Civil War. One could posit that the South could have made up for the North's superior numbers and industrial capacity with foreign support, but then a great many other factors would have been different as well. Counterfactual thinking can lead us into considering causal factors separately from their context, such that we interchange them like weights on a scale instead of accounting for how each cause arose in a specific environment and would have been different at a different time or place. But a historian's job is to explain interlocking factors while acknowledging their links to each other. Counterfactual questions can be good mental exercise, but remember that the ultimate goal is to better understand what actually happened, not to write a novel (at least, not for your history class; feel free to write a novel on your own time!).

- **Cause versus intention/proximity.** Causes are mechanisms that drive change. They can be confused with proximity—that is, factors that were present at the time change occurred, but not influential on making the change happen. Causes are also easily confused with intentions, which is what people hoped or planned for. Just because a person did X in order to make Y happen doesn't mean X isn't the reason Z was the result. Similarly, if we are looking for the causes of Z, we could overlook the person who caused it because that person intended to make something else happen. Intention is logically different from causation, though both are often worth discussing (in cases where we can know what people's intentions were). Also related is the difference between rhetoric and reality: what people say about their reasons is not the same as their real reasons, and what people talk about is not the same as what actually happens.

- **Monocausal explanations and binary thinking.** Because history is the study of the whole past, with all the richness and complexity of life as we live it now, there is never a single cause for an event or phenomenon. No single causal explanation—even if you can argue that it is the most decisive cause—can explain everything. For this reason, don't stop looking for causes after you find one you consider plausible. You're not fighting over who has the "best" cause. Academic argument is a series of claims supported by evidence and reasoning, not a fight. We are looking for accurate and full explanations of complex events, so black-and-white or "no mercy" answers that refuse to acknowledge other factors cannot be satisfying.

  Similarly, any event or development in the past was understood and experienced differently by the various people involved in it. Remember that there are always more than one, and usually more than two, ways of seeing an issue. The most useful explanations acknowledge multiple evidence-based perspectives. Binary explanations that allow for only two "sides" to a question are often as inaccurate as monocausal explanations.

- **Biased/motivated reasoning.** We each have our own assumptions and prejudices about how the world works and what is most important. These personal perspectives can become a bias that distorts our work if we cling to them despite evidence, or if we ignore evidence that contradicts what we already believe. Stop and think for a moment about what you believed was the explanation for the issue at hand before you enrolled in your current course. Are those assumptions coloring the argument you're making now? "Confirmation bias" is when you pay more attention to evidence that reinforces what you already believe than to other evidence. If you find yourself making a case to support a belief you held before you began this course, check yourself by going back to your notes to look for evidence you might have missed. It is often more enlightening, and more useful, to compose arguments that run contrary to your assumptions. This can give you a great mental workout.

6.10. Revising: Structure

This type of essay is relatively short, so your introduction and conclusion should be proportionately short. And since the question motivating your essay was already provided in a prompt, you don't need to do a lot of work to explain why your question is important. Since the goal for this assignment is to show you can construct an argument, your argument should drive the structure. Lead with your main claim (your answer to the question) and follow it with the evidence you gathered from sources and your explanations about how that evidence supports your claim. Address any likely counterarguments and, in your conclusion, briefly elaborate on how your main claim answers the question more satisfactorily or usefully than other possible interpretations or what its other implications might be. In an in-class exam where you may need to think through your evidence as you describe it, you may not be able to state your main claim until your conclusion, and this is probably acceptable given those constraints (ask your instructor if you're not certain).

Introductions. Getting to the point quickly is desirable in an academic essay and doing so briefly is important when the overall essay is short. In most cases, the first sentence or two can orient the reader with the "who when where what" that you are discussing (your topic). The next sentence or two can stake out what position you will explain and support in the rest of the essay (your main claim), as well as some statement of how your claim differs from other interpretations or common assumptions about the question under discussion. Be careful to avoid generalizations like the following:

> I answer the question of X, which is so important because it's generally misunderstood.
>
> I claim that X, unlike most people who have previously failed to solve this problem.
>
> I will show how X, which has been a problem for historians since the beginning of time . . .

Instead, name specific counterarguments, assumptions, or points of view:

> Although the totalitarianism school dominated historical interpretations throughout the Cold War, scholars have begun to question its usefulness. I will show several ways in which we can better understand the interwar period by differentiating between its two most murderous regimes.

Paragraph and body organization. The first sentence of each paragraph should be a topic sentence that indicates what the rest of the paragraph will be about. Reading each paragraph of a draft, sum up what it is about in a word or two in the margin. Do the first sentences match the main topic of each paragraph? If not, revise. Is there anything in the paragraph that doesn't belong? Delete or move it.

Scan again the paragraph summaries you wrote in the margin and ask whether the topic of each paragraph is moving your argument forward. The most important pieces of your essay are claims (including subclaims; see section 6.8), evidence, and reasoning. One likely structure for an analytical essay is that each paragraph begins with a subclaim, followed by evidence and reasoning to support it. But this is not the only effective structure. If your main claim can't be logically broken down into parts, each paragraph may explain a different piece of evidence. Alternatively, your claim may rest on just one main piece of evidence that needs to be explained extensively, so each paragraph may be a line of reasoning, an example, or a necessary background story. Whichever structure fits your material, each paragraph should have a clear purpose in supporting your argument. You don't need to have a topic sentence stating, "The purpose of X in supporting my claim that Y is Z" at the beginning of every paragraph, but the keywords in each topic sentence should have a logical connection to your main claim, and each paragraph should add a substantive piece of support.

Conclusions. In a short essay your conclusion might be even briefer than your introduction. It should not repeat your introduction, however. If you are writing your essay in class with no time for revision, your conclusion might be the first time you articulate your main claim, because you developed it as you described the evidence. However, if you have the opportunity to revise, your main claim will ideally be stated in the introduction, and what is left for you to conclude is usually an explanation of your claim's broader implications or relationship to other arguments. As you did with your introduction, you want to avoid generalizations or overly contentious misstatements about the importance of your argument. Consider whether you are impressed by statements like these:

> Having proven that X was caused by Y because Z, no further study of this subject is necessary.

> Unlike the mistaken arguments of X, I have definitively shown that the way Y happened was Z.

> Now that I have shown X, future historians should use my reasoning as they consider how other events happen in other places and times.

Compare those statements to a specific, accurate, and qualified statement like the following:

> When we consider the huge ideological differences between Hitler and Stalin, the differences in how their crimes were carried out and their effects, and consider a broader context where many of their seeming similarities were actually common to other dictatorships or even to Europe as a whole, we should not only look still more closely at the mechanisms of control used in each of these regimes, but remember that extreme politics can arise from a variety of contexts in a variety of ways.

Where does the "background" go? Notice what's been left out of the outline in section 6.8: there's no section there for background, or a chronological story of who did what to whom in the past. You know that your essay should not include too much summary, but at the same time, the causes of events are often a series of people doing things, and some explanation of this complexity is necessary for the reader to understand your argument. The difference between a summary and an argument-driven structure lies in how you frame the details about events and when you bring them in. Compare the following examples:

> In Laurel Thatcher Ulrich's *A Midwife's Tale*, we meet a Maine midwife who balanced taking care of her home with her occupation as midwife, which brought cash into her household. Ulrich uses Martha Ballard's extensive diaries to analyze Martha's daily activities, from weaving to nursing sick postpartum mothers, as well as how these activities were connected economically with her community. From Ulrich's account, women were not the non-economic actors many assume.

> There are many ways women contributed to economic activity even in contexts where they had no individual property rights and few professional opportunities, such as Ulrich's Maine midwife Martha Ballard, a married woman who worked for cash and trade as a midwife while also taking part in community-based textile production.

In the first example, the author has summarized a text first, and then made a point about how it supports her claim. In the second excerpt, the author leads with her claim and adds the evidence much more briefly as an example, including only the details necessary for her purpose. This allows the author of the second example to add further support from other sources or from another part of this source, while the first author might already be out of space before she made her case.

As you finalize the structure of your essay, don't forget to add a title (see section 8.7 on how to formulate a title) or at least a reference to the prompt you have chosen to answer!

6.11. Revising: Showing Your Work

Students often hesitate to explain their thinking on the page, sometimes believing this is similar to including your personal feelings and reactions (which indeed do not belong in your essay). But "reasoning" refers to the logical connections between your evidence and your claims. It's how you explain that your evidence really does show your claims to be true. Without that explanation, your argument is incomplete and unconvincing. To put your reasoning on the page is to show your work, just as in math class, where you need to show the steps you followed from problem to solution.

Which of the following is most convincing?

History is a terrible major. I hated it, it made me feel bored.

History is a terrible major. There's tons of reading and writing, and it's hard to know what you really need to remember, which can make it feel boring.

In the first example, readers have no idea whether they might come to the same conclusion you did. In the second example, you have provided several reasons. Not every reader will agree with them, but each reader can make a conclusion grounded in an objective and logical reality.

It's easy to confuse showing your work with writing a record of your thoughts. The following examples illustrate the difference:

The year 1666 was cataclysmic for Europe, which probably seems surprising, but I'll show how we can look at it that way. 1666 was terrible for England, which was good for its rival the Netherlands. The Netherlands had its Golden Age and took over the English throne in the Glorious Revolution of 1688, and William of Orange consolidated Protestantism and the preeminent place of the navy. So you could look at all these things happening and say these are pretty minor events that just happened in England and involved one other country, but you could also look at this and say that England having a stable, limited monarchy is a pretty big deal over a long period of time, and all that started with William of Orange taking over and combining Dutch and English interests when they were both at their height and that made that kind of strength really long-lasting, when otherwise it might not have been.

The year 1666 was cataclysmic for Europe, even though the most famous and significant upheavals—war, plague, and fire—were specific to England. But I argue that those upheavals were the beginning of the rise of Protestantism and representative government in Europe, even though neither came to fully dominate until the second half of the twentieth century. By crippling England at its height, these events had the effect of strengthening England's naval and trade rival, the Netherlands, which reached the peak of its Golden Age as a result, allowing William of Orange to take the English throne in the Glorious Revolution of 1688, which consolidated European naval and trade power from that time to World War II, and which resulted in a stable, Protestant constitutional monarchy that withstood 250 years of political challenges.

The difference between these examples is mostly stylistic—the content is virtually the same—but the unnecessary rambling (narrating how the author came to her conclusions) in the first example weakens the argument by making the connections between causes and effects harder to follow. The second example explains *why* one event is connected to the other in logical, but not personal, terms.

As you review your essay at this stage, check whether a "because" statement can be added to every sentence: if you can explain your reasoning more fully without repeating yourself, do so. Explain the "why" and "how" that connects each event you mention, but don't describe the thought process you went through to figure out how and why.

6.12. Revising: Identifying Style Problems

The most important principles of style and clarity for an in-class essay are the same as for a short-answer exam essay (sections 4.6–4.7): avoid summing up or simplifying, avoid wasting space with repetition or vagueness, and pack every sentence with as much relevant and accurate information and reasoning as you can. The effectiveness of your essay is judged on whether the words on the page show your mastery of the material and original thinking. If you are running out of time in an exam setting, it is usually better to include relevant details and reasoning in bullet points rather than to leave them out. If the most efficient way to include examples is in parentheses, do so.

If you are writing your essay at home, you will be expected to revise for style and clarity and to use complete, grammatically correct sentences throughout. Refer to sections 5.8–5.12 to make your words more accurate and specific and to delete anything that is not adding value. Next, consider the following more complicated style problems that can arise as we grapple with expressing our own argument.

When we're confused or uncertain, as when we are still fumbling toward an argument, our writing tends to become less clear. Consider the sentence "Henri Dunant wrote *A Memory of Solferino* to incite action into creating an organization to aid the wounded soldiers during wartime." Most readers would stumble over that, but how do we pinpoint the reasons that this sentence is unclear, so we know what to change to make it better? One possibility is not to identify the problem at all, but simply rewrite the sentence several different ways and then use the one that is most accurate, specific, and economical. The most useful strategy, though, that will not only fix one sentence but help you get better at writing more clearly, is to develop your understanding about what makes some sentences more clear than others.

First look for grammatical and other technical mistakes (or work with campus support services or a grammar reference book if you can't do this on your own). In this case, "to incite . . . into" is incorrect. If you look up "to incite" in a dictionary you will find that it's a transitive verb that requires an object (something affected by the action) and means "to stir up" some action, so we can see that "to incite action into creating" is redundant. So we can immediately revise the sentence like this: "Henri Dunant wrote *A Memory of Solferino* to incite an organization to aid the wounded soldiers during wartime."

This still doesn't sound quite right, probably because a verb meaning to "stir up" doesn't fit with something as undynamic as "an organization." When we use a word that's not quite right, often we're trying to remember a different word that sounds similar. Looking through a physical dictionary, where you can browse words that start with the same letters, can lead you to the word you really wanted. Let's try: "Henri Dunant wrote *A Memory of Solferino* to inspire an organization to aid the wounded soldiers during wartime." This is getting closer. We might notice now that there's more redundancy—once we've mentioned "wounded soldiers" it's already clear that we're talking about wartime, so we can leave that out: "Henri Dunant wrote *A Memory of Solferino* to inspire an organization to aid wounded soldiers." The sentence is now clear enough, but still sounds a bit awkward.

When you've checked that each word means what it should and you've removed words that don't need to be there, look for nominalizations. A nominalization is a verb that has been turned into a noun form. For example, we know the verb "to organize." "Organization" is the noun form of this verb. When we talk about "an organization," it is implied that some people somewhere must have "organized" something, and the result was "an organization." If that result is what we're interested in and we don't care who did it, the noun form is what we want. But in this case, we're actually talking about the stage when this organization was formed and the book that inspired people to do that organizing. In other words, the action—organizing—is much more important here than the result. Let's rewrite using "organize" in verb form: "Henri Dunant wrote *A Memory of Solferino* to inspire readers to organize to aid wounded soldiers."

Now that we see the sentence this way, we realize we're trying to say two things at once. Is organizing really the most important part, or aiding the wounded? You'll need to think about what's really happening in your sources and what you're arguing, but here are two possibilities:

Henri Dunant wrote *A Memory of Solferino* to inspire readers to aid wounded soldiers.

Henri Dunant wrote *A Memory of Solferino* to inspire readers to organize aid for wounded soldiers.

Readers of English will have an easier time with sentences that match the grammatical structure subject + verb + object with concrete people and actions (a person + does something + to someone/something). Whenever you see a noun that represents an important action, put it in verb form. This will force you to name the people doing the action (here "readers"), which also helps clarify your sentence and may in some cases prompt you to include other important details you had inadvertently left out.

6.13. Revising: Transitions

A second problem that may pop up as you compose your argument is the difficulty of choosing transitions that reflect the logic of your argument. This mistake usually appears because we are not certain, when we draft, what we are saying or how it fits together. That's fine for brainstorming, but you need to make a conscious effort to adjust your transitions appropriately before you turn in your essay. Consider the following example:

> The Great Depression caused great suffering for the poor, so working people looked to FDR's "Fireside Chats" for hope and reassurance that life would improve. Furthermore, Kennedy points out that life wasn't easy during the Depression.

There are two transition words in this example: "so" and "furthermore." The first makes sense: "so" means "therefore" or "consequently." Whatever follows "so" is a result of whatever comes before "so." In this case, working-class Americans looked to Roosevelt's radio messages for reassurance that times would improve. But the second transition word, "furthermore," means "in addition." It adds something new to a list that has already been started. What comes before "furthermore" here is the statement that American workers hoped for improvement, and what comes after is that "life wasn't easy." That's not something new, it's a restatement of what has already been said, or a contradiction of the idea that there was hope. Try one of the following:

> However, Kennedy points out that life remained difficult for most people through these years.
>
> Despite this hope, Kennedy points out that life remained difficult.

If you're not sure of your transitions, look them up in a dictionary to make sure you know what they mean and look for alternatives in a thesaurus or online list of transitions (again making sure you understand their meaning before using them).

6.14. Proofreading: Past-Tense Verbs

As you proofread for the usual grammatical, punctuation, usage, citation, and formatting errors (see sections 5.9, 5.13, and 8.12 and appendix 1), pay particular attention to verbs. Since we are writing about the past, we primarily use the past tense. However, the English language offers us a confusing abundance of past-tense verb forms (which are particularly challenging for nonnative speakers). The less common verb forms are frequently used in historical writing because we often compare two past events to each other and discuss ongoing processes as well as singular events. And even for those born to English, the difference between the specialized usage of the "historical present" and "literary present" can be perplexing. The following examples show correct usage of all past-tense forms.

There's no need to learn the formal names for complicated verb forms—you only need to know how and when to use them, and for that purpose you can find the example in what follows that matches the logical situation you are trying to describe, and use the forms as you see them here. The formal names are provided so you can look them up for more information or get the right irregular verb form from a dictionary.

When describing events in the past, for the most part we use the *simple past tense*:

> Hitler *seized* power.
>
> Jessica Mitford *wrote* a memoir.
>
> Women *began* to wear less restrictive clothing.

Sometimes we describe an event or process that occurred entirely in the past (it's no longer happening) but went on for some time (*past progressive tense*):

> Hitler *was gaining* power gradually between 1924 and 1933.
>
> Unity Mitford *was toying* with Nazi affiliation during her first trip to Germany.
>
> In the decade following the first world war, women *were working* more and marrying less.

When we compare two events that are both past, and describe a past process that was completed at an unspecified time or an event that took place prior to another specified time in the past, we use *past perfect tense*:

> Before Hitler *seized* [simple past] power in 1933, one could argue the Weimar government *had failed* [past perfect] already.
>
> Jessica Mitford *had denounced* [past perfect] communism by the time she *wrote* [simple past] her memoir.

Feminists of the 1920s *were* [simple past] aware of what their predecessors *had* already *accomplished* [past perfect].

When we compare two sets of events, both in the past, and one of them went on for some time, we use the *past perfect progressive*:

Hitler *had been gaining* [past perfect progressive] power gradually for almost a decade when he suddenly *declared* [simple past] himself Führer.

Unity Mitford *had been toying* [past perfect progressive] with Nazism for years before her parents *realized* [simple past] the seriousness of her affiliation with Hitler.

Women *had been experiencing* [past perfect progressive] unprecedented opportunities since the war, but by the 1930s a backlash *set in* [simple past].

When we compare one point in the past to another point in the past from the point of view of a past actor, we often combine the simple past or past perfect tense with "would" (a modal verb in past form) used to describe "future in the past"—that is, what would have been the future to a person living at the past time we're describing.

Comparing what the Weimar government *had accomplished* [past perfect] by 1933 to what Hitler *would accomplish* [modal past] by 1939, it is not difficult to see why many observers *were* [simple past] impressed.

Although Jessica Mitford *expressed* [simple past] concern about class relations even when she *was* [simple past] a small child, she *would not declare* [modal past] herself a Communist until some years later.

In 1918 propertied women over thirty *were given* [simple past (passive)] the right to vote in the UK, and it *was assumed* [simple past (passive)] that these women's voting patterns *would greatly disrupt* [modal past] election results.

Sometimes in popular or journalistic history writing, the *historical present* is used: this is a literary device where we use the present tense to describe events in the past, to make them "come alive" for the reader. It is frowned upon for scholarly writing, as it can be confusing (especially in the kinds of situations previously described where one point in the past is compared to another):

Hitler *gains* [historical present] power in 1933.

Unity Mitford *goes* [historical present] to a park in Berlin and *shoots* [historical present] herself in the head.

Women's hemlines *rise* [historical present].

Comparing what the Weimar government *has accomplished* [historical present perfect] by 1933 to what Hitler *will accomplish* by 1939 [historical present modal], it is not difficult to see why many observers *were* [simple past] impressed.

Putting the final verb "were" in present tense would make no sense, leading to a sentence where the tense jumps all over the place—doing too much of this can be very confusing. However, we do often use the *literary present* when we write about the contents of a text, as opposed to the act of writing or publishing it, because we're still reading the text, so its ideas are still acting in the present:

Jessica Mitford *wrote* [simple past] a memoir, which *angered* [simple past] most of her family.

But

In her memoir Jessica Mitford *claims* [literary present] that she *began* [simple past] to think about Communism because of the inequalities she *saw* [simple past] around her as a child.

7

Imaginative Projects

Imaginative assignments take an unusually broad variety of forms. You might be asked to write a document from the point of view of a historical actor, such as a diary or memoir, or to create an imaginary historical document such as a treaty or legal brief. You could be asked to prepare a presentation, as in a debate or role-playing game, which may include some writing component, or write a fictional story set in the past.

If you have a choice between a traditional essay and an imaginative one, consider that you need to demonstrate the same knowledge and skills in either. The imaginative essay can be more of a challenge because you need to try something new. On the other hand, because imaginative essays can be fun, they can feel easier even while you're actually doing more work. If you are creatively inclined, an imaginative assignment may help you to shine in ways that you don't get to show in a traditional assignment.

7.1. What's Your Goal?

Whenever you are asked to invent a historical situation, you are still being asked to show change over time, as in traditional academic history. There are two guiding principles:

- **You need to show the same skills and knowledge as in an equivalent traditional essay.** The type and amount of historical substance should be the same as if you were writing an analytical or primary source essay. Only the way you achieve your goals will be different. Rather than focusing on selecting material from the readings to demonstrate your understanding and support your analysis, you will invent plausible and useful details to fit your imaginary character or situation, using the readings to help you find what is plausible and what historical issues would have been relevant.
- **An imaginative essay is an opportunity to explore how identities and perspectives change over time.** Though your instructor may have offered an imaginative assignment in part to engage you in the material, it also serves another purpose. By inventing details to create or explain a historical actor, you are pushed to consider the ways context affects behavior: what

kinds of details about where we live and our circumstances influence the things we do and say? These are central issues in almost any imaginative project, and you will demonstrate your thoughtful consideration of them through the details you invent.

7.2. Types of Imaginative Projects

If your assignment falls into none of the following categories, consider how you can extrapolate from the task you are given to the specific goals, content, and format that will be expected from you in the same way that is outlined here.

Respond as a participant. You may be asked to write a response paper, but as if you are a historical actor who participated in the events described in a reading. Usually this is done with a primary source, as when you are asked to provide the other side of a historical debate by responding to some historical figure's argument—for example, you are asked to compose the British foreign minister's response to the Kruger telegram. Or you could be asked to respond to a historian's account from the point of view of a subject of the work. After reading Rachel Laudan's *Cuisine and Empire: Cooking in World History*, you could write a response to it from the point of view of a cook from a culture and time period you have researched. In this kind of assignment your job is to do one or more of the following:

- To flesh out / add nuance to arguments
- To provide more detail for a specific case
- To address omissions
- To contradict or argue against the author or another voice in the text

Search the scholarly source for particularly strong or provocative points, or points of contradiction, controversy, disagreement, or difficulty, and explain from the perspective of your historical actor why those passages are interesting. Imagine details about the life of your person—such as a slave cook in the Caribbean in the eighteenth century—that might illustrate or complicate what you read, or even points where your character might be dissatisfied with the account of people like her found in your source readings.

Or perhaps you are asked to be a guide for a historical actor: if someone from the past were here with you now, how would you explain our world to her? The first step in that exercise is to identify the major points of change. Make a list of the biggest changes your historical actor would notice. Annotate that list to add your historical person's view or understanding of each of those items. Then add the explanations you would give to this person from the past: what has changed, why, and how? For example, imagine you could take Susan B. Anthony on a walk through Washington, DC today. What would you show her that would most interest her, given what you know about Anthony as a social reformer and activist for women's suffrage? What has changed since her time, and how would you explain those changes?

Create a historical document. When you are asked to create a historical document, such as a letter, diary, memoir, or legal or government document, you might be expected to impersonate a real historical figure and imagine how that person would write the document, or you may be told to invent a historical figure to be the document's author. If you are able to choose whether you write, for example, a diary, memoir, or series of letters, consider the problems and limitations of these forms of documents as you would when reading and analyzing a genuine historical document (see also section 9.5 on identifying and reading these kinds of documents):

- **Diary.** You will compose daily entries, so you will need to decide which dates to include. If a major event occurred that would have closely affected your character, choose at least one entry before and one entry after it to show the changes. Daily diary entries are a good way to reflect the immediate impact of change, but they can also be used to show the details of ordinary daily life. If you assume the diary wasn't intended to be read, you might also assume your diarist would be generally honest, but consider what that person might not want to admit even privately and think of ways to convey that information indirectly.

   Say you are recreating an imaginary diary by Charlotte Corday, a Girondist French revolutionary who was guillotined for assassinating a Jacobin revolutionary, Jean-Paul Marat. Her last entry could not be later than July 13, 1793, when she carried out her assassination, since she was immediately taken into custody, then tried and executed by July 17. Presumably you want to explain her motives in assassinating someone, so you would want to include an entry or several in the period leading up to July 13. But depending on how you want to explain her actions (a form of argument you would be making indirectly), you might also want to include entries from much earlier, when her political views might first have been formed.

- **Memoir.** Writers of memoirs look back at a past time and are able to reflect and make connections about their behavior and beliefs. When you compose an imaginary memoir, you are really comparing two time periods: the time of writing and the time being described. Choose each period carefully to maximize the changes you can show your character experiencing. Consider how much your imaginary memoirist would be likely to remember, and to what degree motivated to be honest. Would he lie about his past? Or perhaps "spin" it in a way that reflects better on himself?

For example, pretend you are writing a memoir by an Italian journalist that was composed in 1960 but focuses on the 1920s–30s, when Italy was fascist. Let's say your journalist established his career by writing sympathetically about fascism. How open would he be about that decades later, after fascism was defeated? Would he say that he wrote as he did then because he was afraid? Or would he explain why he was once a sincere believer? Or something in between? Ask yourself what you know from course readings about the reasons real people supported Mussolini's regime to help you form your answers.

- **Letter.** Letters imply a conversation between at least two parties. Are you allowed to invent both parties to a correspondence, and if so is one person only a reader, or can you write from two perspectives? Or are you addressing a real, known historical figure from the point of view of an imaginary figure? The conversational nature of letters allows you to explore contradictions, disagreements, or differing perspectives. Letters also come with some of the same considerations as diary entries: you will need to choose dates that allow you to convey the most relevant issues for your assignment, and your imaginary author(s) should be caught up in the moment, rather than reflecting over long periods. But as in a memoir, a letter-writer has specific reader(s) in mind and may be motivated to hide or omit information or be outright deceptive. Remember when you choose dates that letters did not reach their recipients immediately: the greater the distance, the more time there would be between letters.

  For example, if you are assigned to write letters between a Jewish immigrant in New York and his family back in Poland in the 1890s, you would need to invent details about who your immigrant was and his life in New York. You would also need to consider what you know about Poland at the same time, and how the contrast between the two places might be highlighted in your letters. You might also invent specific Polish family members and consider what they would want to know about New York. What kinds of events might your immigrant have witnessed or experienced that you could describe in the letters?

- **Legal or government document.** If you are composing a document with no clear author, or with multiple authors, such as a government or legal document, you will need to model your work after a similar real document from around the same time period. What is the purpose of your document? Legal briefs are intended to represent one side in a dispute. To create such a document, you will need to research the dispute and figure out what side you're representing and what that point of view was based on. You will also need to address and proactively refute any claims you think the other side might make. For example, if you were to invent a legal brief written by a populist Kansas lawyer in 1935, making a case to the Supreme Court about the New Deal, what might your lawyer be arguing for and on what grounds?

Diplomatic documents such as treaties are composed by groups of representatives of each participating country. Each side attempts to achieve some advantage relative to the other countries. The result will be a compromise. Think not only about what each country wants, but how they think they can best get what they want out of others without sacrificing their core interests. Similarly, many government documents created within one country are the result of compromise: different departments or interest groups create pressures for or against certain policies, and together they hash out what the government can do. For example, if you were to write a memo from the Soviet Ministry of General Machine-Building Industry to the Politburo in 1989, what concerns would you have to represent? What would this bureaucratic body be asking for from its leaders? What kinds of solutions would they offer for the biggest problems of that time as they affected heavy industry?

- **Drawing, design, object.** If you are asked to create something other than a text, don't worry about trying to be a great artist: your goal is still to explore and explain change over time. Consider how the constraints of the particular form you are creating affect the result. How do you convey an idea visually? What materials do you use? What do you depict, and choose not to depict? What angle do you depict it from? Can you manipulate color or materials? You need to determine what choices would have been available to this kind of creator in the past time you are studying and then ask what choices that historical person would have made and why. How do you reflect those choices and reasoning in your project?

  For example, if you are assigned to pretend you are the Early Byzantine patron of a pilgrimage church and asked to design and describe the building you would commission, you need to consider what message(s) your Early Byzantine elite person would wish to project to pilgrims and how the symbolism of church design in this period could be used to convey that message. If you are assigned to produce a textile that represents how textiles have been used as a means of communication in the past, you might make a quilt square using US Civil War–era patterns that represent rural identities, such as regional flower species.

Write a story. If you are asked to write historical fiction—a story set in the past—your assignment may specify the events and time period to cover (the "setting" for your story) and may determine whether you can or should use real historical people or invent characters. From that starting point, you have two goals that need to be intertwined: to construct a story (which has characters and a plot) and to explain change over time (because this is a history assignment).

A plot revolves around a series of events connected by cause and effect, so look for the causes and effect inherent in a historical change relevant to your assignment or course, whether the change is a big event or a slow development. What were people trying to achieve, or how were they responding to things that happened to them? How did people differ in their goals or responses?

Characters begin as collections of characteristics: age, sex, class, ethnicity/nationality, religion, attitudes, positions, values, fears, expectations. In a story, characters develop in response to challenges posed by the plot. Invent characters that can highlight how historical changes from your course affected various kinds of people.

The easiest way to run into trouble when writing fiction in a history course is to become carried away with your story to the detriment of showing change over time as it relates to issues relevant to your course. Start by thinking through what you want to show or explore about a historical question and let the plot and characters develop from there. Check back in with these goals frequently as you write.

For example, say you are assigned to write a story set in feudal Japan. From your readings you will have learned some of the main concerns and conflicts of that time and place. You might decide that you are interested in the Mongol invasions of the late thirteenth century. From there you could decide to depict the conflict between the Kamakura shogunate and the Mongols, perhaps by telling a story of an ordinary warrior on each side before, during, and after the 1274 invasion. You will invent details about each of your warriors to give them personalities and motives, and you will guess what events they might have witnessed or participated in. Then you will consider how those events could affect each of your characters and how you could use the contrast between them to explore key questions about that time period, such as the rise of the samurai.

One particular kind of historical story you may be asked to write is a counterfactual. This is where you imagine that some historical event occurred differently than it actually did, and then reason out what else would have gone differently based on that one change. Counterfactuals are more or less successful depending on how specifically you pursue the lines of cause and effect emanating from each change. For example, what if Napoleon hadn't sold the Louisiana Territory to the United States in 1803? What would have been different about Napoleon's situation for him to have decided against the sale? In what specific ways would the development of the United States toward the west have been affected by the continued existence of this French territory? How would it affect the development of the West Coast? How might the French have developed their territory differently than the westward American expansion that we're familiar with? From what we know of each country's circumstances and priorities in the early nineteenth century, can we guess how American-French relations might have evolved along a shared border, especially knowing that the French would not have enjoyed the cash payment and cancellation of debts involved in the purchase? Perhaps most importantly, how would continued French control of the territory affect slaveholding there and the debates over slavery in subsequent decades, which would now become an international matter?

Debate. When you are asked to represent a historical person or point of view in a debate, you need to find out everything you can about the ideas you'll represent. If you are allowed to invent a person, consider first what kinds of real people held the point of view you will represent: were they male, female? Of what social class? What nationality or ethnicity? What kind of job did they have? How much education? How would they be likely to come to their position? Invent a personal backstory that shows the kind of person who would be likely to hold this position.

You will usually need to argue for a position that is not your own, whether it is a position you disagree with or simply have never thought or cared about. Put yourself in the shoes of the person you're representing. Consider not only his background and how that influenced his thinking, but what he could know: what information was available to him? What concerns seemed most important at that time to someone in that situation? Consciously set aside what *you* know, your inclinations, beliefs, allegiances, and your knowledge of how this historical situation turned out.

For example, if you are to argue for the loyalist position at the Raleigh Tavern in Williamsburg, Virginia, in 1773, you first need to determine that people arguing in a tavern in colonial America were probably men. Loyalists were often older and more established than patriots and some had personal links with England, so you might decide that you will be a sixty-year-old shop owner who trades in partnership with a brother in England. From there you might decide that your loyalist's main concern was that independence would destroy trade and therefore the colonial economy. From there you could brainstorm a list of arguments to make, the likely counterarguments from your classmates who represent patriots, and your responses to those counterarguments.

Role-playing game. Debates are one kind of role-playing game, but there are many others, and they can become very complicated. Use whatever space you are given to invent details that show how context affected behavior in the time and place you're studying. What difference did it make to be male or female? To be rich or poor? To have one job rather than another job? To live in one kind of place or another?

In a role-playing game you will interact with other students who are also inhabiting some historical persona. Think about how your character's interests combined or conflicted with others'. What did your person need or want to achieve? What would she have been willing to sacrifice? What were her responsibilities and loyalties, as she saw them? Are you representing someone who would be honest with herself and others about who she was or what she wanted? What were her values?

Say your game involves recreating a trial. Each person will have a job: judge, jury member, lawyer, defendant, witness, perhaps journalist. What are the goals, responsibilities, challenges that go with the job you were given? How might this affect your attitude toward the other participants? As much as you can, invent details, facts, reasons, or explanations that help to explain your character's relationship to others and to the central conflict of your game. For example, if you are a prosecutor, what pressures are you facing from your superiors (the state) and what are your personal ambitions? How would you best present your case in a way that appeals to the concerns of the ordinary people on the jury?

Say your game involves people of various social ranks and backgrounds interacting at a social event: you need to know your age, sex, class, nationality or ethnicity, religion or ideology, and occupation and then think about how those facts about you—and any others that might be relevant for the time and place you're working with—would offer you opportunities or limits on how you can behave, and suggest goals for what you could accomplish for yourself or others you would care about. Find out what manners were typical for different social groups and what purposes were served by the kind of event you're acting out. How can you use your character to demonstrate what you've learned?

Imagine a game where you are asked to maneuver against other participants, as in a recreation of a Stalinist purge trial set in a tank factory in 1937. Your goal is to avoid being purged, and perhaps to help purge others in order to get a promotion for yourself. What details would make you more or less vulnerable? Among the other people in the game, who would be likely allies or enemies? What could you do to work with others, or to isolate others, to meet your character's goals?

If you are able to use gestures, accents, or other behaviors to add to your portrayal, this can add to the experience for everyone. Your acting skills are not important, but do make an effort to speak audibly, clearly, and at a reasonable pace. Role-playing games can be an opportunity to express your understanding of the course material in ways that are not possible in a traditional essay. Make the most of this in whatever ways fit your abilities and inclinations.

Writing up a debate or role-playing game. You may be asked to write a summary of your debate or game afterward, to be turned in for a grade. Your purpose in any write-up of an in-class activity is to demonstrate how you prepared and what you learned. It follows, then, that your write-up should include the information you read and invented for your role and how you thought it through. Explain how you chose which details to find or invent. Consider what surprised you or gave you ideas as you participated in the activity in class. But don't give a moment-by-moment account of how you reacted to the whole activity and don't include how much you enjoyed or didn't enjoy the experience. First brainstorm a list of the moments that struck you, then revise that list from first reactions into a list of lessons you learned. For example, if you were surprised by how persuasive your opponent's case was, you might revise "I was surprised by how good X was" to "I was impressed by X's argument that Y, because Z. This was unexpected, because when I prepared my role, I emphasized A."

7.3. Reading for Imaginative Projects

The usual kinds of course materials—textbooks, scholarly arguments, or original documents—can seem useless for an assignment that involves inventing imaginary people or situations. However, your success in this assignment still depends on how closely you use those readings. You will probably not be quoting and may not even be citing your sources in the usual way (see section 7.9), but the choices you make as you invent details need to be grounded in historical evidence and the questions historians ask.

As you prepare for an imaginative assignment, turn to your course materials to look up specific facts or to read explanations of positions held by your character. Beyond that, you also need to glean from your sources the concerns and priorities that would be relevant for your assignment and the ways that various forms of identity affected people's ideas and behavior (for more on how historians understand identity, see section 3.1). To find this information even in sources that were not intended to explain this content directly, look for the people. Scan through your readings to find details about individual historical people and notice what kind of information is provided about their identities, ideas, and behaviors.

You may model a character you invent directly on something you read, but not necessarily: think about what your readings or course lectures say about how identities affected particular situations or questions and then extrapolate from that information to imagine a person and assign details about them that would inform who they were and how they would have acted. For example, if you read about the American western frontier in the middle of the nineteenth century and see that pioneers were mostly single men, imagine what it would have been like to be one of the few women. Your reading should tell you why it was mostly single men who went out to settle the American West and that might suggest a backstory to explain the kind of exception that would lead a woman to go. If she was unlikely to travel to the frontier alone, how might she end up alone once living there? What could the consequences be? Find out as much as you can to answer these questions from the readings and then fill in the remaining gaps—not by inventing at random, but by reasoning from what you do know to what would be most likely to follow from it.

7.4. Brainstorming: What to Know or Invent

Brainstorming for an imaginative project is much like brainstorming for a traditional assignment. You still need to reason from evidence. Your readings inform the possible, likely, and interesting details you can use to show the how and why behind changes in the past. Think strategically about what you need to show, find accurate details from readings, and then invent a scenario to demonstrate those facts and ideas. Use the questions historians ask and especially the list of ways historical identity can affect people's behavior and ideas in section 3.1 to help you brainstorm.

Start with what you want your character to demonstrate. What are the historical issues involved in your assignment? Is it about social mobility? Then you want a character that moves from one social class to another. What are the ways and reasons this could happen? Is your assignment about political ideas? What were different kinds of people were likely to believe and what motivated those beliefs? Try brainstorming a list of questions that your class has been discussing and then add ways characters or situations could help to answer them.

7.5. Brainstorming: Taking a Stand

Beyond demonstrating that you understand the historical issues at hand (in detail and accurately reflecting their complexity), you also need to demonstrate your own thoughtful take on the materials, just as you would take a stand or defend a claim in a traditional essay. Look at the questions you brainstormed: what would your answer be if you were writing an analytical essay or research paper? You probably don't know yet, because as with a traditional essay, you need to work through your evidence before you begin to see what conclusions to draw. Try brainstorming an actual analytical essay based on the most important question raised for your imaginative project, using the methods described in sections 6.4–6.7.

Once you begin to have an idea of what you want to show, one common way to try to insert an argument into an imaginative project is to have your character say what you think, as in this example:

"What we need is a defense of privacy!" argued Alexander Hamilton at the Constitutional Convention.

However, this method can result in anachronism: "Privacy" was not understood in the eighteenth century in the same way we understand it now, and nothing like it was under consideration by anyone at the Constitutional Convention in 1787. So, instead, you need to start with what is known—look up what issues were under consideration at the Constitutional Convention and how the major players thought about them—and work from there to develop a position for your character that follows from known evidence, rather than just inserting whatever you want to say.

It is often more interesting and effective to invent a character or situation as different as possible from yourself or positions you think you would hold. This forces you to think more, therefore giving you more room to demonstrate your thinking. Some of the most effective imaginative essays, like the best fiction, introduce difficulties, tension, or real jeopardy of some kind, because tension brings out the most interesting ways that our choices are affected by our circumstances, our culture, and our identity.

Mind-mapping. Many people like to brainstorm any kind of essay using a mind map. A mind map is a visual way of connecting information: you put keywords down on a page, in different colors as you see fit, then gradually draw connections, adding circles, arrows, or other symbols. There are a variety of apps that can help you to build mind maps digitally. Mind maps may be particularly useful for creative projects that need to be based in evidence and issues derived from your readings and notes. Begin by throwing this information down at random, and then explore connections and possibilities using pictures, symbols, and color to bring out your creative side and free your mind to consider the unexpected.

7.6. Drafting: Playing with Ideas

Drafting should always begin in a freewheeling way, where you don't edit yourself and you let any idea take you wherever it can go, even if it seems ridiculous. This is especially true of imaginative work, since editing is a sure way to tame imagination. Having brainstormed relevant facts and situations that are grounded in the readings, now is the time to see where they might take you. Write whatever comes into your head, with no goal but using as much as possible of the material you brainstormed. Have fun with it. See what happens.

If you are preparing a debate, speech, or other kind of performance, what you are drafting is more of a script or notes. Even though you might not need full sentences, paragraphs, or transitions, and you may not have to turn in this text, draft out how the ideas you brainstormed might sound when you say them aloud.

7.7. Revising: Substance

Once you have drafted a lot of material and followed your inspiration as far as it will take you, it is time to put on your editing hat and review your work. Once again think of your assignment as if it were a traditional analytical essay: find ideas in your draft that represent a historical question and its answer. Where do you show—indirectly—evidence for your answer? How do you show the connections between your evidence and what it means? If you are representing a particular point of view in a debate or role-playing game, what is your character's goal and what does he base it on? Is he prepared for challenges he will meet from the other characters? What would those challenges look like, and how would your character respond?

This is a stage of the writing process where it is helpful to outline: having identified the most important points you want to make, consider how they should be presented to your reader or audience, then eliminate repetition and add support or explanation where it's needed. The form your outline should take depends on the nature of your assignment, but consider one of the following examples. Use your outline to check that you are conveying what you need to meet assignment goals. Then form a plan for when or how each major piece should appear to the reader/audience, which might be drawn out in a more elaborate outline that you create specifically for your project.

Response
Who I am:
What I care about:
How I think:
Why I think this way:

Diary, letter, memoir
Change(s) to show over time:
When change(s) occur:
How the change(s) is/are shown:

Visual project or object
What should viewers understand from this?
How will they understand it?
What choices do I make to execute this plan?

Defense of a position (as in a debate, trial, discussion, some documents)
Goal:
Strategies:
Support:
Counterarguments:
Response to counterarguments:

Story
Setting:
Plot:
Main characters:
Development of characters over time:

7.8. Revising: Language and Style

There is usually no expectation of traditional academic formality in an imaginative essay. But it is important to think carefully about word choice and tone or style in any form of writing. In this case, try to choose and order words as your imaginary historical author might have done. Of course, you are not expected to be expert in imitating a specific historical writing style (unless you are in a rare classroom where this is actually part of what is being taught). Instead, think about how a diary writer—especially one who writes only for herself—would employ an informal tone, whereas a memoir (which is usually written with the assumption that someone will read it) would be more formal and perhaps a bit self-justifying. Letters might be gossipy and share personal information and ask questions as well as narrate events. Government documents would be formal and precise.

Consider the following examples. The first in each pair is written in formal essay style; the second matches word choice and style to the document type.

From the diary of an imaginary colonial American housewife:

Today I wove a cloth that I can sell at the market, because I take part in my village's economy even though I'm a woman.

Finished the weaving today. Thinking of charging more, as it's especially fine.

From the memoir of an imaginary medieval Spanish monk:

My childhood involved a number of formative experiences that explain my vocation, including an encounter with a Jewish peddler.

As I look back on my childhood, I wonder what led me to God's work. I remember the day I met a Jewish peddler and talked to him about God's grace.

The other major concern about your language choices is the same for imaginative essays as it is for a traditional essay: you need to "show your work" with specific language. Compare the following excerpts from imaginative essays:

Dear Vladimir,

Hey, Vladimir, how are you doing? This is your cousin Abram from Petrograd. I am writing you today because there are a lot of political events going on in Petrograd and I thought I would update you. As I hope you know, there is a provisional government in power and many people are not happy. There was a man named Kornilov who tried a coup and attempted to take over the provisional government.

Carlos and I were inspired by Il Duce because he united our beautiful nation after the traitorous betrayal of our so-called allies in the Great War. But, even though we will always have him in our hearts, we became concerned as the new war started to go badly. I remember how rumors spread about conditions in the Greek campaign, where our boys were bogged down in rain and mud and brutally driven back. People said even Herr Hitler had warned Mussolini about taking on a fresh enemy. Sometimes I think Il Duce's wonderful virility asked too much of our people.

The first combines a few facts with vague framing language ("a lot of political events" and "many people are not happy"), conveying little about what the student has understood of the material. The second weaves historical details into an imagined story to illustrate the author's interpretation of the subject (that adverse military conditions rather than ideology made Mussolini lose popularity). Revise for clarity and specificity much as you do for a traditional essay (see sections on revising for other assignments: 4.7, 5.8, 5.11, and 6.11).

7.9. Revising: Special Formatting

Imaginative projects are usually formatted in whatever way is appropriate to the assignment, rather than following the guidelines of a formal essay. Your instructor will inform you whether your notes for a role-playing game need to be submitted in writing, for example, or whether you will be graded solely on your performance in class. If the assignment is turned in, you may be free to amuse yourself by handwriting your document on paper you age by staining it with tea, but in some cases your instructor may need you to submit it online or require typed double-spaced text to make it easier to add feedback. But even when you are instructed to type and double-space your work, the document type will still inform its formatting to some degree: if you are recreating a diary, divide it into entries, each with its own date.

No matter what the details of your particular project, any document you turn in must have your name, the course name, the project name, and the date attached to it somehow, so it doesn't get lost or confused with something else.

7.10. Citing Sources

It would appear strange indeed for a nineteenth-century diarist to include something along the lines of "as historian John Smith said" in the middle of an entry. But you still need to cite any arguments or evidence you find in your readings (but not basic facts, such as "Mahatma Gandhi died in 1948"—see section 10.10). It is usually sufficient in an imaginative essay to incorporate an idea from a source as if it were written or heard by your character and then simply insert a note that cites the actual source. For example, you could write a description of the sensational 1887 trial of Enrico Pranzini by an imaginary right-wing French newspaper reporter, formatted in columns with an appropriate newspaper-style headline, a newspaper name taken from a real French paper of the time, and a name you made up for the byline. But you still include a note and "Works Cited" list that includes "Aaron Freundschuh, *The Courtesan and the Gigolo: The Murders in the Rue Montaigne and the Dark Side of Empire in Nineteenth-Century Paris* (Stanford University Press, 2017)."

8

The Historiographical Essay

Historiography is the study of how history has been written. It includes the study of methods and themes historians have used, and it assesses what has and has not been convincingly established about cause and effect in the past. Examples of historiography include book reviews and reviews of multiple works also known as "literature reviews" or "review essays." More elaborate works of historiography may have an argument of their own about how history has been or should be practiced, based on analyses of existing historical writing. If you are asked to read something written by a historian, to summarize the argument, and to compare that text to others written by different historians, then you are doing historiography. These assignments usually expect you to add your own commentary or criticisms. A book review is more specific than a response paper, asking for certain kinds of evaluation, and a historiographical review of several sources adds still another layer of complexity.

If you are asked to choose which sources to include in a historiography essay, part of your contribution is the thought and judgment that goes into identifying sources that form an interesting "conversation" by relating to each other in some productive way.

8.1. What's Your Goal?

When we analyze what historians have written on a subject, we do the following:

- Ask how convincingly the argument is supported by the historian's evidence and reasoning
- Ask what methods are used and with what results
- Ask how one historian's argument relates to the arguments of other historians on the same questions
- Consider the current state of knowledge on the question being addressed, asking what has been satisfactorily resolved and what directions future research should take

Even if you are reviewing only one author, as in a book review, you will still take into consideration how that author engages with the arguments of others, as all scholars do.

One helpful way to look at this engagement between different scholars' arguments is to see them as a conversation. Imagine a group of historians chatting around the bar at their annual convention (as they do). As they discuss some issue or question of common interest, each offers a perspective, based on original research, and responds to the others. When they disagree, it's usually in a collegial way that is focused more on finding the best answers than on any one voice being right. This is a common metaphor for what all academic scholarship, including history, is about. When we write historiography, we are explaining the nature of this conversation. We identify the question being discussed and distill what each voice contributes—including an evaluation of how convincing or important that contribution is and how it relates to the others (agreeing, disagreeing, adding, etc.). Finally, we come to some conclusion about the nature of the conversation: Has it resolved its question? Raised new issues? Suggested a path for future research?

In a historiography assignment, you are not usually asked to construct an argument of your own. But you still do contribute your own thinking to the essay. Your contribution consists of your thoughtful and reasoned choices of what details to include from each source and your critical evaluation of their arguments and assessment of how they add up.

8.2. Reading Conversations

When you read for a conversation essay, you are reading secondary sources (analyses written by historians), so take notes as you would for a response paper (sections 5.3–5.4). In addition, look for and make note of ways that the texts relate to each other. These interactions between texts can be literal: one author mentions another author, often explaining exactly how they differ. In many cases, though, the connections between texts are not stated outright. Two or more texts can be "in conversation with each other" as long as they are about related questions and ideas. Even if one author's work was published long before another's, as we read them both today we can talk about one as having an effect on the other because of their effect on us as readers. Reading the texts together, we learn more about the subject(s) they have in common, with different contributions from each author adding different perspectives or evidence.

The following is a list of the most common ways one argument can relate to another. Arguments can relate to each other in several different, even contradictory, ways on different aspects of their common question.

- Agree
- Disagree
- Add to
- Refine
- Clarify
- Illustrate
- Revise definitions of

- Undermine
- Quibble with
- Provoke
- Shift direction of
- Shift emphasis of
- Reapply in new context
- Question methods or evidence of

As you take notes, write a brief description of the type of interaction between texts, such as the following:

[Author A] adds to [Author B] by looking at [a different set of documents], but they come to similar conclusions.

[Author A] undermines [Author B]'s claim that X by showing how in some cases, Y was actually more common.

By applying the concept of X in [different context], [Author] clarifies the variety of ways that [concept] could play out.

Though largely agreeing with the main claim, [Author A] quibbles with the way [Author B] selected evidence, suggesting that a broader claim could be supported if X were considered also.

We rarely see any historian saying the equivalent of "I'm right and everyone else is wrong." While you will frequently encounter disagreement among historians, they usually agree on at least some aspects of a question, and disagreement often stems from using a different approach, a different set of evidence, or both. This means both historians may have convincing answers to different aspects of a question. As you take notes on the nature of the conversation made by your texts, be careful not to oversimplify their relationship as more confrontational than it is.

We always pay special attention to the introduction and conclusion when reading a secondary source (see section 5.2 on how to read secondary sources). We judge scholarly works by how effectively they meet their goals, and those goals are usually stated in the introduction, with the conclusion often giving more detail on exactly how they have been met. In introductions scholars also often explain how their work relates to others', though in an article this may also appear in the body. We also pay extra attention to the bibliography and citations, which tell you what kind of research the work was based on and which secondary works the author consulted or is referring to.

About the author. In addition to the usual key parts of a book, a foreword or acknowledgments section may give you valuable information about the author's background or funding that in some circumstances may be important for understanding how the argument fits into the work of other scholars. If you are reading an article or chapter with no acknowledgments, it may be worth your time to look up information about the author online. The identity and background of the author is usually not significant in a work of historical scholarship, so in most cases you will not mention anything about the author in your historiography other than name. This is because academic publications are almost always written by qualified scholars in the appropriate field, who are generally paid by universities to produce scholarship that meets ethical criteria. The peer review and editing process are meant in part to ensure that these criteria are met, and historians' relatively modest funding needs usually preclude conflicts of interest. Because exceptions do happen, however, a brief inquiry is worthwhile. In addition, it is possible for scholars to write very broad works that expand beyond the immediate field of their training, or to retrain themselves in a new, adjacent field. In many cases this makes no negative impact on the work and adds a valuable perspective. But it may be worth asking whether an author's training, language skills, or an entrenched ideological perspective may color the choices made in the research in ways that need to be considered.

An internet search will usually bring up an author's university affiliation and educational background, and perhaps a brief statement about the person in a university department profile. Major authors may have an entry in Wikipedia. Some faculty may have their own website or a profile on a professionally oriented social network such as Humanities Commons. Remember that more than one scholar may have the same name, so read carefully to make sure you're looking at the right person. Once you have identified the author, consider her position, institution, discipline, other publications, and educational background. What languages does she read? What are the dates and subjects of her primary publications? Does she work for a think tank or research center rather than a university? Think tanks sometimes solicit research aimed toward particular results: do an internet search on the institution to see if it has a stated perspective or is explicitly independent. You need to judge whether any or none of this information is relevant to include in your review, and explain its possible significance if you do include it. It is unlikely that you will have enough information to be certain of the impact of an author's background on the text, but you may raise it as a question, phrased in appropriately speculative language, such as in the following examples:

> Given that [author] was trained in the history of Ottoman Turkey and is fluent in Turkish, he presumably had to rely on translations of the Greek and Slavic sources.

Though this broad-ranging, cross-Atlantic study brings to light valuable comparisons, the author's specialization in US history may raise questions about the depth of research on the African side.

8.3. Drafting: Conversations

When you begin to write about a "conversation" among historians, the most important thing to remember is that the conversation—the relationships between each author's arguments—is the focus of your essay. You don't want to use all your space summarizing each text in detail. One way to maintain focus on the conversation is to begin by writing the key points of the conversation in script form. Imagine your authors together at a party, having an informal chat about their question. Try to have each author state a main idea or most relevant contribution in language that shows a natural flow from one idea to another, as in this example of how some economic historians have addressed the question of why Britain led the Industrial Revolution (simplified for the purposes of this example):

Joel: Britain took the lead because of the Enlightenment. Its unique scientific culture allowed Britain to take advantage of its human and physical resources. That is, superior scientists created useful knowledge, which was then exploited by skilled craftsmen who also had the right kind of institutions (secure property rights, free trade, etc.).

John: That sounds great, but the Enlightenment happened all over the place and started long before the Industrial Revolution. Also, these inventions were made by people who knew little or no science.

Robert: It wasn't the knowledge or skills! It was simply the right economic conditions. New technologies were invented in Britain because they were profitable there, but not elsewhere, like France. Usually it's expensive to invent stuff. But in Britain, the risk paid off because wages were very high, borrowing money was cheap, plus England had plenty of cheap coal.

Gregory: But coal was cheap in a lot of places. And if wages were high, wouldn't entrepreneurs first try to save on other inputs before doing all the complex, risky inventing? Besides, wages were high for about a century before all the inventing actually started!

Nicholas: Greg, it works if you combine what Joel and Robert are saying! Joel explains where innovations came from and Robert explains why they were actually adopted. This is getting us somewhere, though yours and John's objections are noted. We need more work to flesh out the details.

By distilling each argument to its essentials and imagining the authors interacting directly even when they don't do so in their texts, you highlight the nature of their relationships. The following bolded words describe the ways that each author relates to the others: John **doubts** Joel's claims. Robert **agrees** with John and **adds** a new possibility. Gregory **disagrees** with Robert. While Nicholas **concedes** the truth of both John's and Gregory's criticisms, he **shifts focus** to the combined effect of Joel's and Robert's claims and **suggests** further research.

Once you've made these relationships clear to yourself, you are in a good position to begin drafting formal prose that describes how each author contributes to an overall conversation. Begin by summarizing the nature of the whole conversation. What are the questions they all address? What is the state of our knowledge on those questions after reading all the texts? In what ways has each author contributed to our understanding? From that point, you will know what and how much to distill as you consider each author in turn, to show how each author contributes in the way you already distilled rather than just listing separate, complete summaries of each author.

8.4. Drafting: Book Reviews

If your assignment is a book review, you are still doing historiography, and there is still a scholarly conversation to consider, though the relative weight of each portion of your essay will be different, and a book review requires some additional elements. The purpose of a book review is to tell scholarly readers whether this book will be worth their time. Readers want to know whether it addresses questions and offers new evidence or interpretations that relate to their own research. Readers may also want to know whether a book would be suitable to assign in a course or is so important to understanding their field that they should read it even if it's not directly related to their research. Your goal is to explain how valuable the book is for what purposes and what questions and contexts it is relevant to, so your readers may decide for themselves if they need to look at it. Avoid a "book report" that simplifies its content, merely passing on "the gist" or summarizing everything from beginning to end. A review does something more complicated and thoughtful. It selects the key details that convey the most important factors potential readers need to know:

- **Selection of sources.** Are they sufficient and representative enough to answer the stated questions?
- **Use of sources.** What methods were used? Are they reasonable methods to meet the stated goals? (See section 8.5.2.)
- **Clarity of argument.** Are the claims clearly stated and fully explained?

- **Value/importance of stated goals.** Does the book contribute something new that resolves debates of interest to others, or have influence on other questions?
- **Effectiveness in achieving goals.** Does the book do what it says it will do? Will it be more effective for some kinds of readers than others?
- **Audience.** What is the most appropriate audience for this book? Who would be interested?
- **Omissions and alternatives.** What did the author leave out? What could have been done differently?
- **Context.** How does the book compare to other books on the subject or broader field? What is this book responding to, or what gap is it trying to fill?

Your review should address all these questions with examples, explanations, and quotes from the book. The final point, the context of the book, is where the "conversation" fits in even when your essay is based on only one main text. Authors may specifically mention other works they are engaging with, but in some cases you will need to figure out how the text responds to broader questions of interest to the field. Look for the places where the author states the main claims and pay particular attention to language that points to previous assumptions or research, including terms such as the following:

- Contrary to
- Unlike
- As opposed to
- While
- Whereas
- According to..., yet

Next, examine the notes to or near the main claims. These are often citations to related works, and authors may explain the exact relationship between their own work and others in the notes rather than the main text.

8.5. Evaluating Contributions

Beyond distilling the most relevant arguments from each author and how they relate to each other, a historiography essay must also evaluate each of these contributions. We ask whether each author's argument is convincing, but also which contributions are most significant or useful in improving our overall understanding. You will often see the authors you read similarly evaluating the work of other authors.

When we evaluate scholarship we avoid expressing our personal judgments, since our purpose is to help the whole field come to a better understanding, not to make an individual choice for ourselves. We also try to avoid thinking of scholarship in terms of "good" or "bad." Truly bad scholarship is that which misrepresents or omits evidence, includes significant factual errors, or employs faulty reasoning with the intention to deceive. If you find such tactics, condemn them accordingly.

We are looking for arguments that are useful, convincing, or satisfying—they add something new to our understanding of a significant question or issue. Arguments that are effective meet the goals stated by the author. Arguments that are significant or important change how we understand an issue or question. We often ask, "What's at stake?" in order to focus on how a study contributes to larger questions. Sometimes we talk about whether evidence has "explanatory power," meaning it offers a satisfying explanation that we didn't have before. We tend to like scholarship that "unpacks" complicated terms and concepts by taking them apart and explaining their meanings and origins.

Published scholarly work should be original in the basic sense of saying something that hasn't been published before, thereby filling a gap in our knowledge. Most published works present new evidence or a new interpretation of familiar evidence. But we tend to praise scholarship as original or pathbreaking when it goes beyond that to offer a new way of thinking about a subject or convincingly undermines established assumptions or accepted wisdom. A study that is unusually thoroughly researched or that usefully deploys broad contextual knowledge may be praised as erudite, while arguments that pay especially close attention to logical consistency are rigorous. Some studies may not be fully convincing, and yet we can still appreciate them if they provoke fruitful new directions in the conversation or disrupt existing narratives in useful ways.

When we evaluate a work of scholarship, we need to recognize and use some specialized terms that define genres and common methods. Other terms are frequently used as criticism, often in specialized ways that you may not need in an undergraduate essay but are likely to encounter in the readings. These terms signal important ways that historians distinguish their arguments from each other and weigh the value of each contribution.

8.5.1. Genres

Many historical works can be described as taking a certain overall approach based on which aspects of the past they pay attention to (or the questions asked; see section 3.1). There are a few established categories, or genres, that describe the most common approaches, although recent studies are likely to combine several of them. Today we tend to worry that a work that too closely follows any one genre or method can err by leaving out important context and connections.

- **Political/diplomatic/military history.** From the beginning of professionalized history in the late nineteenth century until about the 1960s, most academic history was primarily political, diplomatic, or military, which meant it was focused on the actions of people who held political power or on how political power was decided in war. Much of it centered on the lives of rulers, politicians, diplomats, or generals and the movements of armies and ships. In the mid-twentieth century, when this understanding of what counts in history began to be re-evaluated, political and diplomatic history dropped off in popularity for a long time. Changing understandings of the importance of categories such as gender, race, and nationality, and the agency of people without obvious power have led to re-evaluations of how political power has been wielded (noting, for example, that even absolute rulers were constrained by their populations in various ways), and to much more wide-ranging studies (for instance, how armies cultivated notions of masculinity, or how the social networks of diplomats affected their political strategies).

- **Social history.** Starting around the mid-twentieth century, historians widened their perspective to focus on groups other than the powerful. Traditional political history had seen these others as being acted upon: rulers and generals taxed them, made the laws they abided by, and sent them to war. Social history restores agency to "ordinary" people—those who do not hold extraordinary direct power over others—by exploring the ways that groups (such as serfs, slaves, workers, the middle class, soldiers, women's rights activists, intellectuals, etc.) act, collectively or individually, to achieve their own goals or to adapt to conditions imposed on them. (See also agency, section 8.5.2.)

- **Cultural history.** Coming on the heels of social history as a critique of "traditional" political history, cultural history encompasses the study of how people's attitudes, mentalities, manners, habits, traditions, affiliations, and beliefs contribute to how we understand and evaluate the past, to how people defined themselves and behaved in the past, and to how external forces (such as laws, institutions, and religion) shaped individuals. Where social history focuses more on groups of people, cultural history can be more focused on individuals or ideas and meanings, but this is not a clear-cut distinction.

- **Legal/institutional history.** Some historians focus on laws (in theory and practice) or on specific institutions, such as the early American bureaucracy, European public radio in the interwar period, or international peacekeeping missions. Others work on institutions in a conceptual sense such as marriage, prison systems, or the press. In these cases individual actors are of less interest than the ways people who are connected to an enterprise act collectively or interact with each other. The earliest institutional and legal histories focused on how institutions distributed power from the top down, but later works are part of the overall postmodern trend: thinking about how people throughout society behave, not just how people in power act upon others.

- **Intellectual history.** The history of ideas, or intellectual history, ranges from the study of how influential ideas (such as socialism or utilitarianism) have developed over time to the history of individual thinkers (such as Einstein or Machiavelli) and their context—how they became who they were, how their ideas developed, how their ideas were received in their time and later (reception studies)—to the social history of ideas, which is the history of how ordinary people applied and adapted great ideas. Intellectual history also includes histories of how certain schools of thought or whole disciplines, such as the history of science or the history of human rights, have developed.

8.5.2. Methods

The following terms describe some of the most common methods that historians use. These terms are neutral: they do not in themselves imply any criticism. But one of the ways that historians often set their own work apart from others is to disagree not only about evidence or reasoning, but also about methods. The following terms describe particular ways of doing history. (Note: you can hear the correct pronunciation of specialized words like many of these on forvo.com if they are foreign or howjsay.com if they are in English.)

Quantitative history. Some forms of historical analysis may be based primarily on quantitative data. Typically such studies have used demographic records (births, marriages, deaths, census reports), voting or polling records, and other numbers to understand the behavior of groups of people. They are especially likely to do this in cases where direct documentation is unavailable, but also to answer different questions, such as "Were people better nourished in X place at Y time than in Q place at R time?" which has been addressed through military records recording the height of each new recruit. Quantitative history enjoyed a brief heyday in the 1970s and 1980s but is rarely an exclusive method today. Increasingly it has become part of new digital methods that may also employ linguistic and other kinds of analysis.

Psychohistory. Another trend of the 1970s–80s was the application of categories and interpretations from psychology to the historical assessment of individuals. For example, Michael Paul Rogin wrote a psychoanalytical study of Andrew Jackson that argued that his actions as president toward Native

Americans stemmed in part from childhood traumas. However, this kind of history was heavily criticized by psychologists as well as historians: psychologists are unwilling to diagnose someone they have not met, and historians argue that such diagnoses are anachronistic when applied to a time before anyone thought in modern psychological categories (that is, what could it tell us about the person's views or how other people reacted to them to label them schizophrenic, for example? The diagnosis itself, setting aside its accuracy, is not of historical significance). Psychohistory did have a positive influence in pushing historians to consider personal aspects of the lives of power-holders in history, such as their private relationships, childhood, education, and upbringing, which have proved to be useful avenues of inquiry.

Marxist history. Marxism refers to the ideas of the social theorist Karl Marx, with emphasis on his prediction that capitalist working classes would organize themselves and revolt against property owners to seize the wealth that is the product of their labor. A "Marxist" in a general way refers to a follower of Marx, usually presumed to be someone who thought his prediction was accurate and desirable. A Marxist revolutionary works toward making Marx's prediction come true by organizing labor or protesting capitalism.

But a Marxist historian is someone who follows Marx's interpretation of history or definitions of historical categories. Marxist historians may not have an opinion regarding revolution. But they do believe that economics determines most of what we do; that capitalism is inherently exploitative and creates class conflict; that because economics defines class divisions, class divisions are one of the driving forces in society. Today few historians are dogmatic followers of Marx's principles of historical progression, and most criticize his ideas as overly deterministic (see section 6.9). However, most historians also see Marx's influence on the development of historical understanding as useful: we usually accept that economics is a fundamental influence, that class divisions are important social categories that help us understand human behavior, that middle-class supremacy and wealth is neither inevitable nor a pinnacle of civilization, and that capitalist development had a dark side.

Revisionism. A revisionist history is one in which the historian significantly revises or re-envisions a subject that was thought to be understood. Although all histories add to our knowledge and alter what we believed previously, we use the term "revisionism" for work that fundamentally alters the terms of an existing conversation. For example, some of the latest military history re-envisions accepted narratives by looking at them again through the lens of social and cultural history, such as *Public Health and the US Military: A History of the Army Medical Department, 1818–1917* (Bobby A. Wintermute), which examines how military doctors helped to transform public health during the Progressive Era, expanding our notion of both policy and military spheres. Revisionism can be used in another, negative, sense, but that is more easily distinguished as negationism or denialism (see section 8.5.3).

Thick description. Borrowed from anthropology, thick description is a method of analyzing ritualistic or theatrical events or behaviors (as opposed to texts or objects, though historians often rely on written descriptions of such events, since they took place in the past). The historian connects the way people moved or dressed, or the symbolic associations of their clothing or spaces they inhabited, to what those gestures or visual representations signified to the people around them. For example, Richard Wortman wrote a monumental history of the Russian monarchy, but rather than writing a traditional biography of each emperor, he analyzed coronations and processions to explain each monarch's "scenario of power," or the story monarchs presented to the public to legitimize their reigns.

Deconstruction/postmodernism. Something is constructed if it is created by human culture, as opposed to the natural world. Photosynthesis is not constructed. Definitions of "traditional marriage" are constructed, because they change over time and place and are created and altered by people. To deconstruct a text or a narrative is to tease apart or "unpack" these culturally constructed meanings so we can fully understand them.

Deconstruction is part of a broader approach to knowledge, known as postmodernism, that developed in the mid-twentieth century. The term "postmodernism" applies in many ways to many contexts, but in history it is usually understood as a skeptical approach to received narratives and assumptions of absolute truth, morality, objectivity, or progress. But "postmodernism" can also refer simply to the period of time following "modernism," which is roughly 1960 to the present (see section 5.10.4).

Theory. This very general term, common to most social science and humanities disciplines, describes any methodological premise that may guide a historical study. For example, Edward Said's theory of Orientalism (see section 8.5.3) has been used by historians as a lens to understand any context where one culture creates perceptions about another for its own purposes. A historical work may be described as "theory heavy" if it seems to the reviewer that the methodological framing is so dominant that it gets in the way of a clear interpretation of evidence. Alternatively, a work may "lack theoretical grounding" if it ignores established and useful ways of framing questions or evaluating evidence. In general, though, historians are less theory dependent than other disciplines. "Theory" in the social science or humanities sense is much closer to the everyday definition of the term as "a series of interpretive claims" than it is to the scientific use of "theory" as the most accepted explanation based on already thorough testing.

Discourse. This term describes a specific way of talking observed in a certain group. For example, the term "rape culture" captures, in part, a modern

American discourse in which women are described as bearing some responsibility for their own rapes because of the way they dress or behave, even though evidence shows that rape is an act of violence and assertion of power, not a sexual act based on lust or attraction. This particular way of talking is not the only way to talk about rape—sociologists and law enforcement professionals who study rape speak about it differently, for example, as do people in other cultures—which means that rape culture discourse is constructed, and therefore historical. So "discourse" is not just a fancy word for "talking"; it describes a pattern of speech that reflects conscious or subconscious attitudes and is observed in one group but not others, or at one time but not others. Examining discourse is one way that historians can find evidence of attitudes or assumptions that people don't explain outright. The adjectival form is "discursive."

Postcolonialism. Colonialism was the process by which Europeans exerted control over other territories around the globe to extract resources and impose their own practices. "Postcolonialism" or "postcolonial studies" refers to research about how colonized places were affected by these processes and also to the effort of scholars to study colonized places without the assumptions, ideologies, discourses, or biases that stem from colonization (such as Orientalism; see section 8.5.3).

Subaltern history. Derived from postcolonial studies, the term "subaltern" refers to people who are left out of dominant power structures and institutions. In general usage it also refers to any category of people traditionally left out of history's "master narratives" (section 8.5.3). When we do subaltern history today, we are trying to restore to the historical record the actions, values, attitudes, and agency of women, people of color, people of all gender identities and sexual preferences, the poor, people with disabilities, and other previously excluded social groups. When we do this, we often find that a previously accepted master narrative actually omitted important changes, causes, and effects. So subaltern history does more than resurrect forgotten people. It critically reassesses our whole understanding of history. Subaltern history is a form of social history that emphasizes how social categories are constructed, performed, resisted, and defended, and what that means for all people, and what it says about societies.

Intersectionality. A person who is marginalized because of her gender may also be marginalized because of her race. Intersectionality refers to the *compounded* effects of being marginalized by more than one category of identity, differently and in addition to how either form marginalization operates by itself.

Agency. When a person acts deliberately, for her own reasons, that person is exhibiting agency, or acting as an "agent" who shapes events. Traditional political historians often assumed that people without political power (virtually everyone before the late eighteenth century, and most people until the twentieth) lacked agency, at least so far as human activity was recorded in histories. People without power were left out of history or were described only as reacting in response to what was done to them by those with power (whether they rejoiced, suffered, or were indifferent). More recent work often has a goal of "restoring agency" to these groups: that is, showing the ways in which even some of the most powerless people have acted in their own interests, adapted circumstances to suit themselves, and accommodated or resisted outside pressures in their own diverse ways.

Reading the silences. "Reading the silences" means finding ways of learning about the lives and ideas of people who did not leave behind direct textual evidence of their views and experiences. A political leader such as Julius Caesar, Mao Zedong, Catherine the Great, or Winston Churchill is not "silent": people like that leave behind texts attesting to who they were and what they thought. In contrast, a slave girl from the ancient Mediterranean, a medieval peasant in Japan, or a factory floor worker in Lyons in 1870 is said to be "silent" in the historical record in the sense that they were probably illiterate and most likely no one else wrote about them.

How do we reconstruct anything about how such people lived? There are many creative ways to "read the silences." Using previously ignored piles of round rocks found in nearly every archaeological site, Elizabeth Wayland Barber reconstructed much of women's and children's labor in the ancient world (they spun thread on spindles, using those rocks as weights). Knowing where these objects were found allowed her to reconstruct the relative status of, conditions for, and methods used by these people.

In other cases we simply look harder. In obscure archives or other repositories from which the "important" documents have been removed to a central location, one can sometimes find documents written by the types of people we usually assume were silent. This may require that we carefully extrapolate from very small pieces of evidence to draw tentative conclusions.

In still other cases we painstakingly gather tiny pieces of disparate evidence embedded within typical sources to construct a coherent picture of a whole. Laurel Thatcher Ulrich took one seemingly uninformative diary by an early nineteenth-century Maine midwife and spent ten years researching her community and everything referenced in the diary to reconstruct this one woman's world, and from that demonstrated how her evidence could speak to women's roles in economics and medicine in that period.

Microhistory. This is a method of historical inquiry where one small case is studied in great depth in order to shed light on the larger context. For example, when little is known about French peasants in the fourteenth century, a historian might focus on a single village that happens to have left rich documentary sources (as Emmanuel Le Roy Ladurie did in his groundbreaking work *Montaillou*). Though that single village cannot be representative of all French peasants of the period, knowing a great deal about the one case allows us to make more out of scant evidence from other contexts.

Mentalities. The influential German word *Weltanschauung* means "world-view." The same idea is captured by the French term *mentalité* or, in English, "mentality." A person's worldview or mentality is the whole range of ideas and attitudes that inform her interpretation of what she experiences in the world. Another translation could be "philosophy or conception of the world." Your worldview may be composed of your religious and political beliefs, the common values held by social groups with which you identify (by your ethnicity, religion, age, urban/suburban/rural identity, fashion identity, and so on), specific forma-tive experiences you've had, and your hopes or aspirations about what is possible or how things work. Cultural historians attempt to reconstruct the worldviews of specific individuals or groups in the past.

Prosopography. Prosopography is a form of collective biography, in which the life stories of some group are studied together. Often it emphasizes the network of relationships between people or draws general conclusions based on demo-graphic or other trends, in order to reveal more about a population than a study of one individual life could yield (especially when sources may be too few for a traditional biographical approach). Prosopography is becoming increasingly useful thanks to digital tools that help to analyze large amounts of data.

Comparative history. When you compare a phenomenon or institution in two different places, you hope to learn more about both contexts from the exercise. Examples include a comparison of slavery in the United States, Cuba, and Brazil or of the revolutions that occurred across the Atlantic world in the late eighteenth and early nineteenth centuries. Generally, one hopes to isolate which factors in a given environment caused or influenced the ways a common phenomenon varied from place to place (this helps us to understand the mechanisms of cause and effect), or to isolate factors that are common across different environments and that therefore may have a more general underlying cause.

Transnational/global history. Not to be confused with comparative his-tory, transnational studies focus on historical phenomena that cross borders. Examples include international institutions (such as the League of Nations, but also international charities or radio networks or activist groups), cultural phe-nomena (such as Dada, or the popularity of cocktails and the new kinds of social interaction that came with them), or the study of movement across borders (such as migration or diaspora communities).

Transnational history is understood as a corrective to studies that too often focused on only one nation, even when examining a phenomenon that was not limited to that place. This usually occurs because of limitations in the researcher's language abilities or the availability of source materials, such as when someone writes a book on French cubism even though cubism was an international movement because he can't read Spanish or travel to Spain). Transnational history is also a corrective to studies that have been bound by modern definitions of a region even though those boundaries might have been much less significant at the time being studied. For example, we think now of Germany and Austria as two distinct places, and they have distinct historiographies, but before 1871 there were dozens of German-speaking states, and even as late as 1939 many Germans thought of all German speakers as belonging to the same "nation," while many others whom we now call "Germans" actually thought of themselves as "Bavarians" or "Prussians."

Transnational history has developed in part because our society is increasingly interested in globalization as it affects our daily lives. But globalization did not come out of nowhere: there is a history to our global trade, to ideas of international fairness and human rights, and so on, which is being studied by global and transnational historians. Global history examines phenomena that take place around the world, such as political imprisonment, food culture, the use of public spaces, or the cotton trade.

Imagined community. Coined by historian Benedict Anderson, this term originally described a population that perceives itself as a nationality—that is, people who do not actually know each other or interact personally but "imagine" themselves as part of a coherent community based on an abstract notion of a "nation." The term can describe any group united by a collective sense of identity rather than by literal personal interactions.

Longue durée. Coined by the Annales school of French historians in the middle of the twentieth century, this phrase for "long lasting" signifies a historical analysis that emphasizes slow-changing phenomena (from culture to climate), in contrast to medium-term changes such as social developments or short-term changes such as politics. Histories that make arguments involving centuries of time are focusing on the longue durée.

Big history. A relatively new trend, big history re-examines the idea of what can be studied historically by taking a much wider view to encompass "prehistory" (before written texts), the history of climate, and even the history of the planet and solar system. Big history weaves together and asks questions about all the interconnected aspects of our world, often focusing especially on interactions between the environment and all the flora and fauna that inhabit it, including but not limited to humans.

Begriffsgeschichte. Translatable as "conceptual history" or the "history of concepts," *Begriffsgeschichte* is the history of how the meaning of key terms changes over time. It is a method of intellectual history. For example, the history of the changing meanings and uses of "freedom" is a *Begriffsgeschichte.* The term also refers to the notion that all history should be written with awareness of the way conceptual understandings change. For example, when we read about a

Baltic German diplomat's wife writing about her love for her "native" country, Russia, in the 1810s, we must recognize that the concept of nationality was not then fully developed as we understand it now, as connecting ethnicity and linguistic background intrinsically to nationality. *Begriffsgeschichte* calls on us to avoid this anachronism and to strive to understand historical concepts as they were understood by the people using them.

Oral history. If the people being studied are still alive, can be reached, and are willing to talk, a historian might be able to ask them direct questions. Making and using such interviews is called oral history. Oral historians act more like sociologists or anthropologists (and have borrowed some of their methods) in interviewing subjects, polling them, or observing them in their usual activities and environment. As in these other disciplines, there are some ethical complications in oral history that we don't have to worry about with documents left by people no longer with us: do you name your living subjects? How much of their private information—perhaps shared with you in a moment of intimacy—is it right to publish?

Memory. Some historians study how people memorialize the past. Memorials, statues, and monuments reflect the importance to a culture of some earlier event, person, or group. This form of historical memory tells us not about the time being memorialized, but about the people who are memorializing and their time. This is because people often remember the past with nostalgia, or historical memory selects parts of the past that are deemed important by the memorializers, thereby ignoring other aspects of their real past. That tells us a lot about what the memorializers value and how they cope with difficult aspects of their past and present.

The closely related concept, nostalgia, is not a longing for the actual past, but a longing for an image of the past based more on wishful thinking or selective memory than the real past. The consciousness that the real past is gone forever and can never be fully recovered is sometimes considered another aspect of the yearning of nostalgia. Part of the history of memory can be a study of how people have longed for and/or (mis)remembered earlier periods.

Digital history. Digital history refers to scholarship that answers historical questions using (at least partly) digital tools. Databases and other digital tools can perform analyses that humans cannot or that would be prohibitively time-consuming to do in analog ways. Digital tools can analyze links in a social network by name, family, rank, location, and occupation, or compare the use of words and syntax in a text to help identify the author, or any number of other tasks that involve comparisons of huge data sets. Digital tools can also be used to gather evidence more widely than would otherwise be possible, to organize and record or annotate evidence, or to exhibit or distribute the results of historical research.

8.5.3. Terms of Criticism

The following terms represent ways that an argument—or one of its elements, such as a piece of evidence or line of reasoning—can be unsatisfying or unconvincing. When you see these terms used, they are almost always at least implying a degree of criticism, and in some cases they can be damning or even hostile. In addition to the following terms, you might also encounter those described in section 6.9, which represent forms of faulty logic.

Loaded. A word or phrase is loaded if it implies a judgment beyond its literal meaning. For example "tyranny" describes a type of government but with implied criticism. Some terms have a neutral meaning, but can also be used in loaded ways when misapplied or deployed with hostility, such as "Zionist" or "feminist." Historians try to avoid terms that are always loaded and to be scrupulous in defining others that are sometimes deployed in controversial ways. You may see a term described as loaded in order to criticize it for being used judgmentally or uncritically rather than analytically.

Reductivist / essentialist. An author who "reduces" or simplifies an idea or theory down to its essentials might be accused of being reductivist or essentialist. A reductivist explanation loses so much detail that it is no longer accurate. For example, if we try to summarize the theory of Orientalism as "the way western people talk about the east," we have been reductivist, because we left out key points that accurately define the theory and make it useful.

Problematic (versus "to problematize"). A text, idea, interpretation, or narrative of the past is "problematic" if it raises more questions than it resolves, obscures understanding, inaccurately or incompletely represents sources or ideas, or introduces unnecessary confusion. A historian's narrative is most likely to be described as problematic if it simplifies the past or leaves out significant people or ideas. "To problematize" has a different meaning: to dig deeper into the complexities of an issue to explain them. This is something historians consider useful, so when someone says, "This needs to be problematized," she is suggesting that the author needed to raise more questions or inquire more deeply.

Master narrative. This is an interpretation of major events that has become widely accepted throughout the public consciousness. Much of what historians do today is to revise previously accepted master narratives to take better account of evidence that has been ignored or misunderstood. For instance, a now-discredited master narrative of modern European history is that over time people got more political power and personal freedom. We sometimes assume that anyone would be happier living in the developed world today than at any time previously (and that the farther back you go in history, the worse it got). But it is a fallacy to imagine that history is a progressive march toward the present and thus that we are the pinnacle of civilization. Middle-class, property-owning men have indeed gained power and personal liberty in Europe and the United States over the last two centuries or more, but often at the cost of the power and personal liberty of many others, including women, the working poor, and anyone who is not white. Moreover, that trend is not a straight line, nor is any other.

Descriptive/narrative/antiquarian. When academic historians accuse a work of being "descriptive," "narrative," or "antiquarian," they mean the work lacks an original argument that contributes in new ways to our collective understanding of the past. Since this is the entire goal of academic history, naturally a purported academic work that does not meet this goal is considered unacceptable. No work that is exclusively descriptive would be published through a normal peer review process, but you might see a criticism of a work as "too descriptive" or "containing too much narrative," which is not saying no argument exists, but that it is crowded out by other material that merely tells a story. A work described as "antiquarian" is being accused of addressing questions of no general significance or of fact-finding rather than interpreting.

Positivist. Positivism was a nineteenth-century effort to base history entirely on empirical evidence. Positivists believed that no truth could be gained except from the physical laws of the universe and sensory experimentation. This notion is still an influence on history today (and is the reason it is considered a social science as well as a humanistic endeavor), but over time historians have demonstrated that strict positivism offers limited, if any, understanding of many aspects of human motivations and culture. Since those realms are crucial in understanding human behavior, we must use other tools in addition to empirical observation. You are most likely to encounter the term "positivist" used critically to describe a work that restricts itself to empirical data, ignoring the contradictory but overwhelming influence on the past of human whim, belief, emotions, habits, culture, assumptions, and unconscious drives.

Teleological/linear/Whiggish. To see history teleologically is to imagine a purpose in historical events: an end that all developments are heading toward, such as the Christian notion of time moving toward a second coming of Christ. We also sometimes use the word "linear" to describe this sense that history is moving forward in a more or less straight line, toward ever greater progress. This is a mistake we make when we look on the past as leading toward ourselves, when in reality our lifetime is just another passing moment, all events are contingent on each other, and nothing is inevitable. Teleological writing sometimes uses the word "history" as if it were a person rather than a field of study, saying, "History leans toward . . ."

Another term sometimes used to capture a teleological view of history is "Whiggish," which takes its name from the British political party. A Whiggish view of history sees all events as working toward a goal of progress and historical actors as either heroes who help events move in their inevitable direction, or villains who inhibit that progress. Whiggish histories tend to look back on events before a certain big change as unimportant or preparatory to what came afterward, rather than as significant in themselves at the time they occurred.

Ahistorical/historicize/historicity/historicism/historism. When someone describes something that changes over time as if it were universal, we say the description is "ahistorical" (as in the opposite of "historical"; see section 5.10.6). By contrast, when we "historicize" some idea, concept, institution, or phenomenon, we show how it changes over time. We usually talk about historicizing something that is generally assumed to be universal or natural (such as race) and we show it to be in fact "constructed," or created by people in different ways in different times and places. In a sense, all historians are historicizing in all their work: the word describes the process of doing history. It is usually scholars in other fields or journalists who are criticized for being "ahistorical."

The related term "historicity" refers to whether something is a factual part of the historical record, as opposed to myths, legends, or fiction. For example, we can ask about the historicity of Scottish kilts: did people really wear them, or were they invented by the novelist Sir Walter Scott? (It's complicated.)

You may see still other terms that are confusingly similar, such as "historicism" and "historism." Historicism is a philosophical tradition (a way of thinking not limited to historians) that emphasizes the importance of context in our understanding. It has been used both positively and negatively; if you come across it, you will need to look closely at the way it is being used and the specific thinkers associated with it in the text you are reading. Historism is a school of historiography (a way of doing history) that places more than usual emphasis on the changing nature of human behavior and traditions and explains each event or action as entirely a product of its context, as opposed to being explainable or predictable as part of a pattern, system, or grand unifying theory. For example, Leopold von Ranke, one of the founders of the modern discipline of history, favored the "historist" view that human agency—the decisions and actions of individuals—drive history, in opposition to Friedrich Hegel, a philosopher of history who saw an overarching pattern of "thesis, antithesis, synthesis" driving events, with human agency largely irrelevant.

Sonderweg. A German word meaning "special path," when used in a historical context *Sonderweg* is a theory that German history developed differently from a "normal" West (usually understood as France and Britain, sometimes including the United States). Specifically, *Sonderweg* has referred to Germany's unique version of democracy in the Weimar Republic, then to the Nazi notion of Germany's special "mission" in the world (to dominate it), then to historians' assessment of what went wrong in Germany that allowed Nazism to develop. However, the approach to history encapsulated in this term (and sometimes applied to other countries by extension) is now frowned upon as inaccurate and unclear.

Backwardness. During the Cold War, scholarship on eastern Europe often assumed or tried to explain why this region was "behind" or "backward" compared to western Europe. The term refers most specifically to economic development, but is sometimes applied much more widely. By extension, the same concept is sometimes used for other regions. The concept has been questioned, however, because it assumes western Europe presents the norm rather than the exception and because eastern Europe was not as different or as homogenous as previously assumed. Since the Cold War ended, historical scholarship rarely invokes the concept except to explain where or how it doesn't apply, or to accuse another historian of assuming it does.

Eurocentrist. When a historical study makes claims about "the world" or implies that claims apply more widely when they are in fact based on Europe, we describe this as Eurocentrism. The term can also describe a worldview in which Europe is entitled to a leading role, politically, economically, or otherwise. Because Europe has been an economic and political center for (only) several recent centuries, it still dominates popular and scholarly understandings of the world. Indeed, many of the conventional terms described in this book are derived from European history and should be used carefully or altered for the history of other parts of the world.

Orientalist. Coined by scholar Edward Said to describe how westerners imagine "the East" (which is not, in reality, one coherent thing), "Orientalism" is also used more broadly to describe the image or stereotypes of one culture held by another culture, or the act of conceptualizing another culture not by observation, but in contrast to one's own self-image. The term is used to distinguish perceptions from reality, but also to shift focus from the object of such descriptions ("the East") to the creators of these images (Europeans), because what they want to see tells us a great deal about them but nothing about the culture they are inaccurately trying to define. When a historian's work is described as "orientalist," that means the historian is confusing perceptions with reality in this way, while "orientalizing" refers to the process of creating such images on an imagined "other."

Negationist/denialist. When "revisionist" is used as a pejorative, the work could also and more accurately be termed "negationist" or "denialist." Negationism or denialism refers to a historical narrative that rejects or ignores accepted historical evidence for some purpose, often political or cultural. For instance, in the Southern "Lost Cause" narrative of the Civil War, Southern whites re-envisioned the war as a fight for freedom against the supposed tyranny of an industrially advanced North, even though abundant evidence makes clear that the war was in fact fought to defend and protect slavery. This form of revisionism is a rejection of the principles of academic history (and used very differently from "revisionism" as a method within academic history; see section 8.5.2).

Biased/subjective. Historians can be accused of bias (the noun) or of being biased (adjective) if they have some prejudice or conflict of interest that causes them to emphasize certain evidence unfairly over other evidence, or that drives their interpretation in a particular direction that does not take all relevant evidence into account. Biases may range from someone being paid to write history slanted in someone's interest to having a particular affinity for a country or ideology that causes the historian to ignore evidence that sheds a negative light on it. Nothing authored by humans can be truly objective, but we aim for transparency about where we insert ourselves into a text, including in our selection of evidence. When we criticize scholarship as "subjective" we usually mean that the selection or framing of material is not transparent or shows a personal or idiosyncratic slant.

Nostalgic/idealized. Historians who portray a past time and place in an positive light by ignoring negative or uncomfortable aspects may be accused of idealizing the past. One of the impulses that can drive historians to idealize is nostalgia, the yearning for an imaginary version of the past that is comforting or lacks problems that concern us today.

Reified. To reify is to describe something that is symbolic, imagined, or feared as if it were actually real. For example, a historian who describes a whole group of people as having certain qualities or opinions that people commonly assume about them reifies those assumptions—he writes about them as if the assumptions are reality.

Structuralist. Structuralism is a method more common in other disciplines, including linguistics, anthropology, sociology, economics, and literary criticism, and at its height dates to the first half of the twentieth century. It is based on the notion that separate elements can be better understood as part of a larger system, and often looks to identify underlying systems or structures that have not been consciously recognized. In history, structuralism looks for patterns in how institutions or groups work. However, one of the most potent criticisms of structuralism—which began to fall out of favor in the 1960s—was that it can often be ahistorical. This means the emphasis on identifying an underlying pattern or system can lead to a false sense of a structure being unchanging or more similar from one context to the next than it really is.

Other/othering. When you separate a person or group of people as outsiders, you make them an "other." This process can be described by making "other" into a verb: "to other" someone is to define the person as an outsider (and therefore your own group as "inside"), and the "othering" of a culture when you define people simplistically or as less than equal or significant because they are different from your own culture. Many historical studies describe processes of othering, but it is a criticism if the historical study itself presents some group as lesser than another because of its difference or foreignness.

Dehumanizing. To remove or ignore someone's individuality or agency is to dehumanize them, in contrast to "humanizing," which is part of what history can do at its best: to humanize people is to show their actions and choices in context as part of the range of human behavior, without judgment.

Totalizing/universalizing/zero-sum. When historians "totalize," they are looking at the past through an extreme lens that views the world as more black and white than it is. A totalizing view can also be described as "all-or-nothing," or "zero-sum," as in a "zero-sum game" where you win either everything or nothing. In this case a historian may be overstating how broadly her evidence applies or oversimplifying a historical reality. Sometimes a work may be described as "universalizing" when it attributes actions or attitudes more broadly than is justified.

8.6. Finding Your Contribution

Having understood each voice in your conversation and how they relate to each other, and having begun to consider how effective each argument is, begin drafting some overall assessment of the nature of the conversation. Your assessment may take any of the same forms that historians use to respond to each other's arguments. For example, you may write that you

- are not convinced
- are convinced but want to know more about X
- quibble with small points while accepting others
- appreciate the contributions of these authors and suggest future directions for research
- suggest ways of applying ideas from these texts in new ways or new contexts
- compare/contrast the texts and observe what we learn from that process
- weigh evidence from multiple sides and add it up to make some larger point
- weigh and compare the relative significance of each text (see section 4.5)
- apply a conceptual framework to illuminate or test the results of the works you are reading

A conceptual framework is an idea, term, concept, or method that can be employed to explain different scenarios, understand evidence, or organize information to make better sense of it. For example, perhaps one of the scholars you have studied asks whether certain behaviors were coerced by a leader or represent a consensus of what people wanted. You might, in your historiographical essay, borrow this interesting opposition and apply it to the other texts to see if it sheds light on those other sets of arguments and allows you to compare how well they all hold up.

Whatever form your contribution takes, it remains a commentary on the arguments of others, not an argument of your own, because you do not support your claims with new evidence of your own and because you organize this essay around the sources instead of your claims. Contrast this to a research essay (chapter 11).

8.7. Composing a Title

Every formal essay needs to have a title. "Historiography Essay" is not a title; it is the assignment type. A title should capture the content of your essay, telling your reader what to expect. Compare the following examples:

An Essay about Several Sources on the Industrial Revolution

Debating the Industrial Revolution: Sources on Women's Textile Labor

Debating the Impact of Women's Factory Labor on the Industrial Revolution

Sally Goes to the Factory: How Women Textile Laborers Fueled the Industrial Revolution

Women's Textile Labor in New England: A Regional Comparison

New Directions in the Study of Nineteenth-Century Women's Factory Labor in New England

The first example is vague, giving little sense of what the essay will say. The other examples are all specific enough, but each suggests a slightly different emphasis in what will be covered in the essay. Some of the titles hint at what your take on the debate will be ("a regional comparison"), while others emphasize that you will describe a debate rather than present your own research ("debating," "sources"). Other than the first, all of these titles are acceptable for a formal essay. Your title is less important than what comes afterward, but it does make a first impression, so put a little thought into crafting a title that is accurate and specific and at least hints at what makes your essay different from other essays on the same subject. Be sure to format it correctly (see appendix 1, section A1.6).

8.8. Revision: Structure

At this point you should have a lot of writing on paper and be fairly sure of what you want to say. The next step is to revise for structure. Put all the pieces you have gathered into an order that will be easy for your reader to follow, as opposed to the order in which you discovered the material. This is a good time to outline. For a historiography essay where the "conversation" forms the backbone of the essay, label each of the voices in your conversation as A, B, and so on, or just use the authors' last names in place of Source A, Source B, and so on, in the outlines that follow.

There are two broad approaches to presenting a conversation involving several sources: either take each source one at a time, or organize it by major idea and discuss all the sources' treatments of each idea together. Choose one of these approaches depending on the nature of your material. If all your sources work on very closely related questions, each with a different contribution, the "conversation led" structure may work best. If your sources each address a very different aspect of an issue that links them only loosely, the "source led" structure may be better. And if you have some combination of those cases, you may need to combine the two outline types.

Once you have chosen an overall outline type, consider the order of sources within that outline. It often makes sense to address sources in the order they were published, but you might also follow the chronological order of the events they cover, or some other sequence, such as the steps in a process (for example, by first addressing a book about policing and surveillance, then one about the court system, then one about imprisonment). Try several outlines to see which seems to let your material fall neatly into place. If you find yourself frequently referring to earlier parts of your essay or repeating yourself, try a different structure.

Source-led outline

Introduction
- Explanation of the problem addressed by all sources
- At least a hint of the current state of resolution of that problem by the sources you will consider in this essay (name the sources here)

Source A
- Argument (claims, evidence, reasoning)
- Your critical evaluation

Source B
- Argument (claims, evidence, reasoning)
- Your critical evaluation

Source C
- Argument (claims, evidence, reasoning)
- Your critical evaluation

Nature of the conversation
- Connections between texts explained, compared, contrasted
- Your critical evaluation of how the sources as a group address their common question/problem

Conclusion
- Your conclusions on the "state of the field" in answering the common question/problem
- Suggestions for future research

Conversation-led outline

Introduction
- Explanation of the problem addressed by all sources
- At least a hint of the current state of resolution of that problem by the sources you will consider in this essay (name the sources here)

Conversation point 1:
- Source A (argument, your critical evaluation)
- Source B (argument, your critical evaluation)
- Source C (argument, your critical evaluation)

Conversation point 2:
- Source A (argument, your critical evaluation)
- Source B (argument, your critical evaluation)
- Source C (argument, your critical evaluation)

Etc., as needed

Conclusion
- Your conclusions on the "state of the field" in answering the common question/problem
- Suggestions for future research

They say / I say outline. Still another way to conceive of your historiography essay is to imagine it as alternating between what "they say" (the authors of your sources) and what "I say" (your own observations or criticisms). Some students find this a more intuitive way of outlining the body of an essay, like this:

Evidence point 1:
    They say X
    I say Y
Evidence point 2:
    They say X
    I say Y
    Etc.

Or:

Historian A:
  She says X
  I say Y
Historian B:
  He says X
  I say Y
  Etc.

This format is borrowed from the book *They Say, I Say: The Moves That Matter in Academic Writing* (Graff and Birkenstein, New York: Norton, 2018), which is an excellent reference on the rhetorical moves typical of academic writing in any discipline.

Book review outline. Book reviews tend to follow a fairly standard structure, beginning with what the book accomplishes, followed by criticisms if any, and ending with a general assessment of which readers will find the book most useful, for what purposes. Try outlining in the following way, but moving the parts between the introduction and conclusion to most sensibly reflect the book's content, strengths, and weaknesses. This outline suggests you add your critical evaluation in each section of the body, but instead you might discuss the key points of the book neutrally and add a separate section of your own evaluation toward the end. All but the first body section could come in any order that seems appropriate to your material.

Introduction: Provide the full name of the book and its author, and a brief, one-sentence summary of what it's about (adding whatever key information is not already in the title).

- *Goals*: State the author's goals and your assessment of how effectively the goals are met.
- *Argument*: Restate the major claims, evidence, and reasoning in your own words, including any questions or concerns you have about them.
- *Sources*: Explain in your own words what kind of sources were used. Archival? Published memoirs? Newspaper accounts? Etc.
- *Methods*: How does the author go about achieving her goals? State whether you think her method was appropriate to meet her goals, or whether some other strategies might have added something important.
- *Context*: How does this book fit it with a larger discussion of the issues at hand? In what ways does the book contributes something significant? What questions are left open?

Conclusion: State who the intended audience for the book is, and whether the book would satisfy that audience's needs. If appropriate, suggest other purposes the book might serve or people who might be interested in it.

8.9. Revision: Subject and Verb Tests

As you revise your essay on the sentence and paragraph levels, refer to previous sections on style and clarity (sections 4.7, 5.7–5.12, 6.11–6.13). After completing those revisions, this longer and more complicated essay is a good opportunity to also examine your draft in a new way. The following exercise is based on research about how readers of English process text and the excellent lessons in style developed from it by Joseph Williams (see Williams and Joseph Bizup, *Style: Lessons in Clarity and Grace*, New York: Pearson, 2016).

1. In each sentence of your essay, circle the main grammatical subject and underline the verb it belongs to. The exercise depends on doing this accurately, so if you need to review grammatical parts of speech, do that first, preferably with a tutor or a thorough grammar manual such as *The Bedford Handbook*. If you need only a brief refresher, see appendix 1. It is often easier to first cross out parts that are not the main subject or verb (any phrases following a preposition, anything ending in -ly, and so on).

2. Glance through your whole draft, reading only the string of circled subjects. Ideally, that string of grammatical subjects should represent the most important people, events, or ideas in your essay. In a historiographical essay, where the "conversation" is the focus, the authors, titles, and main ideas from each voice in your conversation should be reflected in most of the grammatical subjects of your sentences. Mark any sentences that don't fit this pattern. Sentences with vague subjects like "this" or "it" should definitely be revised.

3. Now look at the underlined verbs that match the grammatical subject of each sentence. How many of them are "empty" verbs like forms of "to have" or "to be"? Most of those will need to be revised. Ideally the verbs should indicate specific actions, and looking at the grammatical subjects and verbs together should give you some sense of what the essay is about. The verbs probably won't be actions in the sense of running and jumping, but they should be specific. Compare the following lists of subjects and verbs:

It was	The authors discuss
There could be	Lingley identifies
Lingley states	Her book argues
Sinicization is	Non-Han Chinese people became
This is	They mean
It follows	Woodfin counters
It was	A reader could assume
Analysis suggests	Woodfin analyzes and suggests

The second list gives the reader a fair idea of what the essay is about from just the subjects and verbs. The subjects are concrete "characters" doing specific actions. Revise your sentences so that the string of grammatical subjects and verbs matches the central ideas of your essay. Your readers will not only find each sentence easier to follow, but will sense a flow from one sentence to the next.

In this process you are likely to encounter some nominalizations. Nominalizations are actions described in noun form like "connotation" or "assumption," from "to connote" and "to assume." Change nominalizations back into verbs with their proper grammatical subjects: "The word connotes" or "The writer assumes." Change nominalizations paired with empty verbs such as "Resistance was dangerous" to "Resisters were usually caught, and punishments included torture, execution, or prison camp sentences." Notice how revising the subject and verb often forces you to fill in a much more specific sentence all the way to the end. This is part of why we do it.

If you run into trouble revising this way because the ideas or "characters" you think are most important are often at the ends of your sentences, check how many of your verbs are passive. Passive verbs are a grammatical structure that allow you to leave out the agent ("Mistakes were made") or shift the subject to the end of the sentence ("Mistakes were made by the president").

You may have heard the standard advice to avoid passive verbs completely. This advice is overstated: passive verbs can serve a purpose. We mostly avoid them because they leave out who did the action. Essays that are full of passive verbs can also be hard on the reader, because the construction puts words into an order that feels more remote or complicated. But there are times when we need passive verbs to leave out a grammatical subject that is not actually important. For example, "Aaron Burr was arrested" is a better sentence, despite the passive verb, than "Unknown officials arrested Aaron Burr," because in this case the person arrested and the fact of the arrest are important, but the people who happened to carry it out aren't worth mentioning. The other important purpose of a passive verb is to shift the doer of the main action to the end of the sentence because it gets more emphasis there, as in "Mistakes were made by the president."

The rule of thumb is to aim for grammatical subjects at the beginning of sentences paired with specific active verbs. But if your revision clearly makes the sentence less clear or less effective, check whether you're wrestling with a passive verb that is actually serving a useful purpose in this sentence.

4. Still looking at your verbs, quickly scan to make sure that they're all in the past tense or, when appropriate, the literary present (see section 6.14).

5. Now take a look at what comes before and between your subject-verb pairs. Ideally, English-speaking readers expect to find grammatical subjects and verbs next to each other and near the beginning of sentences. The more you insert other phrases before and between your subject-verb pairs, the less clear your essay will be. Look for introductory phrases that come before your subject-verb pair. Some short phrases that orient the reader provide important information or transitions:

- According to [author]...
- However...
- In the late fourteenth century...

But other phrases may serve little purpose and are best removed. Look especially for common filler:

- It is clear that...
- Clearly...
- Obviously...

If what you're saying really is "clear" or "obvious," the reader should understand it without having to be told.

When you find a phrase between your subject and verb, try shifting it before the subject or after the verb. If the phrase is a brief orienting statement, it probably belongs at the beginning:

Theodore Roosevelt, at the start of the twentieth century, became president following the assassination of William McKinley.

At the start of the twentieth century, Theodore Roosevelt became president following the assassination of William McKinley.

If a phrase adds an important qualification or example, it is probably better shifted to a place later in the sentence or in a new sentence:

Theodore Roosevelt, a famous conservationist and Progressive leader, became president following the assassination of William McKinley.

Theodore Roosevelt became president following the assassination of William McKinley, and became known as a conservationist and Progressive leader.

Theodore Roosevelt became president following the assassination of William McKinley. He would be known as a conservationist and Progressive leader.

If you already have a lot of other things happening in the rest of your sentence, breaking it up into two or more separate sentences is almost always preferable. Group ideas so that each sentence has one purpose.

At the start of the twentieth century, Theodore Roosevelt became president following the assassination of William McKinley, and became known as a conservationist and Progressive leader, as well as being the youngest president and splitting the Republican Party to start his own, the Progressive Party.

At the start of the twentieth century, Theodore Roosevelt became the youngest president in history following the assassination of William McKinley. As president he would be known as a conservationist and Progressive leader. After failing to be nominated by his own Republican Party in 1912 he created a new Progressive Party.

If you're not sure what to try, just draft several possibilities and read them aloud to choose the most effective.

6. Readers of English expect a sentence to begin with concepts that they already understand and introduce new or particularly important information at the end. Consider the following examples:

Sinicization affected non-Han Chinese people, according to historians. Forms of governance, culture, and religion were among the influences brought to such people by the Han Chinese.

Historians have identified a process of cultural change in medieval East Asia called Sinicization. Sinicization describes how the majority Han Chinese came to influence non-Han Chinese people. Such influences included forms of governance, culture, and religion.

Which set of sentences is easier to follow? In the first example, the grammatical subjects are concepts that haven't previously been mentioned or defined, and more familiar information is at the end and feels like an afterthought. In the second set, each sentence begins with a subject and verb that are already comprehended by the reader and end with a new idea. Once introduced, that new idea can begin a subsequent sentence, with more new information again in the emphasis position at the end. Revise your sentences one more time to make sure that new information is introduced toward the end of sentences before becoming a grammatical subject.

8.10. Revision: Using Feedback

Your assignment for an essay of this length and complexity may include some peer review—in which one or more of your classmates reads and comments on your essay, and you do the same for others—or you may have an opportunity to submit a draft to your instructor for comments before turning in your final version of the essay. If either of these opportunities is available to you, take advantage of it, and if not, find a friend or family member, or a campus writing tutor, who is willing to read your essay for you.

Nearly every writer, no matter how experienced, asks for feedback from others in the process of revising. When we work hard on a piece of writing, we become so familiar with it that we can be unable to notice differences between what has been fully realized on the page and what is still in our head. Readers who are not familiar with your sources are especially likely to notice when your essay is not as clear or complete as it could be.

Asking for feedback. If you have to ask someone outside of your course for feedback, give that person some specific instructions about what to look for in order to get the most substantive and useful comments. What instructions you give depends on what most concerns you about your essay. You might ask someone to concentrate on any of the following:

- Is the reasoning convincing? Ask your reader to read without marking up the essay, and then summarize it in her own words. This tells you whether the reader is really taking away what you intended to convey. If the result is not what you expected, go back to section 8.8 to work on how your main subjects and most important new ideas are arranged in your sentences.
- Is the essay complete? Ask your reader to insert questions, question marks, and squiggly lines at any place where she is not certain she understands what you are describing. Revise by adding examples and explanations in each of those places.
- Does the essay meet expectations? Give your reader the assignment instructions you were given, or if these were minimal, have her read section 8.1, then read your essay. Ask that she tells you any area in the assignment that could be expanded, not just if there's anything you left out entirely.

- Is the essay clear and appropriate in style? Ask someone who is familiar with academic writing to mark any sentence he had to read twice or that caused him to stop or look back for an explanation. Ask him to summarize the main idea of each paragraph briefly in the margin, and to cross out any word or phrase that is repetitive, vague, generalizing, or redundant.
- Are there grammatical or punctuation errors or typos? If this is what you want feedback on, don't ask the same reader to also comment on the content. Each reader should focus on just one goal.

Responding to feedback. Ask the following questions as you look over the comments you received:

- Did your reader get an accurate sense of what you wanted your essay to say?
- If your reader understood your essay, was she also convinced by it?

If the answer to either question is no, you know you have some significant work to do, but you will revise differently depending on which problem you have. If your reader gave you specific suggestions for how to revise, you shouldn't necessarily follow them exactly (even if the suggestions came from your instructor). First try to find out how your reader got a different impression from your words than you intended to communicate.

Look again at the reader's annotations. Is there a pattern to the kinds of things, or the parts of the essay, that have a lot of question marks, squiggly lines, crossed-out words, or other suggestions? It may be that you're having trouble with a particular rhetorical move, such as beginning the essay, or ending it, or supporting your claims. Or maybe you just ran out of gas toward the end of the draft. Or you started rough, but found your way by the end. Figuring out which of these is the case tells you what to work on next. If the problem areas are spread out, but of a similar type (lots of generalizations, or quotes aren't handled effectively, or you haven't fully distilled your sources) then, again, you know what is a priority for you to work on next.

Then ask yourself whether your reviewer noticed something you didn't, or made a suggestion for something you hadn't thought of. Do you like the idea? Is it useful for *your* goals for the essay? If the reviewer noticed or suggested something that would pull the essay away from your intended direction, you don't need to follow her advice, but you do need to address how what is currently on paper is not conveying what you intended. For problems involving emphasis, see section 8.8.

Don't avoid making suggested changes because they're too much work. Big changes often involve more big thinking than time, but even if time is a factor, it is what makes the difference between an essay that works and one that doesn't.

If you decide not to make a change suggested by your reader, it should only be because you want to solve the problem identified by making a different kind of change that you think will most effectively serve your goals for the essay.

Make a to-do list detailing how you will revise. Using the most concrete possible language, and breaking down all tasks to the smallest possible units, list the things you need to do next.

- What do you need to look up or find out from your sources?
- What major questions do you need to think about to reframe your essay more effectively? List each one separately, with sub-questions as necessary.
- Do you need to find an additional source?
- Do you need to reword your main claim or subclaims?
- Do you need to change the order of paragraphs?
- Do you need to indicate your transitions from one idea to the next more clearly?
- Do you need to address counterarguments, or do so more effectively?
- Do you need to qualify your claims? Reword them to make sure they're strictly accurate?
- What small changes do you need to make in the text of your essay (choosing more specific words, deleting unnecessary verbiage, formalizing/completing citations, attributing quotes, defining terms, supplying some background)?

8.11. Revision: Grading Yourself

One additional form of revision that may be useful is to take a last look at your essay as if you were grading it (or better, have a very critical friend do it for you). If your instructor has provided a rubric or other details about how your essay will be graded, follow those criteria exactly. Break down the assignment you were given into parts and give yourself a grade or score for each part by going through your essay and identifying specific passages in black and white that satisfy (or don't satisfy) each requirement. If you were not given specific instructions, use the criteria in section 8.1 or table 8.1.

The list of "expectations" in the table includes the content of the essay broken down into parts:

- Have you clearly and fully explained the central problem that all the sources are discussing?
- Is your distillation of the source arguments clear and accurate, including qualifications?

Table 8.1 Grading Rubric for Historiographical Essay

Expectation	A	B	C	D	F
Clarity of central problem					
Clarity of distillations					
Completeness of distillations					
Clarity of conversation					
Completeness of conversation					
Clarity of criticism					
Originality of criticism					
Mechanics of using sources					
Structure and organization					
Style and clarity					
Grammar, usage, formatting					

- Are your distillations of the sources complete, including all the points that relate to the central problem you have identified?
- Have you explained the nature of the "conversation," that is, how each voice is interacting with others (agreeing, adding, quibbling, etc.)?
- Have you fully explained what the "conversation" has and has not established and its significance, without leaving out any decisive elements?
- Have you added your own critical evaluation of individual sources and the nature of the whole "conversation"? Have you made it clear to the reader where you are inserting your own comments, and that these are your evaluation, going beyond what was already said by your sources?

The items in italics in table 8.1 list formal expectations: the elements of the essay's form that convey content to the reader smoothly, according to the standards of formal academic writing.

- **Mechanics of using sources:** Do you quote, paraphrase, attribute and cite your sources appropriately and accurately?
- **Structure and organization:** Does the essay have a clear beginning, middle, and end? Do paragraphs each have a single coherent topic? Do paragraphs transition from one to the next logically?

- **Style and clarity:** Is the tone and vocabulary of your essay appropriate for an academic audience? Are your words accurate and specific, without repetition? Can a reader follow your essay without difficulty or confusion?
- **Grammar, usage, formatting:** Is the essay correct in grammar, punctuation, formatting, and formalities of usage?

Give yourself a score for each expectation, from total absence or failure to meet the expectation on the far left to exceeding expectation on the far right (roughly corresponding to letter grades from F to A). Use this exercise to identify areas where you can still improve your essay before turning it in. It helps you to see where *on the page* you have met assignment expectations, as opposed to the skills or knowledge that may be in your head, but not yet on the page for your grader to find.

8.12. Proofreading: A Checklist

You should now be in the habit of proofreading for spelling, grammar, punctuation, formatting, and usage, using more than just the built-in auto-checks in your software (see sections 5.9, 5.13, and 6.14). Use the following checklist for this or any other long essay. Remember you need to start this checklist while there's still time to correct any omissions.

- Are your name, your instructor's name, the assignment name, and the course title and date on the first page? (If your paper goes astray, electronically or on the floor of someone's office, this information will make it possible for your paper to get back into your grader's hands.)
- Are all names and titles spelled correctly? (There's nothing more embarrassing than misspelling your own name and nothing more ridiculous than misspelling the name of the person grading you!)
- If you are submitting an electronic file, did you put your last name and the name of the assignment in the filename? If you submit a file called "historiography.doc" and so does someone else in your class, one of the two could easily be overwritten by the other.
- Did you save the file in a format that can be uploaded or emailed as required? Files that can't be viewed can't be read and therefore can't receive a grade. Submitting an intentionally garbled file and claiming computer error is an old trick to get an extension on an assignment: unreadable files get a zero. It's your responsibility to check. PDFs are the least likely to get garbled, if your instructor accepts them.

- Do you know where to upload or send the document and confirm that it was received? Double-check that you're clicking the right link. If you are asked to email the file, you won't get a confirmation, but you will have a dated copy in your sent mail file that can serve as proof you sent it on time. If your instructor lets you know that he did not receive it, forward the dated copy from your sent mail or a copy of a submission receipt.
- Does the title of your essay accurately and specifically describes its contents?
- Did you check for spelling, grammar, punctuation, and usage mistakes like "world war 2," which should be "World War II" (see appendix 1, section A1.7)?
- Is the document double spaced throughout?
- Did you insert page numbers?
- Are all quotes and paraphrases accurately cited, consistently using a recognized citation style (such as Chicago or MLA)? (See section 10.10 and appendix 1, section A1.9.)
- Are quotes formatted correctly, with marks, indents, or spacing as appropriate for the length of the quote? (See sections 5.9 and 9.4 and appendix 1, section A.1.5.)
- Did you add a Works Cited page, if you need one? (If you only cited one source, it is unnecessary.) Did you format the citations here in "bibliographic" rather than "footnote" or "in-text" style? (See section 10.10 and appendix 1, section A1.9.)
- If you are using footnotes, check for multiple citations to the same source. A second citation immediately after the first can be replaced with "Ibid., [page]," and later references to a source you already cited can be replaced with a short citation (section see 10.10).
- Are all titles formatted correctly (in title case, in quotations for titles to short works like articles or chapters, in italics for long works like books)?
- Are the margins all set at one inch? Don't use larger margins to make your paper look longer. It just makes it look empty.
- Are you using a font size roughly equivalent to 12-point Times New Roman? Small fonts can be tiring for the reader, and very large fonts make your essay look like an elementary-school project. Avoid unusual font styles like Comic Sans.
- If you are printing your essay, do you have access to a functioning printer that will produce a readable hard copy using black ink?
- If you are printing, did you staple the pages together? Unstapled pages can be lost in the course of being carried around with other essays, and missing pages can't be graded. If you don't own a stapler, buy one!

9

Primary Source Interpretation

If you are asked to write about a text that was created or first published in the historical period you are studying, then you are interpreting a primary source. Such assignments often ask you to "analyze," "interpret," do a "close reading," or "read between the lines" of the text. These assignments usually ask you to read a document deeply and make your own claims about what we can learn from it. Simpler assignments that ask you only to summarize and briefly comment on or ask questions about a primary source are similar to a response paper, so read the relevant parts of that chapter as well.

A primary source interpretation is organized around an argument about what the document means, articulated in a thesis statement or main claim, as described in sections 6.10 and 11.8. If your primary source assignment asks you to compare two or more documents, read sections 11.4 and 11.11 on comparisons as well as this chapter. If your assignment asks you to consider both primary and secondary sources fully in constructing your own argument, work with both this chapter and all of chapter 11.

9.1. What's Your Goal?

When you write a primary source interpretation, you are doing the most elemental task all historians do: you are examining an original artifact from the past and asking what it might mean. When you interpret a primary source, you examine it from three angles:

- **Text.** What does the document say? What message was it conveying to its original readers?
- **Context.** Who wrote the document? Why did they write it? When? Where, how, when, and by whom was it read? What circumstances inspired it? What circumstances colored the way it was read? What influence did it have? In what ways does it reflect on the time and place from which it came?
- **Subtext.** What was being said indirectly, or "between the lines"? What was left unsaid? What can we infer about the author's intentions or assumptions from the way the text is written?

A primary source interpretation uses an exploration of text, context, and subtext not only to explain the document and what it can teach us, but also to answer broader historical questions. The results of this process will be your main claim or thesis statement. Primary sources are a kind of evidence, so a primary source interpretation is a reading of evidence and an exploration of what that evidence might show. That interpretive reading of evidence is how we support our claims.

9.2. What Is a Primary Source?

Primary sources are documents or objects written or produced in the period you are studying. Primary sources are evidence for historical analysis, whereas the analyses written by historians are known as secondary sources. Most of the time, that's all you need to know. However, as you look closely at primary sources and create your own analyses of them, it is worth thinking more deeply about what these terms mean. After all, why don't we just say "original sources" and "analytical texts"? Why use terms that often mislead students to assume that "primary" means first in importance or chronology? The terms "primary" and "secondary" as applied to sources do have deeper meanings with important implications for how we use them.

Let's say you write a paragraph right now about how your day has gone so far. This is a text. Just a "text," with no fancy label. But now let's say that your friend Brian reads your paragraph, and then writes his own paragraph explaining what he thinks are interesting implications of your text. In relation to each other, your text becomes *primary* and Brian's becomes *secondary*. Yours is the original text compared to Brian's, while Brian's text comments on yours, and is therefore secondary to it.

Now let's say that several other people—Mohammad, Natalie, and Pia—also write interpretations of your paragraph. All of these people's essays are secondary, because they are all analyzing the original, primary text written by you. If still another person, Raisa, comes along and writes a summary of the texts written by Brian, Mohammad, Natalie, and Pia, then her text is *tertiary* because it's still another level removed from your original (*primary*) text.

In other words, the status of a given text as "primary," "secondary," or "tertiary" is relative. This relative status depends on how each text is being used and its relationship to other texts.

In most cases, we can correctly say that primary sources are documents such as letters and diaries, secondary sources are historical books and articles, and tertiary sources are textbooks and encyclopedias. But what if we look at a Nazi science textbook printed in 1935 in order to see what it tells us about Nazi ideology? In that case, it is a primary source, even though it is a textbook and summarizes the analyses of people who were looking at original data. Its status as a primary source derives from how and when we are using it.

Now consider *The Age of Extremes* by Eric Hobsbawm. Hobsbawm is a well-known Marxist historian who lived through many of the events he describes in this textbook about the "short twentieth century," meaning the period from 1914 to 1991 (he was born in 1917 and the book was published in 1996). Although it is meant to give readers an overview of world history in that period, Hobsbawm also uses it to make an argument about this period having a distinct, connected meaning, because of links he makes between World War I, World War II, and the Cold War. Is this book a primary source, because Hobsbawm experienced some of the events he describes? Is it secondary, because he is a historian presenting an argument about how we should understand those events? Or is it tertiary, because it mostly summarizes the work of many historians and provides an overview of what happened? The answer depends on how you use it. If you read *The Age of Extremes* in a course to fill out factual background and to look up details, you are using it as a tertiary source. If you cite it in your historiography essay on interpretations of the causes of World War II, then you are using it as a secondary source. If you read it to discern how Hobsbawm's personal experiences and view of history shaped his interpretations as an influential Marxist historian, you are using it as a primary source for your own analysis of Hobsbawm's role in historiography.

Now consider a memoir published in the 1960s but written about the author's childhood in the 1930s. If a primary source is "a text written at the time we're studying," and we're studying the 1930s, can this memoir be a primary source? Yes, it can, though we would read it carefully knowing that the author based it on decades-old memories, which can be inaccurate or affected by what the author learned later. We could *also* use such a memoir as a primary source if we were studying the 1960s, if we wanted to inquire about what made the author decide to write about her past and what was going on in the 1960s that might have inspired, colored, or altered her memories of earlier times.

Contrast this last example to a diary kept in the year 1830 but lost in someone's attic for 150 years before finally being published in the 1980s. This diary can be used as a primary source for the study of the period around 1830, when it was written, but has nothing whatsoever to do with the 1980s, since the text was created in 1830 and unaltered later. It was only made available at the later time, without effect on its contents.

Having explored these complicated exceptions, we can now lay out a more elaborate, but more accurate and reliable, definition of primary, secondary, and tertiary sources:

- If we are analyzing a text (or object or other medium) to use it as direct evidence about what was happening or what people were thinking in the past, it is a primary source.
- If we are analyzing a text to find out what others have learned so far about a past time, it is a secondary or tertiary source. If we are reading such a text for the author's argument or interpretation of the evidence, it is secondary. If we are reading such a text for its summary of what is generally known about the past without interest in the author's own views or interpretations, it is tertiary.

9.3. How Historians Use Primary Sources

The mechanics of finding, quoting, and citing sources are basically the same whether your source is primary, secondary, or tertiary, and for this reason you may not have seen these terms used so much in other courses and may wonder why your history instructors use them often and even define assignments according to which kind of source you're using. Because history is the study of the past, a major distinction between primary and secondary sources is fundamental to the way we work. Primary sources are our only form of evidence (we cannot usually create data sets or design interviews, as a political scientist or sociologist might). Secondary sources are not evidence: we use them only to frame our questions and claims. We have distinct methods for making sense of primary sources and different questions to ask about their reliability than we would employ with secondary sources. Our methods for reading primary sources are also different from the methods used to read similar texts in other disciplines. For example, you might be asked to write about *Huckleberry Finn* in an English course and a history course, but each discipline asks you to consider different kinds of questions about the text and what it means.

9.4. Text: Sourcing Documents

Understanding what kind of source you have, where it came from, and the basic facts of when and where it was produced is vital to everything else you need to do in a primary source essay. This process is often referred to as "sourcing" a document. If you make a mistake at this stage, nothing else in your essay is likely to work. Consider the following introduction from a primary source essay:

> Ellen Schrecker's *The Age of McCarthyism: A Brief History with Documents* describes how many Communists had a hard time during Communism. In Schrecker's document, it seems that McCarthy questioned and sometimes arrested people he suspected of being Communists. Ellen Schrecker is a history professor, with a PhD, at Yeshiva University and an author with a focus of the history of anti-Communism. Her novel was first published in February 1994 and written in New York, NY. Schrecker expects history students who have an interest in American history or anyone interested in American history to read her book. One of Schrecker's documents is Rose Krysak's *Rank-and-File Communist in the 1950s*, October 31, 1979.

Unfortunately, this example gets almost everything wrong about what kind of text the student was reading, and consequently the rest of the essay is as unsuccessful as the introduction, since it is based on false information. The student confused the document he was supposed to be analyzing with the book that the document was published in. Instead of answering questions about the author, date, and publication of a historical document, he answered questions about the book that made the document available to students. Therefore he describes the wrong author—a historian instead of a historical actor—the wrong date—1994, which was not the period being studied in this course—and the wrong place and purpose of publication (New York; for students). Finally, the student confuses this non-fiction collection of documents with a "novel," which is a work of fiction (see section 5.10.1 for definitions of the types of publications).

Professional historians usually get their primary sources from archives, where they may often hold a yellowed, centuries-old, handwritten piece of paper in their hands. As a student in a college classroom, it is unlikely that you will have access to documents in their original state. Instead, you see primary sources that have been edited, translated if necessary, and gathered together in groups by topic and then published in books or on the Web for student use. You may be given a photocopy or digital scan of just the page or two containing your document and never see the collection it came from, much less the original archival document.

The first key to figuring out what you're dealing with is the citation (or the same information from a book's title page and its reverse, which should have been provided to you with an excerpt):

Krysak, Rose. "A Rank-and-File Communist in the 1950s." In *The Age of McCarthyism: A Brief History with Documents,* edited by Ellen Schrecker, 117–118. New York: St. Martin's Press, 1994.

Notice first that there are two author names and two titles. One of the titles is in quotation marks, and the other is in italics—italics denote titles of long works like books, and quotation marks are used for titles of shorter works, including those that appear inside a periodical or book. Your document must be the shorter one, so Rose Krysak is its author. Also notice the words "a brief history with documents" in the book title. Document collections tend to have words like these somewhere in their title:

Document collection	Sources in
With documents	A reader
A documentary handbook	Readings in

Those keywords tell you are looking at a collection title, not the title of an individual document. Another clue to the same thing is the phrase "edited by" in the citation—the person whose name follows is an editor, not an author. An editor gathers sources, chooses portions of them to include, and sometimes adds explanatory notes. This is obviously quite different from the author, who composes the words and ideas in the text itself. Editors may also be indicated in a citation with the abbreviation "ed.," or "eds." for more than one editor. Note also the abbreviation "tr." or the phrase "translated by" in a citation or on a title page. A translator converts a text that was originally written in another language into English so that English-speaking readers can use it. A translator is not responsible for the content of a text and therefore also should not be treated as an author.

In this case, the citation describes an interview with a woman named Rose Krysak who had been active in the American Communist Party in the 1950s (a period when Senator Joseph McCarthy waged a campaign against communism in the United States). The interview was conducted in 1979 and was gathered together with other documents about the McCarthy period by a historian named Ellen Schrecker, who also wrote an essay and put all those things together in one book, called *The Age of McCarthyism: A Brief History with Documents.* Now notice the publication date, 1994. The date of your primary source will either be within the period you are studying (in this case the 1950s), or a memoir/autobiography written later but describing the period you are studying. The date the document was originally written or *first* published—if it was published before being included in a collection for students—is usually in the text itself (as in a diary entry or letter) or provided near the document text by the editor, perhaps in an introduction or footnote, but *not* in the citation. The date in the citation indicates only when this collection of documents was made available in this form.

While you are looking at the publication date, you might also notice there is usually a location as well as a publisher's name. Citations for books require the publisher's name and location (such as St. Martin's Press, based in New York), but this is never relevant to your primary source essay.

The location where your document was actually written is relevant to your essay, but you will not find it in the citation. That means you also need to look closely at the other information you have. Start with the title page and table of contents for the book your document came from, if you have them. The table of contents will list each document, often providing the author names and original dates of writing or publication as well. Look next at what comes right before and alongside the document itself. In collections made for students, the editor often writes a note explaining how, when, where, and by whom the text was originally written, and sometimes when and how it has been published before. Look also for headings, subheadings, or footnotes, which may also provide some information about your document. In some collections, footnotes or a glossary will define obscure words or names for you.

9.5. Text: Document Types

Knowing what kind of document you have informs what kinds of questions you will need to ask about it and is especially important in helping you to identify the author and intended audience. Some document types are fairly obvious: usually the formatting will tell you when you're looking at a diary, and it may also be given away in a title or heading: "The Diary of So-and-So." But in other cases you will need to deduce what kind of document you have from clues in the text itself. The following are the forms of primary sources you are likely to encounter in coursework.

9.5.1. Personal Documents

These are documents written by and about individuals, originally for private use.

Diary/journal. A diary is a personal record with periodic entries, usually not intended to be read by others in the near term. Diaries consist of separate, dated entries describing a day's events or thoughts. "Journal" is sometimes used interchangeably with "diary" and should not be confused with the other kind of journal, a published periodical containing scholarly articles.

Letter. Private or personal letters are usually written by one person to another individual (the recipient is the "intended audience"), though letters written before the nineteenth century were often expected to be passed around to interested friends or family members. Letters are each dated, and usually describe events or thoughts that occurred on or shortly before their date. A group of letters written back and forth between two people is referred to as "correspondence." "Epistle" is a synonym for letter, and the adjective "epistolary" means "having to do with letters," as in an "epistolary novel," a long work of fiction written as if it were a series of letters.

Unpublished note or drawing. Any other document created by a private individual is "authored" by that person and may have no intended audience or a small, private intended audience.

9.5.2. Public Documents

These are any documents created for publication or produced in the public interest by officials acting in their professional capacity, either released publicly, therefore for a "general audience," or circulated among other officials, so that the audience includes people who work in the roles or offices given access to the document.

Memoir/autobiography. Memoirs are written by individuals to describe some period in their past (the name derives from "memory"). An autobiography is an account one's whole life, though the distinction is not always followed closely. Most memoirs and autobiographies are written to be published, and therefore for a broad audience, but some are written only for family members or other narrow audiences.

Interview. Oral history is written based on interviews with people who experienced some historical event or phenomenon. Usually a historian finds and deliberately interviews such people, though sometimes we use interviews conducted at some earlier time, often by journalists. The person being interviewed is the person of interest—the "author" for these purposes—and her words are the "text" being analyzed. The audience is the interviewer as well as those expected to read or use the interview (often scholars and students, sometimes general readers). Consider how the presence of the interviewer and the purpose of the interview (for scholarship or otherwise) may have shaped the account the "author" gave of her experiences.

Fiction (known author). The author is named, and the work was usually published for a general audience in its country of origin. There are three broad categories of fiction; be careful to name the type of work accurately:

- **Novel:** Stories developed over book length
- **Short story, novella:** Short stories are too short to be published in book form. Novellas are between short stories and novels in length.
- **Play, screenplay:** Fiction written to be acted out on stage or screen.

Art (known creator). Artistic works or objects that are not texts or not entirely text-based and can be attributed to specific creator(s).

- **Painting, sculpture, drawing, photograph, poster, advertisement, etc. by a known creator or attributable to a specific organization or publisher.** The "author" in these cases is the artist, or more specifically a painter, sculptor, photographer, illustrator, cartoonist, engraver, and so on, if that person is named, or the organization that made the work available. The "audience" is the viewers who the artist expected would be likely to encounter the work.
- **Music, lyrics, or musical performance by known creator.** The author of a musical work is known as a composer or songwriter. In some cases, a composer writes music and a lyricist writes the words (or a librettist: the words of an opera or storyline of a ballet are known as the libretto, or sometimes "the book," for the spoken lines in a musical). Performers of musical works also have a creative role and might also be considered a form of "author" of the work. The audience, or listeners, might include anyone who could play the piece, listen to a recording, or be present at a live performance.
- **Film, animation, television, or theatrical performance by known creators.** These are works that involve many creative contributors, though the director and screenwriter/playwright are usually considered primarily responsible for the content. When you consider questions relating to the "author" of your work, apply them to whichever person or people are responsible for the choices that you are analyzing, whether that's a director, editor, actor, set designer, or someone else. The audience for a performance might be the general public, if anyone had access to seeing it, or the people who were literally present for a given performance or first saw the work when it was produced. A film made in 1929 was created for an audience that saw it in 1929, not the present-day audience, even though we are still able to watch it.

Cultural ephemera (popular works with no known creator). Jokes, sayings, songs or folklore (oral narratives) without a named author or point of origin can be assumed to be the product of whatever culture where they circulated (in which case that culture is both the creator and audience for the purpose of analysis). If the organization that produced a printed work like an advertisement or propaganda poster is unknown, we try to infer what kind of organization or individuals would likely have produced it. The popular or viral nature of these sources means they usually reflect a narrow time and place (they are "ephemeral," or short-lived), and the lack of attribution to a creator means we can infer that the content represents common assumptions or concerns rather than an individual point of view:

- Jokes, sayings, myths, legends
- Popular songs, poems, oral narratives
- Graffiti, tattoos, or other ubiquitous visual patterns or symbols
- Advertisements, posters, cartoons, event programs of unknown origins

Historical periodical. Newspapers and magazines often name an author for each article they contain, though some will be anonymous or written by multiple people as representatives of an editorial board. You may also be interested in the overall editorial view of the periodical, meaning the choices made by its editor(s) to select or direct its content as a whole, in which case the editors are in the role of "author" for your analysis. Also consider how layout designers, photographers or illustrators, and even advertisers contribute to shaping the contents. Many periodicals are published for a general audience, but others specialize their coverage or style to capture specific kinds of audiences, which you may have to discern from internal clues.

Prescriptive literature. Books or articles written in order to provide advice, guidance, or inspiration for how people should live presume an audience of readers who did *not* already accept the tenets being recommended by the text (otherwise they would not need the advice). The author of such works is sometimes anonymous or hidden behind a pseudonym, in which case you might infer some details about the author from the text itself or the venue where it was published, but will not be able to name the person.

Official document (authored by representatives of a recognized institutional body). Official documents are sometimes authored by named individuals, sometimes by an office or institutional unit. Some official documents do not indicate who literally prepared them (often because it was a group of people working in consultation). To answer questions about the "author" of such documents, consider whichever office or institution took responsibility for the creation of the document. The most immediate audience is whoever was expected to act on the document or be affected by it. Some official documents were only seen by other officials, some were made with an awareness they would be released to the public, either immediately or after some set time:

- **Government:** Products of bureaucracy such as minutes, memos, reports, schedules, and so on. Minutes record what was said and decided at official meetings. Memos are short pieces of communication within an institutional body. Reports are summaries of information collected by some party to inform another party. Schedules are dated lists or calendars of events, meetings, and so forth.

- **Legal:** Laws, proclamations, decrees, or legal codes or regulations written by lawmakers or rulers, or treatises written by legal scholars. Legal documents are enforced by a government or influence the enforcement of law.
- **Other institutional:** Products of non-governmental bureaucracy, such as military, clerical, charity, corporate, or activist records, endorsements, and so forth. These can be similar in form to government documents, being bureaucratic in nature, but their purposes and audience vary depending on the institution that produces them.
- **Individual officials:** Statements, treatises, speeches, or essays by people holding office in a governmental, political, clerical, charity, or military structure and acting in their professional capacity, who may be understood as speaking at least in part as representatives of the organization they work for. Speeches often have two layers of audience: the live audience that was present when the speech was delivered, and a secondary audience that was able to read it if it was transcribed and published or otherwise circulated.

Non-fiction. Authored by someone other than representatives of a recognized institutional body (essays, treatises, articles, reportage, speeches, academic writing, interviews with public figures). This category covers any form of writing with a known author acting on his own behalf and intended for public consumption. Therefore the "author" is usually named, and the intended audience is usually the public of whatever place where the document was produced, though in some cases like speeches it might primarily be the people present when it was delivered, or some smaller group if the text was not widely published.

9.6. Reading Primary Sources

Primary sources selected for students are often much shorter than secondary readings or textbook chapters, but they are more difficult to read. There are two main reasons primary sources are unusually difficult.

First, the language may be old-fashioned and perhaps not listed in common dictionaries. Look up unfamiliar terms in the *Oxford English Dictionary* and look for "archaic" definitions, being careful to note the dates the word was in use. Just because a definition is old does not mean it is the one being used in your document; you need to find the definition that was in use when the document was written and that makes sense in the context you found it. There may also be names, events, or other historical phenomena named that are not familiar to you. Look these up in your course materials or an encyclopedia. If you are looking up a term in a general encyclopedia, again be careful that you do not accept the first explanation you come across; look for the one that fits your time period and context. A specialized reference work, such as *The Bedford Glossary for European History*, will give you more relevant information than Wikipedia. To find an appropriate specialized reference, browse your library's reference section or consult a reference librarian (section 10.2).

The second reason primary sources can be more difficult to read is that by definition they were not written for you. They were written for someone else, or for no one, so you will have to do some extra work to put yourself in the place of the original author and audience. You need to use everything you know from class and other readings about the time and place where your document was written to put yourself in the shoes of the author: What was she concerned about? Why would she put pen to paper to produce this document? What was the author hoping the document would accomplish? Who would have read it first? What might that first reader have thought about the document? Why would she read it? Using these questions, try to read the document as it was understood in its time, looking up whatever information you need to help you follow along.

Sometimes you will be asked to read a single book-length primary source, usually a novel or memoir. Dive straight into the whole book beginning to end (unlike the way you approach a secondary or tertiary source). As you read, mark any passages that strike you as relating to course questions or themes. After you've finished, go back to those passages, and think over the work as a whole, to consider what ideas or passages raise historical questions or answer questions that have been discussed in class or addressed in your secondary readings.

Any source must be read skeptically, but primary sources require us to consider a few common ways a source can be unreliable or misleading that are peculiar to the source type. When reading fiction we are looking for what the text can tell us about the assumptions, values, beliefs, concerns, or material culture or manners of the time it represents. The same is true for any artistic works: the brushstrokes or perspective of a painting may tell us something about the artist's interests or goals, which are indicative of assumptions, values, and other aspects of the work's historical context, but we are not interested in the choices, effects, or techniques that make an artwork significant regardless of its time and place.

Memoirs and autobiographies are often written long after the events they describe, and most interviews similarly ask the subject to recall events that are long past, so we need to read these with an awareness of how the author's memory may be faulty, or how subsequent events might cause the author to want to explain or justify some period of their past in a way they were not aware of at the time.

Prescriptive literature is frequently mined by historians because it is often focused on the habits and customs of everyday life that are otherwise elusive, but it must be read not as evidence of how people actually lived, but how the advice-givers wanted people to live, which implies that the reality was otherwise. Similarly, other works that told people what they should do or want, like political campaign material, public service materials, or advertisements, can tell us what the creators hoped for and also that the audience was assumed *not* to be living up to that hope. Some government and legal documents should also be read as prescriptive: telling people what to do or intending to shape behavior through instruction or regulation, which indicates that the government was concerned that real behavior was otherwise. Any bureaucratic or organizational text may serve a similar function but be aimed at a narrower audience; a company might issue directives to guide employee behavior or innovation in a desired direction, for example.

9.7. Afternotes for a Primary Source

When taking notes on a primary source, you are looking for different kinds of information than you did when reading historical analyses. Use the following categories to record the most important information about each primary source you read. The more detailed your notes are, the more material you have for your first draft.

- **Citation.** Enter the full bibliographic citation, which shows where you got the document from and will be needed to cite the work in your essay.
- **Author(s).** Enter the name of the historical person who wrote the document, *not* the editor or translator who made it available to students. Add any identifying information about the author, such as occupation, nationality, age, and sex, as far as that information is available and relevant to your reading of the document.
- **Document type.** Enter a document type using sections 9.4–9.5. Be as specific and descriptive as possible, not just choosing the correct type from the list but noticing any variations or additional details unique to your document.
- **Date written.** Enter the date the document was first written, not when it was most recently published. This might be only a year, or an exact date—enter the date as precisely as it is provided.
- **Date read.** Enter the date the document was *first* published or read. Some documents, such as diaries, were not published or intended for any reader at the time they were written, so enter "n/a" for "not applicable."

- **Author purpose.** Explain what you think the author(s) intended to accomplish with this text. This is not always stated outright. In many cases you have to deduce the author's purpose based on what you read and what you know about the context.
- **Intended audience.** Who did the author expect would read the document? Who was it for?
- **Reader response.** If known and relevant, explain how the document was received by its original readers (was it influential, did it change minds, was it controversial?).
- **Vocabulary.** Enter any words you don't know that are keeping you from understanding the text. Look them up as needed and enter the definitions here.
- **Immediate context.** Explain as much as you know or can find out about the immediate context (see section 9.8).
- **Broader context.** Explain as much as you know or can find out about the historical, comparative, and historiographical context (see section 9.8). Make note here of references to course readings, lectures, or your research as needed.
- **Key passages.** Quote (with page number) any passages that strike you as particularly important, interesting, strange, contradictory, or striking.
- **Subtext.** Explain as much as you can guess, extrapolate, or speculate about the possible subtext (see section 9.9), especially what is implied by the key passages you noted above. Include pages numbers whenever you are referring to a specific passage.
- **Questions.** Add any questions you have about the document after reading it, including anything you don't understand, need to find out, or wonder about.

9.8. What Is Context?

Context is the environment that surrounds a subject. A person lives in a time, a place, a culture, a society. A state (government) exists at a specific geographical location, at a given time, with a given set of relations with its neighbors and the rest of the world, and expectations and participation from the people it governs. A text was written by some person, at some time and place, intended to be read by some people for some purpose. These are all examples of contexts.

The interwar period in Europe cannot be understood without recognizing that everything that happened then was to some degree a reaction to the Great War that preceded it, and cannot be interpreted clearly without recognizing that we look at it today through the lens of our knowledge of World War II (thus coloring the interwar period as a "buildup" to World War II, even though at the time there was no certain knowledge of what was coming or inevitability that it would come). Historians always want to know the context. History itself—the study of the past—is about establishing that one kind of context: what came before, that got us to where we are now?

It is possible to study the characters, plot, and themes of John Steinbeck's *The Grapes of Wrath* and appreciate what it tells us about human nature, as well as its artistry, without caring much about when it was written, by whom, or for whom. But historians care primarily about what that novel can tell us about the Great Depression, dustbowl migration, and class in America. We use the novel as evidence to better understand the time and place where it was written or read.

Some facts about context can be definitively known, and you must find those facts in order to understand your document. Other aspects of the world that brought about your document are a matter of interpretation. If definitive answers are not available, speculate what the likely possible answers are based on the information you do have. If likely answers are unknowable, consider whether just raising a question may add something to our understanding of the document.

The following sections define the four major types of context we consider when making sense of a primary source document. As you begin to brainstorm your essay, write down everything you can find about the context of your document.

Immediate context. All primary sources need to be understood in light of basic facts about how they were produced, so far as those facts can be known.

- What was the author's social and/or professional position, what were his abilities, what did he know or not know, what were his goals? What circumstances may have restricted or defined the nature of what he wrote (did he have money, education, leisure, was he censored, was what he wrote about a dangerous topic, etc.?).
- When and where was the document written? What was going on at those times and places that may have affected the writing?
- When and where was it published (if it was published), in what format? How might the circumstances of publication have affected the writing, or the way it was read? How did the original readers react to it?
- Is the document you read part of a larger text, such as an excerpt from a book? If so, what part does it play in the whole?

Historical context. Our interest in these documents stems from their connection to related historical events, so we must always make as many connections as possible between the text and the time and place it was produced or describes.

- What broader historical phenomena was this text a part of? If it was part of some debate, development, or trend, or was written during or after some big historical event, in what ways does the text reflect those phenomena? Do you see references to these events on the page?

- What can this text teach us about the historical context that surrounded it? Does the text tell us something about key actors, or reflect attitudes of a given group, or provide evidence to settle some significant question(s) about the past?
- Does the document express a common or widely accepted point of view, or a minority view? To what degree did people pay attention to this document at the time it was written? To what degree did it influence others?

Comparative context. You may not be able to address comparative context if your assignment does not involve reading other, related primary sources. Comparing your document to another primary source can help you see aspects you did not otherwise notice, help you see how some aspects stem from differing contexts, or help you judge the degree to which your document is representative of others. Comparative context can also help you judge the impact of a document. Your goal is to find out how this text is like or not like other texts that might be expected to be similar in some way, and then to draw conclusions about the reasons for both similarities and differences.

- What do you learn if you compare this text to another written by a similar person but in a different place or time?
- Or compare your main text to another written in the same time or place by a person in a drastically different social position or who holds a very different point of view?
- Or compare it to a very similar text from a similar place and similar author, to begin to judge how representative it might be of that category of people at that time and place, and perhaps to judge how the time and place caused certain patterns of reactions?
- Or compare it to a similar text by a similar person in a similar time or place but addressing different aspects of the problem/event, in order to help you fill out a more detailed picture?

Historiographical context. If your assignment involves reading related secondary sources, consider the following questions about how the interpretations already made by other historians can help you understand your document:

- How could your primary source help to support, undermine, complicate, or further explain what historians already know about the historical events or phenomena to which the document relates?

- Are there particular historians' arguments to which we could relate this document? Would the document help us to better understand a certain historian's argument, or criticize it, or add weight to it?
- Is there a debate or controversy among historians to which this document is relevant? If so, how can the document help you to weigh the various sides of the debate? Does it support one point of view more than others? Or perhaps it suggests we should look at the debate from a different point of view altogether.
- Does this document show us a historical point of view or phenomenon that historians have not considered, or have not considered fully enough? Does it suggest a direction for future research?

9.9. What Is Subtext?

Subtext refers to meanings associated with a text that are not spelled out in black and white. Subtext is what we mean when we talk about what is "between the lines" of a text. Subtext is not invented or imagined and does not include our feelings about a text as we read it. Subtext is a matter of interpretation, but it is grounded in what is on the page rather than the personal associations of individual readers.

Consider how jokes work: when you hear a joke and laugh, there is something that makes it funny beyond the literal words. There is some knowledge that you share with the person telling the joke. For example, if your professor posts a picture on the classroom screen of Professor McGonagall that says, "It's on the syllabus!" in the same kind of font usually used for internet memes, she is assuming that you are familiar with Harry Potter characters and with memes. When you view the image you figure out that she is presenting herself as the stern but supportive teacher, like Professor McGonagall, and reminding you of your responsibilities. All of those facts are definitely true, even though they are not written out or explained. The text could have said just "Remember to read your syllabus!" with no image, but it would not have been as effective. Someone unfamiliar with Harry Potter would not be able to identify or understand this subtext, but it is still there, and it is knowable.

The following are common types of subtext that we look for in historical primary sources. As you read your document, go through the list and look for each kind of subtext. You will not always find something significant in every category, or even more than one, but in any complex document there is some kind of subtext. See also sections 9.5–9.6 for complexities that are specific to certain document types.

Motivations. What did the author want to achieve with this text? Is there evidence on the page that the author was aware of her goals, or should we assume the goals were subconscious? What clues do you see on the page that point to the author's goals? What other clues could help us figure out what the author intended? What kinds of values or priorities guided the author to make her choices?

Assumptions, beliefs. What does the author seem to believe is true, even if he does not say so outright? Look for claims and ask: "If this is true, what else must be true?" The answers are the author's assumptions. Ask what the author seems to expect from his reader(s)—those are assumptions. Ask what the author must believe about the world in order to describe it the way he does—those are assumptions. Beliefs are premises we accept in the absence of evidence. A person can believe in a higher power without seeing hard evidence, but people also have many other kinds of beliefs, from believing in ghosts to believing that life is essentially fair.

Point of view. How much information was available to the author at the time of writing? What did the author know or not know that influenced the text? Separate what you know from what this author could know at the date of writing. How did the author's point of view on the world—the information she was able to access—shape what she wrote?

Bias. A bias pulls you in a certain direction despite known evidence, as opposed to a belief, which is a view held in the absence of evidence, or a position, which is a view drawn from evidence. Does the author hold views that contradict or ignore evidence that was available to the author at the time of writing? Those views are biases or prejudices. Biases tell us a great deal about the author's mindset, personality, and goals.

One kind of bias is a conflict of interest: if it will help a person financially to support X, she may say that X is terrific even if she knows otherwise. If a person may get into trouble because of Y, he may speak out against Y even though he otherwise has no opinion on it. Prejudice is another kind of bias—for example, a view that a certain group of people tend to behave in a certain undesirable way, regardless of how people in that group actually behave or the legitimate reasons they may have to behave in ways that others interpret negatively. (A prejudice can also be positive: I can insist that my children are the cutest children that ever lived.) Another kind of bias is a habitual or professional bias, where the author sees everything through the lens he is most accustomed to, rather than taking in new evidence or new ways of looking at an issue.

Seek the reasons for biases rather than judging or dismissing them. In casual speech we talk about bias as a reason to dismiss something: a text might not be worth reading if it is biased. Do not reject a text or a passage in a primary source because it is biased: it is a useful clue. Ask why it is biased and what that bias says about the author and his message.

We can also confuse enthusiasm with bias: a person might be passionate about her opinion, but that does not in itself tell you whether the opinion is supported and rational or based on prejudice—you need to examine her evidence and reasoning to determine that. Sometimes we confuse bias with representativeness: if a person represents a certain group, for example, when we read the diary of a factory worker to represent what life might have been like for laborers in that time and place, that worker is not necessarily biased in favor of labor. To represent means only to be a typical example of something.

Position. If the author's claims are supported by evidence and reasoning, or the evidence available to the author at the time of writing seemed to reasonable people to support his claims, then do not to refer to these claims as "biases" or "beliefs." They are "views," "positions," "reasoned opinions," or "perspectives." You might analyze the effectiveness of the author's argument the same way you would assess a secondary source, but also discuss how the author's position influenced his behavior or his effect on readers.

Omissions. What does the author not say that we might have expected to see, or that might have been relevant to his goal? What are the possible explanations for why a relevant point was left out? Could it have been deliberately left out (for what reason?) or was it likely an oversight? If so, what does that suggest about the author's motivations, biases, assumptions, or inattention?

Passing mentions. In works of fiction especially, but also in diaries, letters, memoirs, and other primary sources, you might find passing mentions where the author unintentionally revealed something about her world. Descriptions of people's manners, customs, habits, or assumptions, mentions of objects and how they were used (collectively referred to as "material culture"), and other details can give you clues about what that time and place looked like or felt like, and how people behaved or thought. These kinds of statements describe aspects of the world that people take for granted, because they seem unchanging while they surround us. But read later, such details may no longer be familiar. Noticing those things that seemed natural and inevitable to the people reading and writing the document, but that are no longer true for us, points us toward something that has changed: something historical.

Self-Awareness. How well equipped was the author to achieve his goals with this text? That is, was the author educated enough to make conscious and careful choices of words and rhetorical devices, so that we can assume each choice was deliberate? Did the author put time and care into composing the text, or was it written casually? How aware was the author of uses to which this text might have been put at the time? Did he expect it to be published? Who did he expect would read it? Did he expect it to have an influence on readers, and if so, what kind?

Style / tone / word choice. What do the choices of words, organization, style, and tone of the text tell us about the author and her intentions? If the choices seem haphazard, illogical, or ineffective, perhaps that indicates an author who was not in control or not serious about her text. If the choices seem to come together to create a coherent effect on the reader, this effect was almost certainly created by the author: Consciously or unconsciously? To serve what purposes? If the choices seem to shift, creating a certain effect in one place and a different effect in another, what can this pattern tell us about the author or her goals? Was the author agitated or uncertain? Or trying to sound that way? Or did she change views in the process of writing? Or is the author trying to elicit different reactions to different aspects of the topic (for example to pull focus toward one aspect and away from another)?

Consider each choice the writer made: what is the effect on the reader? How did the original readers respond to it, if we know? How might the author have expected readers to respond, knowing only what the author knew at the time of writing? Individual words might reveal associations with other subjects or ideas. Words and phrases connect ideas to other contexts in which they have also been used. If you are reading a work of fiction, consider how the literary devices the author chose convey information about the author's views and her expectations of readers. Any single choice may have great or little meaning, but *patterns* of choices almost always have something to tell you.

Stick closely to the choices you see on the page, rather than an overall "feel." If you identify a tone, you should be able to support that reading by pointing to words and syntax that create that tone for most readers.

If your primary source was translated into English, there is a limit to how much you can ask about word choice, style, and tone, since these aspects of a text are not equivalent from one language to another. If you notice something about the language that may be significant but may have been altered in translation, include it in your essay with a qualification, as in the following examples:

Assuming the original Japanese carries the same connotations ...

The word X in the translation may suggest Y.

9.10. Brainstorming: Context and Subtext

Your first step when you begin to write about a primary source should be to notice anything strange, interesting, striking, or unusual about your text, and to ask questions about what is or is not on the page and why. Throw as many of these observations down on paper as you can, in any form.

Many people find it easier to brainstorm this kind of thinking in mind maps rather than lists (see section 7.5). Just spill everything you're noticing onto a big piece of paper or the screen. After you have put down as many thoughts as you can, take a break and then add more. After you have exhausted your ideas, add color or other symbols to make connections between ideas, in preparation for drafting. If you are more comfortable with lists, try making three big lists, for text, context, and subtext. Under each list, write down what you see in your document to answer each of the questions raised for each category in this chapter.

9.11. Drafting: Analyzing Subtext

Analyzing subtext means making the jump from noticing "what's between the lines" as defined in section 9.9 to figuring out what all that means. In large-scale research projects, historians usually combine multiple methods of analyzing primary sources. Historians often perform a qualitative or simple numerical analysis of large sets of sources, where, for example, we ask the same question across a set of documents; compare, group, and distinguish between categories within a source base; or count the instances of a certain mention or phenomenon and look for patterns behind when it appears (such as how often a diarist mentions work tasks at different times of year, to understand the seasonal nature of her work). These kinds of examinations of documents are often done without elaborate statistical training or software, but still require access to large numbers of documents, so students usually do this kind of analysis only in independent thesis projects, if ever, not coursework.

The most common method of analyzing primary sources, however, is manageable even at a very small scale and is therefore the main way you are taught to approach them. The term for this method, "close reading," seems to imply that we simply read the sources extra carefully. This is somewhat misleading: close reading is actually a process of questioning and writing as much as it is about reading, and it is a systematic form of analysis, not just a matter of close attention.

Close reading a text. Close reading is a way of reading self-consciously, as if you are reading and at the same time watching yourself reading, questioning how the word choice, associations, and structure of the text shape your understanding. Close reading equally involves *writing*: putting into words what you are seeing in and around the text you're studying and what those clues add up to.

If you have ever tried to read between the lines of an email or text to draw conclusions about how the writer really feels about you, you were doing a close reading. Psychoanalysis is partly the close reading of various "texts" such as dreams, fears, and fantasies in order to explain aspects of our feelings or behavior. The following three steps are all necessary parts of a close reading:

- Read small pieces of the text at a time, slowly, and repeatedly. Notice what stands out: strange or unusual language patterns or words, anything that is repeated, passages that are placed or worded in such a way as to indicate that they are particularly important, analogies or metaphors, or any other striking details. Anything that you don't understand or that bothers you is a potential clue. If you have already brainstormed lists of words and passages that point to the forms of subtext defined in section 9.9, then you have already gathered these clues. Systematically check the list of subtext types in section 9.9 to make sure you didn't miss any.
- Question and explore: Looking over the clues you brainstormed, now consider what these clues might add up to. For each clue, attempt to form an exhaustive list of possible meanings or explanations (don't settle for the first that occurs to you). Remember to ask historical, not literary, questions. If this becomes confusing, review the list of historical questions in section 3.1.
- Assess, organize, and describe in words what you find from this process of noticing and questioning. Explain connections between what is clearly written (text) and what is implied, assumed, or suggested (subtext), assessing all the possible explanations and organizing the patterns made by these clues. Make decisions about which explanations make the best sense of all the evidence you have gathered.

Close reading a visual source or object. If you replace the word "text" with "painting" or "object" or any other artifact from the past, replace "author" with "creator," and "reader" with "viewer" or people who used the object, you can use the same methods to ask the same questions about a visual source or object.

For a painting, you might consider framing, color, shadow, lines, shapes, and brushstrokes rather than word choice or organization. For an object you may consider how it was made and the choices that were involved in its production. For a film or television show, ask about editing, cinematography, acting, soundtrack, and so on. In every other way, the process is the same as when analyzing a text.

9.12. Drafting: Significance

Noticing, questioning, and explaining what you see in your document is a key step, but it is not yet a full interpretation of the primary source. Next you need to suggest what may be significant about the text, context, and subtext you have analyzed, and its implications for our understanding of history.

Review section 4.5 on what historical significance is. In casual speech we more often discuss influence, which is when a document matters because it "changed the course of history." History is always changing, however. The importance of a document for historians lies in *why* and *how* it influenced people or events. It is also easy to confuse significance with relevance, assuming a document is significant because it relates to a topic of discussion in the course, but this is a mere starting point.

Since significance is a matter of why and how one historical fact affects others, try the following exercise: using any material from your document, brainstorm five sentences using the word "because" and then add "how?" after each, and fill in an answer.

X because Y. How? Answer:

Compare the following excerpts, each attempting to show the historical significance of something noticed in a primary source document.

> The interview with a protestor is significant because he was involved on the day and can tell us how important it felt at the time.

> The protestor's testimony shows that the Party was not a small group of radicals without popular support, as many wanted to believe, but that in fact they were responsive to a mood on the streets.

The first sentence does not really explain significance, it just claims it (twice). The second shows what lessons can be learned from the document and how those lessons help to resolve an existing historical question.

9.13. Revising: Claims

By now you should have generated many ideas and observations about your primary source and what it might mean. They might be more than you need for your paper (that would be ideal, since you probably need to edit them down). For your first round of revision, identify the most interesting and significant of those ideas. Read all your notes and drafts and circle any statements that add an idea that was not already in your document or talked about in class. You should have at least two or three of these.

Now assign a highlighter color (or a symbol you can put in the margin) for each idea you circled. Reading through your draft again, highlight or mark any other place in your writing where you are referring to, alluding to, or expanding on the idea assigned to that color or mark. This should show you how much you have already written on each main idea. Much of what you highlight is likely to be repetition: you were developing ideas, and we tend to circle around a notion as we figure out how to articulate it. But you might also have important discussion of what that idea means, and hopefully you have identified several areas in your primary source that support each idea. When you revise for structure, you will group each idea in its own section, together with all the appropriate evidence from the document.

Begin to draft a thesis statement or main claim that in a single sentence explains your interpretation of the document. Look through the ideas you have highlighted from your drafts: What do they add up to? What has this document taught you that you didn't know before? Try to fill in the following blanks:

[Document] shows why/how _____.

A close reading of [document] reveals _____, which we couldn't have known from a first glance.

[Document] answers [some question from your course] by showing _____ or explaining _____.

Refer to section 11.8 and revise your statement until it is contestable, specific, and substantive and makes only one major claim (though it may be broken down into a variety of smaller, subordinate claims that you support throughout the paper).

9.14. Revising: Structure

The structure of your essay should not follow either your thinking process as you explored the document, or the order ideas first appeared in the original. It needs to be structured for your reader, who needs to know that you have something worthwhile to say and to get through each point without repetition or wandering. This stage of turning a large amount of disorganized drafts into a coherent essay crafted for your reader is a good time to outline. The following suggested outline assumes you are analyzing one primary source (perhaps with some context provided by others), rather than comparing two documents with equal attention to both. If the latter is the case, see also section 11.11.

Introduction. Where the source comes from, what it is, why it is interesting, what it can tell us (= text + immediate context, thesis statement).

Body. These elements could fall in any order within the body, and in any amount, including skipping one or two, depending on what your particular document and other sources, if any, can tell you. The order and number of subpoints for each point should also follow from the peculiarities of your material and what you want to say about it. Consider these five possible ways of organizing a discussion of subtext and context in the body of an essay.

1. From small to large (can be reversed):
   Subtext
   Larger context
   Historiographical context

2. Point-by-point close reading:
   Subtext 1
     (explained with additional context)
   Subtext 2
     (explained with additional context)
   Subtext 3
     (explained with additional context)

3. Point-by-point contextualization:
   Context point 1
     (subtext, if any, used to explain links from text to context)
   Context point 2
     (subtext, if any, used to explain links from text to context)
   Context point 3
     (subtext, if any, used to explain links from text to context)

4. Integrated close reading:
   Subtext 1 + context
   Subtext 2 + context
   Subtext 3 + context

5. Thematic, organized by points of historical significance rather than parts of the text:
   Subclaim 1
     (supported with context/subtext as needed)
   Subclaim 2
     (supported with context/subtext as needed)
   Subclaim 3
     (supported with context/subtext as needed)

Conclusion. State again what the document can tell us, but explain it now more fully and with appropriate qualifications, adding its significance for answering other or broader questions.

9.15. Revising: Quoting Primary Sources

When you do a close reading of a document, you quote it extensively. Contrast this to distilling secondary sources, where you want to paraphrase as much as possible, because exact wording of secondary sources is rarely important for meeting your goals. The opposite is true when you are exploring subtext. The exact wording of the document is the focus of your attention, and it is how you support any claims or observations you make or questions you ask.

On the rare occasions where it's worth quoting a secondary source, we usually do so in passing with an attribution: "According to X, this term can be defined as 'Y.'" Sometimes we quote a phrase or maybe a sentence or two that provides a precisely worded definition or explanation because we want to capture exactly how the original source used the term or phrase, but we rarely question it or explore any unintended meanings in the secondary source. With primary sources, questioning and exploring unintended meanings is the goal. Therefore, we tend to quote in different ways. Rather than quoting in passing, we want to stop and explore the words closely. This results in two basic ways of quoting. Revise your draft now to make sure you are quoting when you need to and in an appropriate form.

Quote sandwich. In a so-called quote sandwich you provide your reader with a whole passage from the original text, usually a few sentences. This is the "meat" of the sandwich. The bread on top is your attribution: you explain who authored the quote and why we should care about who she is, or how the author's identity helps to make sense of the quote. You might need to explain details about where the quote came from in the larger document, or its original purpose. The bottom piece of bread is your close reading of that quote: your exploration of its subtext.

Because analyzing the choices in a passage is a process of explaining and asking questions about each piece, naturally an analysis should be longer than the passage being analyzed. It's not an absolute rule, but you can expect the analysis to be longer than the quote itself. If it is not, consider whether the passage you quoted is interesting enough to quote at that length, or whether there is more you can say, guess, or ask about the passage.

Quotes that are longer than two or three lines need to be formatted differently than a short quote. They are called "block quotes" and set off from the main text to make it easier for the reader to distinguish your words from the ones you are quoting. Block quotes are indented at the left or on both sides, single-spaced, with a blank line above and below the whole quote. Do not use quotation marks, because the block quote spacing already marks it as a quote. The footnote belongs at the end of the block quote, not in the attribution that comes before it or your discussion that comes after.

Consider the following examples, only one of which is an example of proper formatting and a full "quote sandwich." See if you can name the error(s) in the first two examples and explain why the final example is the most effective as well as the only correctly formatted one.

Example 1

Unity Mitford wrote:

Such a terribly exciting thing happened yesterday. I saw Hitler. At about six last night Derek rang me up from the Carlton Teeraum & said that He was there. Derek was having tea with his mother & aunt, & they were sitting *just* opposite Him. Of course I jumped straight into a taxi, in which in my excitement I left my camera which I was going to take to the shop. I went & sat down with them, & there was the Führer opposite. The aunt said "You're trembling all over with excitement," and sure enough I was, so much that Derek had to drink my chocolate for me because I couldn't hold the cup. He sat there for 1½ hours. It was all so thrilling I can still hardly believe it. If *only* Putzi had been there! When he went he gave me a special salute all to myself.[1]

This quote shows just how excessively Unity admired Hitler, almost as if he was a rock star, which is deeply disturbing, since he was actually a mass murderer.

Example 2

As a young woman studying in Germany the year after Hitler came to power, Unity Mitford wrote a striking letter to her sister that reveals the depth and nature of her admiration for the Nazi leader: "Such a terribly exciting thing happened yesterday. I saw Hitler. At about six last night Derek rang me up from the Carlton Teeraum & said that He was there. Derek was having tea with his mother & aunt, & they were sitting *just* opposite Him. Of course I jumped straight into a taxi, in which in my excitement I left my camera which I was going to take to the shop. I went & sat down with them, & there was the Führer opposite. The aunt said 'You're trembling all over with excitement,' and sure enough I was, so much that Derek had to drink my chocolate for me because I couldn't hold the cup. He sat there for 1½ hours. It was all so thrilling I can still hardly believe it. If *only* Putzi had been there! When he went he gave me a special salute all to myself."[1]

In this letter Unity capitalizes her pronouns when referring to Hitler, as one would normally do only to refer to God or Christ, suggesting she saw Hitler as god-like or as all-important. She describes being so nervous she forgot an expensive camera and actually trembled so hard she couldn't physically hold a cup. It is unlikely that anyone not suffering from a severe medical condition could really be shaking so strongly: she was exaggerating to express her tremendous excitement (using the word "excitement" or "exciting" three times in one short passage).

Example 3

As a young woman studying in Germany the year after Hitler came to power, Unity Mitford wrote a striking letter to her sister that reveals the depth and nature of her admiration for the Nazi leader:

Such a terribly exciting thing happened yesterday. I saw Hitler. At about six last night Derek rang me up from the Carlton Teeraum & said that He was there. . . . Of course I jumped straight into a taxi, in which in my excitement I left my camera. . . . I went & sat down with them, & there was the Führer opposite. The aunt said "You're trembling all over with excitement," and sure enough I was, so much that Derek had to drink my chocolate for me because I couldn't hold the cup. He sat there for 1½ hours. It was all so thrilling I can still hardly believe it. . . . When he went he gave me a special salute all to myself.[1]

Unity capitalizes her pronouns when referring to Hitler, as one would normally do only to refer to God or Christ, suggesting she saw Hitler as god-like or as all-important. She describes being so nervous she forgot an expensive camera and actually trembled so hard she couldn't physically hold a cup. It is unlikely that anyone not suffering from a severe medical condition could really be shaking so strongly: she was exaggerating to express her tremendous excitement (using the word "excitement" or "exciting" three times in one short passage). Unity is particularly pleased that Hitler saluted her personally, which she emphasizes by adding the phrase "all to myself" to a sentence where she had already specified that he gave "me" the salute. Her emphasis on having been personally noticed, and her detailed attention to Hitler's whereabouts (she didn't run into him by accident, but was alerted by a friend and dropped everything to go see him, she specifies where he sat relative to her and how long it lasted) together seem more like a young person meeting a famous romantic hero, like a film star, rather than a political leader who had not at the time done much beyond gain power unexpectedly. Much of this behavior might be attributed to Unity's young age—she was only twenty in 1934—but on the other hand, her almost hysterical excitement seems too young even for twenty. It is behavior that might be expected in a young teen, so we must look elsewhere to explain her obsession.

This quote analysis would normally be followed, in a full essay, by another paragraph that offers new evidence and speculation about the source of Unity's obsession.

Quoting keywords. In example 3, the author referred back to especially important words in order to explain what they implied:

> Unity is particularly pleased that Hitler saluted her personally, which she emphasizes by adding the phrase "all to myself" to a sentence where she had already specified that he gave "me" the salute.

You can refer to keywords from a block quote you have already provided, or you can just point to key phrases or words while paraphrasing the gist of a passage you never quote fully. Block quotes can only be justified when your interpretation of the text depends on the reader getting an overall impression of a whole passage, as in the Unity Mitford quote. In other cases where most of the text is straightforward, you are better off paraphrasing, with only occasional quotes to capture the most important words or phrases. For example, having examined the Mitford letter as we have seen, that writer might discuss other letters by Unity later in her essay, but mostly paraphrase them, this way:

> By the end of 1935, Unity felt herself to be a legitimate member of Hitler's circle, writing long, newsy letters to her sister filled with details of party politics that she picked up at social occasions. By this time she had ceased to capitalize pronouns referring to Hitler and her tone shifts from obsessed teen fan to political insider. She recorded conversations, saying Hitler was "in his best mood" and "asked after you" to demonstrate her intimacy with the Führer, and dropped hints of her increasingly extreme political views, as in the disturbing statement, "[h]e talked a lot about Jews, which was lovely."[2]
> 2. Ibid, 68.

Shortening and correcting quotes. Refer to section 5.9 and appendix 1 for basic quote formatting. As you quote more extensively and use unusual sources, you will come across new and more complicated formatting questions. Note that in example 3 the quote was cut down to only the most significant passages that would be analyzed. Less relevant sentences or phrases were replaced with an ellipsis (" . . . "), which discloses to the reader that something was cut. Shortening quotes allows you to highlight only the passages that matter without misrepresenting the quote as actually including only those parts. In some cases, you may need to complete sentences, change pronouns, correct errors or archaic usages, or add explanations in order to make a quoted passage coherent for your reader. Show that you are editing a quote by making these changes inside square brackets, as in these examples:

"At about six last night Derek [Hill, an English art student and friend] rang me up."

Unity wrote that Hitler "gave [her] a special salute all to [her]self."

...as in the disturbing statement, "[h]e talked a lot about Jews."

In the last example, the original version of the quote was the beginning of a sentence, so it started with a capital "H," but here it appears in the middle of a sentence, so the initial letter is made lower-case in brackets to show it was an editorial change.

Other than changes like these, marked in square brackets, we quote documents with their exact original language. In old documents, that language can often be strange or considered incorrect to modern eyes, so you may need to add "[*sic*]" after a word or phrase that the reader might think was your error in copying the quote. It is a Latin abbreviation that tells the reader that whatever mistakes, or seeming mistakes, that preceded it were in the original. If the original document used emphasis (such as italics in typed text or underlining in a handwritten document), include it in your quote and add "original emphasis" in the footnote or parenthetically in your discussion of the quote. In other cases you may want to highlight a word or phrase for your own purposes by italicizing it even when it was not emphasized in the original. Add the phrase "emphasis added" to the footnote or in parentheses in your main text.

9.16. Revising: Learning from Models

Previous chapters have explored ways of revising for clarity and style (sections 4.6–4.7, 5.11–5.12, 6.12–6.13, 8.9). Review these now and do further rounds of revision on your primary source essay accordingly, including getting feedback from a reader if possible. One further way to look at your draft with fresh eyes is to compare it to examples, both successful and unsuccessful (and in-between) of similar essays. Keep in mind, though, that your goal is not to imitate an essay that has been successful before. Your goal is to analyze the text, context, and subtext of your primary source document in your own way for your course. So be careful with examples: less effective example essays can instill a false sense of confidence, while the most effective examples can be intimidating. Either way, they can push you to imitate others rather than to discover for yourself, and that's the wrong direction.

Instead, look closely at the details of how other writers have handled difficult moves like beginning, ending, or close reading, and consider the different choices authors made that led to more or less effective results, in order to expand your toolbox of choices. The following examples compare key passages in primary source essays. Consider which example of each pairing is more effective, and why. Consider, too, how even the more effective examples could be improved and ways that the less effective examples show promise that could have been developed further. Try to describe these choices and their effects using the terms explained throughout this book.

Notice that the pairings are not very different in length and all of them are grammatically correct and on topic. The differences between the more and less successful passages depends on how specific the language is, how much substance the authors managed to convey clearly in the given space, how they used their sources, and how much they demonstrated their own thinking about the sources.

Introductions

George Orwell, a British writer, wrote his book, *Homage to Catalonia* (1938), which was written by George as he wrote a tribute to the loyalists who fought against the fascists during the Spanish Civil War during the interwar period. He expressed his anti-fascist opinions in his book. He was experiencing war during the Spanish Civil War in 1936 and 1937 by being a witness of a social revolution there in Spain. Here's an excerpt of his book, *Homage to Catalonia* (1938): "The Spanish war and other events in 1936–37 turned the scale and thereafter I knew where I stood. Every line of serious work that I have written since 1936 had been written, directly, or indirectly, against totalitarianism and for democratic socialism, as I understand." (Orwell)

The Spanish-American war and its aftermath forced the United States to confront its own values and what it means to have an empire. Because of widespread American belief in isolationism, the news media of the day used crude stereotypes, lies, and half-truths to sway the American people toward a war with the Spanish government. The illiteracy rate at the turn of the 20th century was 10.7%. Because of this, cartoons and pictures were often very helpful in getting any particular point across to a reader. Newspapers such as the New York World, The New York Tribune, The New York Herald, and the New York Journal were instrumental in influencing public opinion with regard to the Spanish government, the Spanish-American war, and the actions of the American government following the war.

Close readings of subtext

I notice in the image that the Cuban soldier only has one knife to defend himself and the Spanish soldier has two. This image makes me have sympathy for the Cubans, but I still see them as the heroic figures in this. Although they are not able to defeat such a strong army, they are still willing to stand up for themselves and make an attempt to gain independence. As a political commentary this image could be partially effective. Like I said before, this image makes me have sympathy for the Cubans. This could politically motivate America to help Cuba gain independence and get more people involved. Although I don't believe this message will be effective today's day and age. Instead I feel like people today will look at it as a fighting match and wait and see who's going to win. Elements in this photo may also be offensive to the Spanish and Latino-Americans or natives today.

In the background of the film are a series of advertisements that seem mundane, for museum exhibits, fashion houses, and Coca-Cola. The typical viewer probably did not even notice the hidden messages in the background behind the characters. These advertisements were directed at women, who were usually the shoppers in a traditional Italian home. The women depicted are dressed in pristine clothing and bright lighting, and look confident and assertive even though this is the height of the war. Mussolini was showing the world that his country was prosperous and managing its crisis. Viewers should walk away from the film with a positive feeling and associate that feeling with fascism. The ultimate plan was to get women to channel their energy into the war without being directly told what to do, how to act or what to believe in.

Context

Despite the fact that *Mein Kampf* was influential to Hitler's rise to power, Winston Churchill, a British politician, and Kenneth Burke, a scholar, criticized *Mein Kampf*. In Churchill's *The Second World War*, he stated that "no other book deserved more intensive scrutiny." He believed that *Mein Kampf* demanded "vigilant attention." Churchill summarizes *Mein Kampf* and states that the thesis of *Mein Kampf* was that man is a fighting animal, a nation is a community of fighters, pacifism is a sin and that the German race is more superior than any other race. Churchill compares *Mein Kampf* to the Koran and called it "the new Koran of faith and war: turgid, verbose, shapeless, but pregnant with its message." Both the Koran and *Mein Kampf* preached of racial supremacy, intolerance, bigotry, totalitarian agendas, and enemies of the individual, Churchill said.

The depiction of women before the war, in 1939, were more sophisticated. The economy had improved since World War I and the country was relatively stable in foreign affairs. Mussolini was still the father of fascism and not yet competing with Germany. These women were confident and relaxed. By contrast, in October of 1941 when *Natura* published pictures of women's wartime fashions women were wearing more casual clothing and standing in front of a magazine rack looking concerned.[2] Although women did in fact go to work during World War II, the women depicted in *Natura* are housewives, which is part of Mussolini incorporating his "new face" of diversity. These women represent mothers or wives that have sons and husbands in the war fighting for their lives. They also represent the women who would reproduce the next generation that would support him. In contrast to the sophisticated-looking women before the war, these women are dressed less fashionably and less assertively due to wartime rations and lower incomes.

Significance

The overall subject of this image is to show how America is a place where immigrants can have a fresh start. In addition, the overall subject of this image is to persuade people that America had immigrants' best interests in mind. The political issue this image represents is immigration and how they are coming to America will hold greater opportunities for immigrants and their families. This image represents Uncle Sam as a savior helping immigrants. Also, this shows Uncle Sam as the good guy wanting to give people coming to America a brighter future. This image is sympathetic because this is supposed to be seen as a helping hand. In addition, this image is sympathetic because it shows America trying to help people of less fortune. This image is very effective piece of political commentary because it shows the perspective of the Americans and shows what they believe they provided for immigrants coming to America.

There are a few things that these jokes all have in common. At first glance, all of the jokes seem like a passive form of resistance towards Germany, and they are. However, I want to argue that although it seems like the Germans saying these jokes were against Germany and its Nazi regime, the truth is that these jokes show just how nationalistic German citizens were. What most of these jokes are emphasizing is not the terrible anti-Semitism the Nazis were promoting, not the inhumane treatment Hitler enforced toward other people, and not the racist political ideology of the Nazis. The jokes all emphasize the bad physical state Germany had gotten itself into. They emphasize the destruction of their land, the lack of food, and bad leadership. By emphasizing their disappointment in the physical state of Germany we can clearly see how nationalistic the German citizens were and how much love they had for Germany. The second their precious country was starting to fall apart, they turn their backs on its leaders, even after tolerating years of that same government starting wars and murdering innocent civilians.

Conclusions

There were several important factors causing fascism, which can be gleaned from the extant literature on the topic. First, the article "Revisiting Spanish Memory" (Muruno, p. 34). This suggests that fascism eventually spread out toward Germany and then Spain. This interesting new conclusion, thus, supports the idea of fascism and so we are left with a sense of understanding why fascism is a unique type of political ideology that was ruled by a fascist dictatorship.

The Roosevelt Corollary, which built upon the foundation of the Monroe Doctrine, was conceived just six years after the Spanish-American war, further entrenching American dominance and interference in the Caribbean. The period in which the American government overtly searched for foreign territory to claim would last until around 1914, when the Panama Canal opened. The Spanish-American War began this pattern of American imperialism through the manipulation of the American population by the newspapers, which shows how effective propaganda and patriotism can be on the human mind.

9.17. Revising: Grading Yourself

Take one last look at your essay from the grader's perspective while you still have time to make changes. If your instructor gave you a rubric or other specific expectations, use those to grade your essay, or ask a trusted and knowledgeable friend to do it (or both). If you don't have more specific expectations for the assignment, try the rubric in table 9.1, which can be filled out as described in section 8.11.

The expectations described here reflect the elements of any standard primary source interpretation essay. Some of these, such as historiographical context, might not be relevant to your assignment, so you can skip those. Remember that you are looking for evidence on the page of each item being addressed; the items don't need to and likely won't appear in this order in your essay:

Table 9.1 Grading Rubric for Primary Source Interpretation

Expectation	A	B	C	D	F
Main idea(s)					
Immediate context identified					
Historical context identified					
Other context identified					
Context analyzed					
Subtext identified					
Subtext analyzed					
Significance explained					
Clarity of conclusions					
Originality of conclusions					
Mechanics of using sources					
Structure and organization					
Style and clarity					
Grammar, usage, formatting					

- **Main idea.** Have you conveyed what the text directly says, accurately, specifically, and in your own words?
- **Immediate context identified.** Have you not only accurately named the author, but explained anything else about who she was that might relevant to interpreting the text, as far as you can know? Have you explained what the author intended to accomplish, identified who the intended audience was, and explained or guessed at the reaction of readers at the time the document was written? If your document was published during the time period you are studying, have you explained the date and nature of its publication? Have you accurately identified the time and place where the document was originally written or created and, if relevant, when and where people first read it?
- **Historical context identified.** Have you accurately identified relevant events or concerns that were happening when this source was created that might have affected its contents or how it was received by its first audience?
- **Other context identified.** If relevant to your assignment, have you considered how comparing your document to other primary sources could help you to understand it better? How could your document add to, test, or undermine conclusions historians have made? Does your document raise

new questions that historians have not yet considered? Are there historical analyses of related sources that could shed light on this one?

- **Context analyzed.** Have you commented in your own words on how this document teaches us something about the time and place it was written and read?
- **Subtext identified.** Have you considered what's going on between the lines of the document as thoroughly as possible with the information available to you?
- **Subtext analyzed.** Have you thoroughly and thoughtfully explored the possible connections, implications, patterns, or other meanings associated with the document that are not stated in black and white?
- **Significance explained.** Have you explained what this document, and your reading of it, can teach us about specific, significant historical questions of general interest?
- **Clarity of conclusions.** Is your own contribution—your interpretation of the document's meaning and significance—clearly stated?
- **Originality of conclusions.** Have you contributed your own thinking beyond what was already stated in the document or in class and other readings?

The expectations in italics in table 9.1 are standard for any formal academic essay, as explained in section 8.11.

9.18. Proofreading

Before you turn your essay in, consult sections 5.13, 6.14, and 8.12 on how to proofread it.

10

Historical Research

If you are asked to identify sources for a project beyond the texts that were assigned for the course, you are doing research. This can involve searching library databases, searching the internet, physically visiting a library or archive, or all of the above. Most research assignments in undergraduate coursework are linked to a long essay assignment, often where you develop your own question in relation to secondary sources and answer it by constructing an argument, supported by primary sources and original reasoning. Chapter 11 covers this kind of long essay. In some cases, though, you will be asked to research only primary sources, for a primary source interpretation essay as described in chapter 9, or only secondary sources, for a historiography essay as described in chapter 8. Or you may need to look up background information to support an imaginative project, as described in chapter 7. This chapter covers undergraduate-level historical research of any kind and should be paired with whichever other chapter addresses your assignment. If you are asked to submit an annotated bibliography, you will find instructions in section 10.11. If you are developing your own research question, it is especially important to also consult section 11.2 before moving further on the research part of your task.

10.1. What's Your Goal?

A research project asks you to practice several distinct tasks:

- Use finding aids to identify and locate appropriate sources
- Distinguish between high-quality sources and lesser-quality sources
- Identify which sources are most relevant for your project and how they may help you
- Annotate and keep track of your sources

Many basic facts about the nature of student research are not well known: much of the most useful information is not available freely on the internet. The high-quality information that is available on the internet is not likely to be found with a single search in an all-purpose search engine such as Google. Doing historical research well often requires physically visiting your university library and sometimes interacting in person or online with a librarian. When you find a source on your topic, you have only just begun; you will still need to decide whether it is relevant, reliable, or useful for your project. Research is a process of exploring, re-evaluating, and editing. There is no straight line from entering a search term to picking up a source to finishing your project.

When you do research for a course, your grade may be based on your participation in a library visit, on a list of sources you identify, on an annotated bibliography you turn in separately, or be combined with your grade for the paper for which you are identifying sources. It doesn't really matter which of these ways you are graded, because the unique thing about research is that you do it entirely to help yourself. The more thoughtfully and thoroughly you conduct the research stage of your project, the better the materials you will have to work with, and therefore the better your chances of success with your essay.

10.2. Using Your Library

The best sources are carefully researched, written, vetted, and edited by trained professionals. Most scholarly research is published and distributed through libraries and bookstores. Universities pay academic presses to get copies of scholarly books and journals to put on library shelves, or e-books that you can check out temporarily to your digital device using your student ID. Universities also pay fees to private companies that build and maintain databases to help you find and access digital copies of articles from scholarly journals, as well as primary source collections and dissertations (unpublished scholarly theses). Whether you visit your library in person or use its resources through your library's website, you will need your university ID or the barcode number on it to gain access.

Increasingly, some high-quality scholarship is made freely available through "open access" publishing, but to find these sources you are still likely to need to do a specialized search. Open-access repositories are usually subsidized by universities or government entities and accessed through an institution's website. Digital history projects may be similarly useful in providing primary sources or data for your project, but in both cases you cannot Google keywords or research questions. If you know the author and title you are looking for, a general internet search might bring you to it if it is available through one of these kinds of collections. If not, you will need to do a search for the collection, first, or be referred to a specific repository or digital history project by your instructor or librarian, and enter your search terms in the specialized database hosted on the institution's website.

Librarians have exceptional training in finding and sorting information. University librarians are trained in how information is categorized, how finding aids are organized, and how to search them effectively; in the different kinds of sources available and their various uses; and in research methods. Librarians are also likely to be the only people who have constantly updated knowledge on what resources are available: library collections and the technology used to access them change continually, and your instructor may keep up with only what she happens to use in her own research.

University librarians that you are likely to encounter include the following.:

- **Reference librarians.** Librarians staffing the reference desk at your university library are there to answer your questions about how to find sources, yet most of them, sadly, spend a lot of their valuable time directing people to the nearest restroom. Perhaps you're not sure what to ask or afraid you'll sound like you're asking the librarian to do your work for you. The librarian's job is to help you figure out how to identify and locate sources, while your job is to know what your assignment is and what questions you're interested in. So if you say, "I'm writing a paper comparing Soviet and American views of Fidel Castro. Can you help me identify some sources?" the reference librarian can then direct you to the right databases and suggest useful search terms to help you find what you need. Be prepared to answer further questions about your assignment. If you have written instructions for it, bring those with you.

  Many university libraries offer live chat with a librarian through their website, or provide a library reference email address. This is the online equivalent of the reference desk, so use it for the same kinds of questions. However, online chat or email cannot fully replace the interaction you would get in person, when the librarian can help you formulate and refine your questions by talking them through with you and can sense when you are not entirely following what she is saying.
- **Area specialists/subject librarians.** University libraries also have specialists who are particularly well versed in a certain area of knowledge, and are often active researchers themselves. In some libraries, the area specialists are divided by discipline, so you would want to consult the history librarian for this project. In other, larger libraries, specialists may focus by region, so there could be librarians for US history and culture, Western European, Slavic and Eastern European, the ancient Near East, African, South American, East Asian, and so on, and you would choose the appropriate librarian for the subject matter of your project. Area specialists help you find unusually difficult or obscure sources in their area of expertise, so for many projects you might not need to consult anyone beyond a reference librarian. However, for a significant research project like a senior thesis or a subject that depends on unusual sources (such as visual objects or a topic on which

nothing has been published for sixty years), an area specialist will be your new best friend. If you're not sure whether you should consult a specialist, ask a reference librarian first.

Your library's website also probably contains "research guides," often divided by discipline. Look for links to "research" or "guides" and find "history." These guides usually list the most relevant disciplinary finding aids and other reference works that your library has access to, and may contain details on how to cite sources as well as explanations of different source types and which databases to use for which purposes. These guides are terrific ways to find out what is available, but they cannot replace interacting with an experienced librarian who can answer your questions as you go.

Finding aids are exactly what they sound like: tools that help you find things. Think about the sheer amount of information available to us today: all the books ever published, all the newspapers and magazines and scholarly journals in every subject, and all the flotsam and jetsam that fills the internet. You can't just browse everything. Even if you want to begin with some browsing, you still need to identify a starting point.

You have probably already typed search terms into a box on a computer screen and seen results pop up that you hope will be helpful. But how, for example, does typing "soccer" into a search box yield results that include sources on football—as soccer is known all over the world besides the United States—while excluding sources on American football? Google won't do that for you in any reliable way, but library databases can.

Search terms help us to find the right results by looking through metadata. Metadata are bits of information that are attached to a source in order to classify it and make it findable in databases. Metadata includes the title and author, but also subject headings, dates of publication, the language of publication, and more. Databases are collections of information, such as the metadata for a particular set of books and periodicals. You could find a book about soccer in Italy in a relevant database even though the word "soccer" never appears in the book's title or even in its contents because that book was tagged with the word "soccer" by a library cataloger. The tag is an example of metadata. All books cataloged by the Library of Congress also get classified into standardized categories, called Library of Congress subject headings, so that you can not only search for the words "soccer" and "Italy" to get that book, but you could also browse through all the books on sports in twentieth-century Italy or all the books on international soccer competitions. Subject headings are another kind of metadata. Many databases search only metadata, not the full text of books or articles.

Databases are the most common type of finding aid, and today most college students will use them exclusively. Many libraries now offer a "one search" box that looks like an internet search engine and appears to be a one-stop way of searching everything the library has. If you are looking for a specific author and title, that box will probably get you to it fastest. However, in order to find out what's available in answer to a research question, you will need to dig deeper, often consulting several different, more specialized databases and using some of their advanced features to narrow your search.

Your library will have its own online catalog, which is a database of the books and periodicals it owns. You may also be able to search WorldCat, a catalog of nearly every book ever published, so that you can identify a book your library doesn't own but may be able to borrow through interlibrary loan. Some libraries also subscribe to collections of e-books, usually provided by the largest publishers—for example, Oxford Scholarship Online and Project Muse—so that you can read a scholarly book even if your library does not own a hard copy. Such books may be available only on your desktop, or may expire after a certain period even if you have downloaded them to your own device.

Library catalogs contain references to periodicals as well as books, but these tell you only which issues they own of a certain title, such as the *New York Times* or *American Historical Review*. There are separate databases for scholarly articles, such as JSTOR, that will allow you to click through to access the whole text. Databases for articles are created by companies that pay publishers for access to their periodicals, so each database contains different titles. Sometimes the hosting company started or stopped paying for a certain title at some point in time, so it may not have everything ever published under that periodical title. For this reason, you may have to search more than one database to be sure you are finding all the articles that may be relevant for your research question (that is the kind of issue a reference librarian might help you with).

Article databases specialize by discipline or subject matter, so, for example, America: History and Life is a database that will identify articles relating to the United States, including both history and other topics. The database called Historical Abstracts will find articles on non-US topics, but only in history. A very general database such as Academic Search Complete can scan for articles across a broad range of disciplines, but does not include every journal ever published (despite the name) and does include non-scholarly publications. Other periodical databases specialize not in scholarly journals but in newspapers and magazines, which might be useful as primary sources in a history course, such as the 17th–18th Century Burney Collection Newspapers.

Still other databases contain references to sources such as government documents or even private documents such as letters and diaries. Some of the entries in primary source databases will tell you only where to locate the source, and it may not be possible to borrow it (some exist in only one hard copy in an archive), whereas others link to documents contained in published collections you could borrow from your library or to online collections that allow you to view or download your own copy. For example, Nineteenth Century Collections Online contains a variety of sources that you can access directly, but it is also mostly restricted to US and British documents. Some databases may have a narrow range of topics, such as European Views of the Americas: 1493–1750. If there is a specialized database relevant to your research project, it may be all you need (that's the kind of shortcut a librarian is often able to point you toward).

Some universities also subscribe to a database called Dissertation Abstracts that includes references for master's and doctoral theses registered at hundreds of universities. Theses are not published, so you can access them only by finding them in this database and then either downloading a PDF copy (if available) or requesting it via interlibrary loan. Since many doctoral theses later get revised and published in book form, look for books first. But on some obscure topics, the only scholarship that exists may be a thesis.

There are at least two kinds of print finding aids you might also need to consult. While print finding aids are becoming rare, historians are among the last people still using them, since we are often interested in very old sources. These old sources include primary documents, but also scholarship: since history is the study of change over time but unrestricted by period or place, there are many topics of historical research that literally only one person has ever written on. It is possible to develop a research project where the only scholarly source was published so long ago that your library has not yet digitized the record. This is more likely to be the case with a primary source like an old, obscure memoir or periodical, especially if it is in a language other than English.

If the records haven't been digitized yet, you may have to look for them in a card catalog—the physical precursor to your library's online catalog. Librarians are usually delighted to help you find these kinds of sources and to navigate the card catalog. A more common but often overlooked form of print finding aid is the published bibliography. You may have only come across the term "bibliography" as the list of works you cited at the end of your paper or as part of an annotated bibliography assignment. There is actually a technical difference between a bibliography and a "Works Cited" list, and your student essays will usually include only works cited. "Works Cited" is simply a list of every source you used in the essay. In contrast, the broader term "bibliography" comes from the Greek for "the study of books." There are many forms of bibliography, from the works "cited" to works "consulted" (meaning everything you read for your essay, not just the sources you quoted or referred to), to systematic lists of all the works that exist on a certain subject or in a certain collection, to "annotated bibliographies" that list the works relevant to some theme and add brief summaries and other notes.

A bibliography can be published all by itself as a reference tool and finding aid. In these cases, a researcher identified a discrete set of sources on some theme so that other researchers could refer to it. If such a bibliography is annotated, it can be especially useful for narrowing down your search before even looking at individual sources. Bibliographies can range from lists of the contents of a private collection, such as the *Catalog of the Fifteenth-Century Printed Books in the Library of Trinity College, Cambridge* to lists of the output of a particular author, like *J. K. Rowling: A Bibliography, 1997–2013*, to lists that put sources in a particular order, such as the *Oxford Chronology of English Literature*, to lists of sources by research topic that serve much like a library database but are thoughtfully curated and therefore more useful, like *A Selected, Annotated Bibliography of Sources in the Kansas State Historical Society Pertaining to Kansas in the Civil War*. Print bibliographies are usually shelved in the reference section of a library and can't be loaned out. Consult them in person, take notes on what you find, and then use databases or a card catalog to find out where to find a copy of the sources you have identified as useful for your project.

Some bibliographies are now maintained online and constantly updated, but it can be difficult to distinguish a reliable online bibliography from a hobbyist's list of sketchy web sources. This is again a case where you need to consult a librarian.

Search strategies. To search a database, you enter one or more words into the search box(es): these are called search terms. For any research project, you will need to enter several search terms into each database (but never whole sentences or questions). In addition, in many cases, you can also use the "advanced" search options to further limit and sort the results.

Before you begin searching, think through a list of search terms and write them down, since you will need to go through your whole list in each database. Your search terms should include all the keywords related to your subject, plus alternate spellings, synonyms, and closely related concepts that go by different names. Then add the appropriate place names, people's names, and time periods or dates. For example, if you're writing an essay on how Mussolini's regime used football competitions to unify the public behind fascism, your search term list might look like this:

football	sports	fascism
calcio	nationalism	interwar
soccer	Mussolini	1920s
competition	Italy	1930s
sport	Italian	

In each database, you'll try several combinations of these terms, and notice when a particular combination gives you way too many or two few results, so you can refine your next search accordingly.

Beyond identifying search terms, look at the options each database offers for other ways to limit your search. You can usually limit results to materials in certain languages, so you might as well search only for sources you can read. In databases of journal articles, you can exclude book reviews, or when the database includes other kinds of periodicals, you can limit it specifically to peer-reviewed articles. You can limit the results by the date they were published, which may be most useful when you're searching for primary sources, to get results covering the time period of your project. In most cases you shouldn't limit the results for scholarly articles by their date of publication, since even very old work may still be the most recent available or still influential or significant even if other historians have written on the subject since. You can limit your results to articles that you can access in full text online, but you may miss valuable sources this way.

Many databases will allow you to combine your search terms using Boolean search operators, meaning words like AND, OR, and NOT that combine terms to get results that meet more than one criterion at a time. This way you could search for "Italy AND sports AND fascism NOT cycling" if you find that there aren't very many articles specifically on soccer, and too many articles about cycling. With those search terms, you'll get articles about fascist Italian sports that include football, but not the cycling ones.

If you're having trouble thinking of search terms that get good results, examine the results you are getting to identify related terms that will expand your search. For example, if you search for "football" and "Italy" you might see the Italian word for football, *calcio*, pop up in some titles. Then if you search *calcio*, you might find another source or two that didn't come up in the first search.

The other main way to search databases besides using search terms is to browse Library of Congress subject headings. This is a good strategy if you're not yet sure what you're looking for or you're not finding anything and need to think about your subject from a new angle. If you find at least one result related even partly to your subject, click on the full entry and look for "subjects" or "subject headings." Click on a relevant subject, and it will show you other sources cataloged under that heading. Browsing in this way is much like wandering through the stacks in the actual library, which is another useful way to explore related works. Many databases have a "browse" tab that helps you to do the same thing.

Once you have identified an article worth investigating further, look for a link to download the full text. Make sure to save the resulting file to an appropriately named folder on your own computer, in a cloud storage account, or on a portable USB drive. If there is no full text available for download, look for a note in the record saying whether your library owns the hard copy of the periodical your article appeared in. If so, identify the call number for that periodical. If not, consult a reference librarian about obtaining a copy from another library or look for a link to "request it" and follow the directions. If you identify an article that is not available in full text through your library, try a general internet search for the full author and title: sometimes authors individually make their articles available on their own websites, through Humanities Commons, academia.edu, or their institutional repository (where their university hosts publications produced by its own faculty).

Call numbers. When you identify a book or periodical volume in an online or card catalog for your library, the next step to get your hands on it is to note the call number. This will be listed in the digital entry for the source (click through to the full entry) or on an index card in a card catalog. Most call numbers are based either on the Dewey decimal classification system or the Library of Congress cataloging system. Most libraries use one or the other, but some libraries use one system for one collection, and the other for a different set of materials.

Both call number systems organize materials by subject and assign a unique code to each book. This code allows you to find a single book even in an enormous library with millions of titles spread out over several stories of a building and also allows you to browse a single shelf or aisle to see all the books a library owns on a given subject.

Dewey decimal call numbers use only numbers: the first three digits (before a decimal) represent broad classes of materials, like 800s for literature and 900s for history. The numbers that follow the decimal make finer distinctions, right down to the individual author and title.

Library of Congress (or "LC") call numbers combine numbers with letters. The first, capital letter represents broad classes (so instead of ten major classes as in the Dewey system, there are twenty-one), such as "D" for World History and "E" and "F" for American History. A second letter can narrow these broad classes down further, so that "DT" represents African history. Letters are followed by numbers that narrow the category down still further, followed by a decimal and further numbers and letters that identify individual volumes.

Look for an entrance to the "stacks" or a specific reading room or "Periodicals Room" if you were directed to do so in the record for this item. Near either entrance you should find a map showing where each class of call number is located in the library. Inside the stacks, you need to find another sign or map showing which aisles contain which call numbers. In some cases one aisle of shelving contains all the books in a certain class (like all the 900s) or in a subclass (like all the 940s). In very large libraries, one long aisle might contain only books from DS401.1 to DS401.2, so you will find yourself walking quite a distance from one subject to another.

A rule of thumb for finding a book on library shelves is that "nothing comes before something," so DS401.1 will come before DS401.11. Beyond that, you simply follow numerical and alphabetical order until you get to the exact call number you need. If you find the exact spot on the shelf where your book should be and it's not there, first take a look around the general area: people often put books back in the wrong place. If it's not anywhere near where it's supposed to be, you will have to fill out a form to request that the library track it down

Borrowing from other libraries. You are not limited to the books owned by your campus library and the articles available in full text from your library's databases. You can get almost any book in the world through the interlibrary loan (ILL) system. Most libraries are connected through this network, but rare books and reference works may not be available for loans.

Once you have identified a source you need and confirmed that your library doesn't own it (by checking its catalog), you may need the author, title, and possibly ISBN (International Standard Book Number) to request it from another library. The ISBN will be shown in the full entry for the book or periodical in whatever database you found it. Look for a link on your library website for making a request.

Many university libraries not only participate in the interlibrary loan system, but also have a parallel arrangement with nearby or institutionally related libraries to exchange their books more quickly. Usually you can request a book without worrying about where it comes from and you'll be informed by email when the book is available. However, it is worth knowing that books available from a local network will arrive within a few days, whereas ILL orders can take a week or two, which may sometimes be too long for your project.

If the item you need from another library is rare, or you need only an article from a periodical that does not circulate in its entirety, you may be able to request that a scan or photocopy of the item be sent to you. You may need to pay some amount to cover the cost of such a service. These services are usually described on your library's website, and may be described in the record you find for the source in a library database. If you're not sure, ask a librarian.

Internal bibliographies. If you have identified at least one good source for your research question, one of the best ways to expand your search is to examine the internal bibliography and citations in the source(s) you have. These will necessarily refer to all the most closely related sources and may also point to other directions or connections you hadn't thought of. Of course, they can't include works that were published later than the one you have in your hands, so this can't be your only strategy. It's most useful as a way of quickly getting to the most relevant literature, from which you can get a feel for the way questions have been asked and answered so far and glean more search terms to expand your database searches in specific ways.

Archives and special collections. Some universities have their own archives or special collections of rare documents. In other cases, your university library may be able to help you access archives in your town, even if they aren't formally affiliated. These kinds of collections are not usually necessary for ordinary coursework, but if you have a particular interest in the subject of an accessible collection or a desire to practice more advanced research skills, it may be worth while to consider using such collections in a large project like a senior thesis. Special collections and archives have their own, specialized finding aids and rules for how and when you can access their materials. Start exploring these possibilities by first asking a librarian at your university, who will likely direct you to a specialist librarian or archivist who works with that collection.

10.3. Managing Information

One of the most challenging tasks in research is keeping track of what you find. As you search for sources, you will get long lists of results. You'll gradually narrow those results down to items worth looking at, and as you look at individual items you will take notes about whether and how each item might relate to your project, then narrow those materials further to the ones you will read for your essay, and then you'll have notes on that reading. Throughout this process, keep careful, accurate records. You may need to backtrack to sources you had earlier rejected or use details from sources you already came across to refine further searches. Notes on why you rejected a source can be as important as the notes you take on sources you will use in your essay.

To keep track of your sources, develop a system from the start, rather than squirreling everything in a pile as you encounter it and hoping it will still make sense when you look at it later. The old-fashioned way to manage sources was to fill out the most important information for each source on an index card. This is still a viable method: write out the full citation for each source on one card and give that card a number. Write any subsequent notes you take from or about that source on other cards with the number from the source card in the same place on each one (such as the upper right corner). Being able to shuffle the cards around as you work can help you organize your thoughts, but be sure to keep them together with a rubber band or clip when not working with them.

For greater mobility and flexibility, you can recreate this method digitally using basic word-processing software or specialized applications. If you expect to do research projects often, learn at least one form of specialized bibliographic software. Programs such as Endnote (which may be made available through your university) or Zotero (a free browser plugin) are databases that are set up specifically for tracking and taking notes on sources. Most library databases allow you to export source records straight from the database into your bibliographic software, so that all the information you need for the citation and to locate the source are already organized. You can then sort and rank these records in your own way, or group or label them according to how you plan to use them. You can also add notes to each record.

Bibliographic software also allows you to copy and paste citations into your word processor for footnotes and works cited lists. Be careful with this: the computer will simply output a citation that follows the rules it was given, even if the source was formatted inappropriately or was garbled on its way to you. You must clean up the data you exported into your software to make sure titles have correct capitalization and no extra spaces or garbled special characters. You also need to check that you select the appropriate citation style that you need for your project, not just whichever one was set as the default (see section 10.10).

You can do your own simplified version of bibliographic software by entering the citation, notes, and any other information you need into a blank word-processing document, which you can then search using Control-F. This works best for small sets of sources; it would quickly become unmanageable after you have gathered more than about ten titles.

Navigating physical sources. When you are holding a text in your hands, first examine its cover, title page, the reverse of the title page, the table of contents, and index. These key portions of any publication provide all the information you need for your citations and to understand what kind of source you're looking at (even when you only access a source electronically, the language used to describe it derives from its origins in print publication, so it's useful to know how to navigate print sources even when you rarely use them directly). Titles give you clues about the nature of a publication:

The Czar's Madman
The Professor and the Madman: A Tale of Murder, Insanity, and the Making of the "Oxford English Dictionary"
The President's Czars: Undermining Congress and the Constitution

Simple titles with no subtitle (the part following a colon, or in smaller print under the main title on a cover) often indicate a work of fiction, as in the first title above. Look for the telltale word "novel" on the cover or "fiction" in very small print on the spine or back cover. Subtitles that provide further detail about what is covered, like the third example, are often scholarly; subtitles like the second example that are exciting but not much more specific than the main title may indicate a work aimed for a general audience. You can confirm the difference by checking the publisher (in this case the second title was published by Harper, a mainstream press, but the third by the University Press of Kansas). Refer to section 5.10.1 for other keywords like "sources in . . ." that indicate different types of publications, like a collection of primary sources.

The title page or its reverse will give the full name of the publisher of a book or journal, helping you to identify whether it is a peer-reviewed press (see section 10.4). The copyright date is stated on the reverse of the title page with the © symbol. This is usually the first, and therefore most important, publication date, since some books are reprinted many times after initial publication, but the original publication date is what allows us to draw meaningful conclusions about what context the source was composed in or is responding to. A title page for a journal, as opposed to a mono-graph, will contain a more specific publication date than just a year—usually a month or season, as well as volume and issue numbers. These indicate you're looking at a periodical (see section 5.10.1 for definitions of these terms).

The table of contents lists sections within a bound volume. If you see author names as well as titles in the contents list, you know you are not looking at a book written by one person, but a collection of some kind. Closer examination of the titles, authors, and dates of each piece should indicate whether you are seeing a collection of scholarly essays (secondary sources), documents (primary sources), or a combination of the two.

The index at the back of a book lists the contents in a much more detailed way: each significant term or concept that appears in the book is listed, followed by page numbers for each place where that term is referenced. This is an excellent way to navigate straight to what you need, but scanning the whole index can also give you a rough idea of what topics are covered and what aren't, in more detail than the table of contents.

Once you are certain you know what you're looking at, refer to section 5.2 on reading secondary sources and section 9.6 on reading primary sources for spe-cific reading strategies. Take notes on all sources you read for your essay. In addi-tion to "afternotes," add a note on how you will use each source in your essay (see section 10.11). For some books, you might write an afternote for the whole book, and also a modified version of the same notes for each chapter (or each chapter you'll use in your essay). In each chapter afternote, record the goal for the chapter and how it connects to the overall goal of the book, as well as what content or chronological or geographical territory it covers.

10.4. Secondary Source Types

For a historical research project, you want to use only scholarly secondary sources or primary sources (see sections 9.2–9.5 on how to identify primary sources). One of the most important tasks you have as you sort through the results of your searches is to make sure the secondary sources you find are schol-arly, rather than "popular" works of history, tertiary sources (see section 10.5), or primary sources such as newspaper articles from the time you're studying.

. Any text published by a scholarly press, whether a book or article, has by definition passed the peer review process, but that does not mean the text is without errors—since peer reviewers are not fact-checkers—and it does not mean everyone agrees with the conclusions made in the text. Arguments are claims supported by evidence and reasoning: the claims are arguable, the evidence are "facts" but often open to interpretation, and the reasoning must follow the laws of logic. That leaves a great deal of room for disagreement even with very reliable and well-vetted texts.

Most assignments in history classrooms restrict you to scholarly secondary sources because popular histories may lack citations, leave out important details, or even introduce imaginative elements that make for a good story but cannot be relied on as evidence for your work. In some cases, however, as when no scholarly source is available on a topic, your instructor may allow you to work with a popular (non-peer-reviewed) work of history. These vary enormously in quality, so if you are considering using, for example, a biography written by a journalist because no scholarly biography exists of a person you want to write about, consult your instructor. Be wary of using any passages that are novelized—that is, where scenes or dialogue appear, but on close examination of the citations you see that there is no primary-source evidence that particular actions or words ever existed outside the author's imagination. The other problem with many popular historical works is that they may have little or no original argument of scholarly significance, which makes them useful to you only for background information, not to frame your own argument (see chapter 11).

If you're not sure whether a book or article you found is scholarly, follow these steps to find out:

- If you found an article through a library database after selecting the filter to include only scholarly articles, you probably have an appropriate source. If it seems strange, though, show it to your instructor or teaching assistant to confirm it.
- If you have a book or journal issue in your hands, look for the name of the publisher on the title page or its reverse, or look for the publisher name on the electronic record where you located the book. Any publisher with the words "university press" in its name is scholarly. Non-university presses that specialize in scholarly works include Ashgate, Berghahn, Brill, M. E. Sharpe, New Academia Press, Norton, Palgrave, Pearson, Rowman & Littlefield, Routledge, Verso, and Wiley-Blackwell. To find out for sure, search for the publisher's website and then search the website for the words "peer review." A notice disclosing that the press publishes only peer-reviewed works is often tucked into a section on submission guidelines. Some presses have both a scholarly and "trade" line of titles, so you will

have to look into your book more closely and probably show it to your instructor to be sure.

- Another way to determine whether a source is scholarly is to Google the
  author's name to see if he or she is a professor in a relevant field at a college or
  university. If you find this is true, you probably have a scholarly source, but
  if you don't find such a profile, it may be that the author is a trained scholar
  working independently. If you are in any doubt, consult your instructor.

10.5. Tertiary Source Types

Tertiary sources are summaries of scholarship used for teaching or reference,
such as textbooks and encyclopedias. A textbook is a non-fiction work that
collects information from many sources to build a broad overview. Textbooks are
generally intended to be balanced and complete accounts for learning purposes
and usually do not contain individual authorial arguments (although the selection and arrangement of information intentionally or unintentionally shapes the
impression the reader gets in subjective ways). For these reasons, a textbook can
be helpful to give you factual background, but cannot help you frame or support
your own argument. It is rarely appropriate to cite a textbook in an essay, because
it is not customary to cite basic facts (see section 10.10).

Reference works, which include general encyclopedias such as Wikipedia,
dictionaries, and also specialized encyclopedias like *The Oxford Companion to
Black British History*, are also tertiary. They too summarize already-published
research rather than present new arguments and evidence. But instead of
presenting a chronological narrative of what happened, as a textbook does, reference works organize entries alphabetically or chronologically so you can look up
a term or concept quickly. You should not usually need to cite a reference work
(this may be different in other disciplines, where for example you might cite a
physics textbook for the explanation of a certain process).

Reference works published by legitimate presses can generally be considered
reliable, though any published work can contain occasional errors or omissions.
Internet reference works such as Wikipedia deserve special attention, and internet lists or timelines compiled by individuals have not been vetted.

Still another kind of tertiary source is broad overviews or syntheses that are
intended to entertain and inform a general audience, such as popular history
and biography, documentaries, and podcasts, or those that aim to apply scholarly
history to issues of present-day interest like op-eds and blogs or podcasts. These
might spark our interest in a topic or give us ideas, but like other tertiary sources
they don't serve the needs of a research essay.

10.6. Internet Sources

Some popular internet resources can be useful for reference, but must be handled with an awareness of their limitations.

Wikipedia. Wikipedia is arguably preferable to any other general encyclopedia (studies have shown it to be more accurate, it is more comprehensive, and it is constantly updated, including a process of reviewing the changes any volunteer editor can make). Encyclopedias give you more depth in defining terms than a dictionary, but can't give you as much depth as a specialized encyclopedia or textbook. All reference sources, general or specialized, can only give us basic facts, with little or no information on disagreements among scholars, the state of current research, or the intersections between related concepts and how they may be applied differently in various areas of scholarship.

One of the great but often overlooked features of Wikipedia is its vast collection of images and maps from the public domain, gathered on Wikimedia Commons. These may be helpful to better understand your other readings or even to use in your essay. The following are some examples of ways you can use Wikipedia in your coursework that are legitimate and worthwhile:

- Your professor keeps referring to "irredentism" but you can't find a definition in course materials.
- You need to confirm that the Korean War began in 1950.
- You want to compare maps of Israel's borders over time to support a claim in your essay.
- You want to put a picture of Chairman Mao in your research paper on political fashion.

If you are using Wikipedia for basic reference, you still need to make an effort to verify that what you are seeing is likely to be accurate. On some Wikipedia pages there is a box at the top notifying readers that the page has been flagged for controversial, unreliable, or incomplete content. But even if you don't see such a notice, check the "View history" tab in the upper right corner. This tab shows when and how the page was edited. Scanning the history of edits can show you whether the page has been recently edited (perhaps as a prank), or whether the edits have gone back and forth, as when there is some disagreement about what should be included. Although the accuracy of Wikipedia has improved dramatically, it is a simple matter for pranksters or people with an agenda to change an entry. These are usually caught and corrected quickly, but at any given moment you can't be certain without corroborating the content somewhere more reliable (but if you can do that, you don't need Wikipedia in the first place).

Wikipedia defines concepts and lists examples of where they apply, but it does not tell you how and why historians have defined the concept in particular ways, it does not explain the different contexts where the concept may or may not apply and how historians argue both sides, and it does not address how and why those contexts affect outcomes. In short, it does not address anything we are in a history class to learn about. The way information is organized and the principles of what is included or not included are unhelpful for serious research—and as a student just beginning to learn how to do research, using Wikipedia to shape your knowledge is likely to lead you in unfruitful directions.

Do not use Wikipedia for the following purposes:

- As a shortcut to locating scholarly sources, by consulting the citations to print sources at the bottom of a Wikipedia entry. Those sources almost never represent anything close to a complete list of the relevant scholarly sources on the subject, and they often include unreliable or out-of-date sources or a skewed selection of the available literature.
- To cheat on an exam by looking up an ID term on your phone. Besides the unfairness to your peers and opportunity cost of cheating, it's unlikely that you'll find the right information. For example, if given the ID term "Metaxas" for an exam on European history, you will find both an Andreas Metaxas described as "Greek politician" and a Ioannis Metaxas, a "Greek general and dictator," not to mention Anastasios Metaxas, a Greek architect. Even when you find the right term, the generalized content that follows is not the thoughtfully prioritized and contextualized information you're asked for in your course. Wikipedia is not a substitute for having a clue what is going on in class.
- As a source of factual knowledge for exams and essays. You are likely to end up with embarrassing errors.
- As a source for the framing of your essay or to support your claims. Reliance solely on reference sources prevents you from meeting assignment goals even if everything is cited properly, accurate, and to the point.
- In a citation. Basic encyclopedia facts do not need to be cited, because they belong to no one and are generally agreed upon (see section 10.10). It follows that there is unlikely to be a reason to cite from a general encyclopedia such as Wikipedia.

Google. Searching the entire web through a general search engine such as Google has all the same problems as Wikipedia, but amplified several billion times because of the scale and variety of what is accessed through a Google search. General internet searches are mainly useful today for navigation, for example to locate a specialized online encyclopedia or a bibliographic software program.

Google is also a problem for another reason. The algorithm Google uses to rank your results tries to give you what you want. This means that if you type into the Google search box, "Is the Holocaust real?" you will get results from Holocaust deniers as if those are the most prominent and relevant internet pages relating to the Holocaust (they are not! The algorithm just thinks those words are a closer match to the words in your question). If you instead entered "documenting the Holocaust" you would be more likely to get sites about the real evidence for the Holocaust, but not ranked according to their quality or reliability—only according to whether they use the word "documenting" or sometimes unrelated commercial criteria. You may even come across texts purporting to be historical documents that have been faked. By trying to guess what you want rather than what's out there or what's the highest quality, the Google algorithm can give you extremely misleading results. As a matter of basic internet literacy, switch to a search engine that does not distort results in this way, such as DuckDuckGo. However, even those kinds of search engines produce results only according to how closely they use the exact words you put in the search box, and the results are still drawn only from what is freely available on the internet—most of it unvetted.

Google has two other services you may have been encouraged to use, with good reason. Google Scholar is a search engine specifically for public domain scholarship. Many disciplines use it extensively. However, history scholarship is not yet well represented in Google Scholar's database, so it is usually not recommended for students in history courses (if your course is an exception, your instructor or a librarian will tell you). So far history has few open-access journals (journals that allow free public access), and historical research often requires that we look at scholarship published much earlier than what is likely to be available in Google Scholar.

Google Books scans whole books to make them available online, mostly drawing from out-of-copyright titles. For this reason, Google Books may sometimes be the best place to find a copy of an old book we might want as a primary source in an essay. However, this is not often the case for undergraduate coursework, and if it is, a librarian would be the best person to recognize when Google Books might be a good place for you to look. Some more recent titles in Google Books cost money to download in full, but could also be available to borrow for free from your library.

Educational websites. You might naturally assume that something on a website with an ".edu" extension counts as "scholarly" and is therefore eligible for use in an essay. These sites are indeed associated with recognized educational institutions. However, that does not mean that what you find on those sites is useful for your coursework. Many of these sites are for high school classrooms and are too elementary for the work you are expected to do in college. Other sites may contain information written by professors for college classrooms, but unless the page you are looking at was written by *your* instructor for *your* course, what you find is not likely to be relevant to your needs.

Blogs and op-eds. These sources are not necessarily of poor quality or inaccurate, though many are. The problems with them are the following:

- You can't know whether they are accurate or reliable, because they have not been vetted through peer review and their authors may or may not have whatever qualifications they say they have. They may even refer to or present "evidence" that is actually fake or has been misunderstood or taken out of context in order to distort its meaning.

- Many such sources have some vested interest in presenting information with an undisclosed slant, whether because they support a cause or are simply aiming for more clicks and advertising money.

- Most such sources are not analytical and do not adhere to scholarly standards of evidence or reasoning, so they are not rigorous enough to build your own argument on them. This does not necessarily mean they are inaccurate. Many scholars write thorough and thoughtful news analysis in outlets such as the "Made by History" column of the *Washington Post, The Conversation,* or *Contingent Magazine.* These are great sources to read out of general interest. But they are tertiary sources that rarely serve your purposes in a research essay. Authors in these venues are usually not presenting their research directly or engaging fully with the scholarship of others. If you find interesting ideas or sources described on sites like these, find the scholarly published works they are drawn from, and use those for your essay.

- Most aim to relate history directly to present-day concerns, which is usually not among your goals for history coursework.

Plagiarism on the web. Copying anything from anywhere is plagiarism. The type of source you copy from has nothing to do with it. Furthermore, copying from unreliable sources only compounds the problem. Though you can fail a course only once, you vastly increase your chances of being caught and of getting the worst possible consequences when you disregard assignment expectations and ethical student conduct.

There are websites that offer to write your essays for you for a fee. Not only is this cheating, which comes with heavy penalties, and not only does it waste your time and tuition in college by depriving you of the opportunity to learn, but the essays you pay for are usually not very successful. Although these sites advertise writers who are experts in many fields, and some of them may actually be close to expert in one or two fields, none of those people have been in your classroom or know the specific readings and expectations for your assignment. Following directions and engaging in your course is an easier and more reliable, as well as honest, way to produce a successful essay.

10.7. Judging Quality

Even after restricting ourselves to vetted sources obtained through reputable databases and libraries, we still need to consider some additional questions when selecting our secondary sources. Sources that have met a minimum standard of reliability are still not all equally useful for your project. And some texts may be questionable on one or two criteria yet still be useful in your essay. Even a very biased analysis, for example, may not convince us of its point of view, but it can provoke interesting and useful questions.

The following sections refer to secondary sources only, because tertiary sources should be used only for reference, with the appropriate cautions, and primary sources, if they are authentic—as anything made available for student use through library databases or published in collections by university presses should be—are already of suitable quality. There are some legitimate internet repositories of primary sources, such as Fordham University's Modern History Sourcebook, but be wary of finding primary sources through a general internet search. In case of doubt, check with your instructor or a librarian.

Who wrote it and when? Most people think the best way to judge any source for any purpose is to ask who wrote it. This can be a shortcut to avoiding sources that are known to be terrible. But while you might dismiss a source based on the author's bad reputation or lack of relevant qualifications, you can't rely on another source solely because its author has a good reputation. We must ask additional questions about an author's authority (how equipped is he to reliably meet the goals of this argument?) and a source's currency (does this research represent the best we know currently?).

- **Authority.** If your secondary source is from a scholarly press, you can assume the author has relevant training and access to sources. Beyond this, scholars vary widely in their disciplinary specialties, and differences in expertise can be reflected in their work. For example, a specialist on French nationalism might write a book making an argument about how nationalism developed in Europe in the nineteenth century that requires that author to go well beyond her training in the history of France. This does not mean the text is not reliable. Someone who was trained in French history can make convincing arguments about broader phenomena. It means only that you should consider how the author's area of specialization might affect their interpretation by shifting emphasis in certain directions, and perhaps not considering other directions. This helps you to understand and weigh the author's argument. It is not a reason to wholly accept or reject it. These kinds of differences in training and approach are one of the reasons we have to read several good sources on any single question to fully understand it: each author's research and expertise will contribute in different ways.

When considering the basis of an author's expertise, we must also ask about the possibility of bias (see sections 8.5.3 and 9.9). Most scholars are paid by universities to produce scholarship with no incentive toward any particular results other than what the evidence suggests. However, these scholars sometimes get additional outside funding for their research, and other qualified scholars are sometimes employed by think tanks or private companies with particular agendas (though some such institutions are as independent as most universities). Be particularly attentive to this possibility when you are studying any subject that is currently controversial, either in US politics or in any other country related to the historical topic of your inquiry. The acknowledgments section of a book should disclose funding sources, and you can do an internet search on an author's name, institution, or funding source to find out more. If you suspect bias may be a factor in a source you want to use for your essay, discuss it with your instructor.

- **Currency:** In some disciplines, especially those involving technology, the date of a research project can be very important, as some studies can become so out-of-date that they lose their usefulness. The date a historical study was published is rarely critical to understanding it or using it in your own research. But it's still worthwhile to consider possible implications. When you are reading several sources discussing the same subject, read them in chronological order and think about how the later sources were reacting to and building on the earlier ones, while the earlier ones were written without knowledge of evidence that came out later.

  If you are looking at a source written a long time ago, consider how that might affect its usefulness. A book-length historical research project can take ten years to complete, so in this slow-moving field a date in the 1990s may still qualify as a "recent" work on many topics. Some subjects are affected by technological changes, however, that make anything from a few decades ago out of date—this is a problem in ancient history, which partly relies on archaeological research. There are some obscure subjects on which the only scholarship available may have been published several decades ago. History developed as a profession in the late nineteenth century, so in theory a scholarly secondary source could date that far back, and it would not be unusual to have to look to a book published in the early twentieth century, for example, for a biography of an obscure nineteenth-century politician. The older the source the more you should consider how the discipline has changed over time (see section 8.5).

Scholarship on recent events may also be affected by how closely it was written relative to the event it analyzes. For example, works about the collapse of communism from 1989 to 1991 that were written in the early 1990s may lack some of the evidence and perspectives that have developed in the years since those events. Some works of that kind may even be more useful as primary sources—as reflections on what historians were interested in and concerned about in the immediate wake of transformative events—than as analyses of currently known evidence.

Test the evidence. Look through the citations and bibliography of your scholarly sources for an overview of what kind of evidence was used in the study. Some books will have a "note on sources" at the beginning of the bibliography, or an explanation in the introduction; articles may explain something about the selection of sources in the first few pages or the first citation. Consider the following questions to better understand the nature and use of evidence in your source:

- **Is the range of sources broad, deep, or both?** Did the author consult many different kinds of sources from many places (broad research), nearly everything that survives on the immediate subject (deep research), or a combination? Historians work within practical limits: on how much they can travel to access sources, how many sources they can identify using incomplete and disconnected finding aids, and how much time they can devote to tracking down and reading sources. No single historian can read everything that could conceivably be related to any given topic. We aim to consider enough sources to conclude that we are reading them accurately. This means we narrow down what we cover so that we can read everything available, or we select a representative sample from a much larger set of sources.

  Sampling requires us to consider what factors "represent" typical or illustrative traits in these kinds of sources, and how many of those can provide a reasonably accurate picture of the whole. The criteria for "enough" are different for every project, and reasonable people will disagree on where to draw that line. Be careful not to hold any one analysis to an unreasonable standard of proving more than one work can do with available evidence. But it is also reasonable to ask whether a work might have been more convincing if it had considered more or different kinds of sources, or whether a different set of sources used by another historian demonstrates that the first set was not, in fact, representative.

- **How does the author use evidence?** Look through the text for citations to primary sources, which point to places where the author is referring to evidence. Does the author close-read quotes from historical actors? If so, consider how thoroughly the author considers context and subtext (defined in sections 9.8–9.9). Does the author analyze and explain statistics or other "hard" data, or select "representative" samples of documents? In either case, consider the author's reasoning about what his data means or implies and ask whether his conclusions are reasonable and whether there might have been anything else to be gleaned from that data.

Test the reasoning. When you consider an author's reasoning, you are following her logic from assumptions to claims and how she extrapolates from what she can demonstrate with documents or data to what we can guess might also be likely. Be alert for logical errors (described in section 6.9). In addition, reasoning that is logically sound might still be limited or unconvincing in other ways (as described in sections 6.6 and 8.5.3).

Test the methods. Historians do not always explicitly describe the method or theoretical perspectives they used in their research, though you should look for such a statement in the introduction of a book or article. If the method is not explained outright, consider the list provided in section 8.5.2 and the broader genres of historical work described in section 8.5.1. Each method of history comes with its own problems, advantages, and limits, so you need to consider a work in light of how well it succeeds within those methodological constraints. Consider also whether the author chose the most effective methods to get convincing answers to their questions: could a different approach have yielded a more useful result? If so, was that different approach possible with the evidence that survives and is accessible?

10.8. Judging Relevance

When we are gathering scholarly sources the question of relevance to our own purpose is perhaps the most important, yet often overlooked. "Relevant" doesn't just mean "on topic." Some sources that share the same keywords as your project may pursue them in directions that are not useful for your goals. In many cases there are simply too many sources on your general topic to incorporate in the time and space you have, so you need to narrow them down to those that are most relevant.

When you ask whether a source is relevant enough to use, you ask first what the source's purpose was. What is its main argument? Is it responding to others, trying to overturn an existing interpretation, or asking new questions? Knowing this purpose can direct you toward other relevant sources and inform how you will use it in your own essay.

In some cases, a work that has a purpose quite different from yours might be more useful to you than one that seems more directly related. For example, a book that addresses unrelated questions in the same setting (time, place, and social group) as your project might mention evidence that you could use to support your own, different claims. A work that focuses on a totally different setting might present an argument you could apply in your setting. And a work that addresses your research question only tangentially may still offer important arguments that you will want to address.

Try filling in these blanks: [source] is useful to my argument by doing X. It will allow me to show Y.

10.9. Identifying Conversations and Managing Scope

No historical question can be reliably answered using just one scholarly source. Don't look for one "best" source or rank your sources from top to bottom. There are no definitive answers or proofs for these kinds of questions. To approach scholarly questions, we need to identify a consensus among multiple scholars, if there is one, or map out the differences and contributions among several conflicting voices. In short, look for the most relevant "conversation" among existing scholarly sources that relates to your research question (for a definition and examples see sections 8.1–8.2). This does not mean you need to consider every voice that has ever published anything related to your topic, but that you need to identify some coherent set of quality sources that approach your research question in a variety of useful ways. Don't ignore any obviously significant sources and don't exclude sources that make claims contradictory to yours. But do restrict or narrow the framing of your research question to include only the number of high-quality sources you can reasonably handle in the time and space you are given.

If you are forced for these reasons to exclude sources that a reasonable observer might consider essential, insert a footnote explaining the reasoning behind your choice. No project can use all sources, but by being transparent about your reasons, you allow your reader to consider your argument on its own terms.

When you have too few sources. One of the common problems at the research stage of a project is not finding enough quality sources to work with. First make sure you've searched thoroughly. Sometimes an important question hasn't been answered because the evidence just doesn't exist. Unfortunately, sometimes this has to be a stopping point, causing you to change your research question. Sometimes, though, it is entirely possible to continue to pursue the question, but your findings will necessarily be more speculative than they could be if you had more to go on. Try adjusting your goal: instead of "answering a question" or "resolving a problem" think about your task as "exploring a problem." Is there enough of interest here to find out, for example, why the evidence isn't sufficient? Can you use an analogy with another kind of problem (for which there is more evidence) to extrapolate what kind of answers there might be to your question? For example, if you want to explore the personal experience of eighteenth-century marriage through diaries, but don't find diaries by a husband and wife pair, you could compare diaries of married women of the period to diaries of unrelated married men. You will not be able to draw firm conclusions about any specific marriage, but you might identify a range of possible answers to your questions about how men and women thought and wrote about that part of their lives.

When you have too many sources. The opposite and equally common problem is that you have reduced your list to only the highest-quality and most relevant sources, yet you still have more than you can handle in your assignment. Consider whether you can eliminate any sources on your list as essentially repeating what you can get from others, or because they have been superseded by more recent or more comprehensive works. It may not be possible to totally eliminate whole texts this way, but in some cases—such as biographies of very important people—you may be able to incorporate a few key chapters or passages rather than each source in its entirety.

10.10. Citing Sources

By the time you enter college, you are probably aware of the concept of plagiarism and understand it to mean "stealing" from others by copying their work without a citation. This is true enough. However, it is a simplistic understanding of the problem and often leaves students in the dark about the reasoning behind our methods and styles of citing sources.

References to the sources on which we base our arguments show our reader at a glance what kind of research we did. It allows a reader who wants to check or build on our work to go back to our sources to test them or apply them in new ways. It allows a reader to distinguish our arguments from others, to see how much of an original contribution a scholar is making. Footnotes also serve alongside first-person statements like "I argue that . . ." to show who is claiming what, thus distinguishing claims from facts. We even cite ourselves, to direct readers toward related work. Citations map how ideas have developed over time, who has contributed, and how individual contributions relate to the whole discussion.

10.10.1. Plagiarism

In a classroom, teachers emphasize that plagiarism is cheating because we must grade you on your work, so we need to know that what you turn in really is yours (and that it is new work produced for the current course, not recycled work, which is how it's possible to plagiarize yourself). This is indeed a serious matter. In published scholarship, where people's jobs depend on their ability to produce original research, it is even more important that credit goes where credit is due. Copying words or ideas from a source without showing where you got it from is a form of theft.

When you plagiarize, you are not hurting or insulting your instructor. You are hurting and insulting yourself, not only because of the consequences that must follow (a failing grade is usually a minimum), but because you are wasting your time and tuition. Copying someone else's words is not learning, any more than going to a gym and watching other people exercise is getting fit. Moreover, plagiarizing well enough to avoid detection is more difficult than just doing the assigned work. If you have missed so many classes and readings that you are unable to do assigned work, drop the course rather than resort to plagiarism.

The following are all examples of plagiarism:

- Quoting a source (with quotation marks) but leaving off the citation (the footnote or parenthetical reference to the source)
- Using words from someone else without quotation marks or citation
- Using ideas from someone else without citation, even if you put them in your own words (or use paraphrasing software)
- Copying work done by one of your classmates, a friend, or relative
- Copying work done by someone who took your course previously
- Paying someone to write your essay and turning it in under your own name
- Using only parts of someone else's essay in yours
- Copying anyone else's work or failing to cite a source, no matter what kind of source
- Working so closely with a friend that you decide together what you should write and both write more or less the same thing
- Reusing an essay you wrote for a previous class

Most plagiarism cases are clear. However, there are some circumstances that students fear may count as plagiarism that actually aren't. It's *not* plagiarism if you:

- Talk about assignments with a friend, as long as you each do your own writing and come to your own conclusions (to avoid confusion, it may be best to choose different topics or some other way of distinguishing your work)

- Include uncontested, basic facts in your paper without a citation, such as "India became an independent dominion in 1947." It is not an idea or claim "owned" by any one person, and anyone wanting to confirm it could look in any source on the subject to get the same information. Therefore none of the reasons we cite sources applies. Most dates, basic biographical facts of famous people, and the existence of major events are not contested and do not need to be cited. In some cases, a person's birthdate may not be known for certain, and if your sources offer different dates, provide and cite both. In other cases, the author of a textbook or encyclopedia may include, implicitly or explicitly, some argument or point of view beyond basic facts. If you want to include that claim in your essay, cite it.

If you're not sure whether a citation is necessary, the safest choice is always to cite.

10.10.2. Citation Styles

When you cite a source, you do so in one of several citation styles. It may seem pointlessly complicated to have to decide among or learn several styles, but there are reasons why citation styles have developed the way they have. Knowing these reasons may make it easier to remember the details of a given style, or at least feel less annoyed by the picky process of citing sources correctly.

The main citation styles have each developed to serve different disciplines:

- **MLA** was developed by the Modern Language Association and is most commonly used in the humanities. As you would expect from a style that is developed for literary criticism and philosophy, the emphasis is on the author and on keeping the citations from breaking up the flow of the main argument as much as possible. Therefore in-text parenthetical notes include only the author name and a page number if needed. Readers turn to the works cited list to get full details.
- **APA** was developed by the American Psychological Association and is used in most social science disciplines. Social science fields aim to solve current problems and questions, so the currency of a source is information you would want to take into account as you read. APA style therefore emphasizes the date of a work, including it early in the parenthetical notes embedded in the main text and in the full reference in a bibliography.

- **Chicago** was developed for a reference work called *The Chicago Manual of Style*, first published by the University of Chicago Press in 1906. Chicago style is sometimes abbreviated as "CMS" or referred to as "Turabian" after a guidebook for students based on the Chicago style by Kate Turabian. Chicago style is the preferred citation style for history and requires footnotes or endnotes rather than parenthetical in-text citations. This allows readers to see all the information about a source when they first encounter it, because historians emphasize examining and questioning types of evidence as well as authorship and currency. Our work can vary widely in the kinds of evidence we might use and our emphasis on how context shapes change requires us to know and question all the details about who said what, where, and in what ways. So we want that information presented more completely right in our main text. Some disciplines confine most citations to a methodology section with only brief repeated references elsewhere, but historians typically cite large numbers of sources throughout our work (typically one hundred to two hundred citations in one article or book chapter, referring to a mix of secondary, published primary, and archival sources). This is also part of why we put them at the bottom of the page in footnotes or at the end of an article or book, rather than filling up sentences with long in-text citations.

Use only one citation style consistently throughout any essay. Chicago or Turabian style should be the default choice in history courses, but MLA may be acceptable for short assignments where you refer repeatedly to only one or two sources. Consult your instructor.

You can consult the *Chicago Manual of Style* in print or online in your library, or pay to get complete access to its online version, but for most classroom purposes you can find everything you need in the free online "Quick Guide" at http://www.chicagomanualofstyle.org/tools_citationguide.html. Appendix 1 also provides an even briefer reminder of the most common forms. Your university library may also have its own guides to all the common citation styles on its website. If you expect to write many history essays, you might consider getting a copy of Kate Turabian's guide, called *A Manual for Writers of Research Papers, Theses, and Dissertations*, which is less expensive and easier to use than the full *Chicago Manual of Style*.

To cite correctly, first identify the source type you have: book, article, part of a book, website, film, and so on (if you're not sure, see sections 5.10.1 and 10.3). Find the citations for that type of source in the guide and copy the form as it is shown. If you are using new, digital source types, make sure you are consulting a recent edition of your citation guide. If you need to cite something unusual such as personal correspondence or an object from a museum, there is still a form to follow, but you may need to consult Turabian or the full *Manual*. Remember that primary sources are cited according to how they are published, so that historical documents published in a collection would be cited by the editor and collection title, even though it's the historical author and original date of writing or publication that matter in your main text (see sections 9.4–9.5). If you are citing a quote that you found used in another source, footnote the source where you found it, but add "qtd. in" at the beginning, as in the following note for an essay in which the student quotes Lord Cromer, the British consul-general in Egypt at the turn of the twentieth century, saying the British Empire brought about a "moral and material elevation" of its subject peoples:

1. Qtd. in Samuel Moyn, *Human Rights and the Uses of History* (Brooklyn, NY: Verso, 2017), 121.

The attribution in the main text tells readers who said those words (and in what context); the footnote directs readers to where they can find the quote if they want to know more about it.

10.10.3. Notes versus Bibliography

All citation styles include two sets of rules: the form of citation that goes in the text as you refer to the source and the slightly different form that goes on your "Works Cited" list at the end of your essay.

Citations in the main text—here referred to as footnotes in accordance with Chicago style—include a page number unless you are referring to a work in its entirety. Footnotes list the author's name in the order we read or say it, first name first, and connect the pieces using sentence-like punctuation (parts are separated by commas or parentheses), to be less disruptive for the reader. Each footnote is numbered, and this should be done automatically by your word processor (use the "insert" menu to get footnotes properly numbered and formatted at the bottom of the page).

Traditionally, after the first footnote to a given source, subsequent notes to that same source are shortened. If the second note comes immediately after the first, it can be replaced with just "Ibid.," a Latin abbreviation for "the same as above." If it comes after intervening references to other sources, it includes only the author's last name and a shortened title, along with the page number (as in "5. Moyn, *Human Rights*, 144"). Abbreviating repeat citations saves typing, which was significant in the days of manual typesetting and typewriters. With word-processing software it is actually easier to copy and paste the full citation than to abbreviate, but most publishers still prefer shortening because it saves space. You may see other Latin abbreviations in the citations in your sources, such as "viz." ("namely"), "cf." ("compare to" or "consult"), "et al." ("and others"), and *passim* ("throughout"). These were common at a time when most scholars studied Latin. English equivalents are becoming more common, so there is little need to learn them. If you come across a Latin word or abbreviation in your readings, a quick internet search will yield a definition, but you may want to bookmark the list of terms and their definitions maintained by the University of North Carolina at Chapel Hill (http://writingcenter.unc.edu/handouts/latin-terms-and-abbreviations/).

The citations that appear on your "Works Cited" list have a slightly different form because of their different purpose. This form can be referred to as "Bibliography," but the most accurate title for your reference list is "Works Cited." A works cited list allows your reader to evaluate the whole range of sources you used all at once. It also allows readers to quickly look up the full details from a shortened footnote by scanning for it in the works cited list. For these reasons, sources are listed in alphabetical order by author's last name, with the last name first, the first line flush left, subsequent lines indented, and are not numbered. Each part of an entry is set off from the others by periods, making it easier to scan titles, dates, or publication details from top to bottom.

10.10.4. Print versus Online Sources

You are likely to encounter print sources, sources published in print that you read online, and online-only sources. This range of ways sources can be accessed is still relatively new, so citation styles that were originally developed for physical media are being adapted. All the citation styles have added forms for digital media, and these are frequently updated as our media landscape continues to change. There is still disagreement among publishers and scholars about whether print sources that you access electronically should be cited according to the form for the print original or in a form that includes information about where and when you accessed it. One of the difficulties of citing online sources is that they may be altered at any time, so that your citation becomes out of date. For this reason it is usually preferably to cite a print source when that is an available alternative.

Citation forms for online-only media also vary in whether a "DOI" number is considered necessary. A DOI is a "digital object identifier," a unique number for any digital source. Chicago and other citation styles recommend including the DOI; however, many scholars and publishers find these numbers are not worth the space they occupy, since looking them up is cumbersome and usually only brings you the URL and other information already provided in the rest of the citation. You can always ask your instructor, but in many environments the DOI is considered optional.

Digital media are still new, and scholarly conventions are adapting slowly to these changes. You may see citation forms change dramatically in your lifetime, perhaps being replaced entirely with hypertext in a digital-only environment. But for the present you need to follow the forms as they are recognized by most readers.

10.10.5. Historiographical and Explanatory Footnotes

Footnotes are not only for citing sources. They are also a place where we can comment on or add further information that does not belong in the main text. Historiographical footnotes provide background information on how historians have studied the subject and how different sources relate to each other. Explanatory footnotes add definitions or explanations that are not essential, but may be helpful to some readers. They can also offer explanations about choices you made as an author, such as when you say you left out a discussion of a related topic because it was beyond the scope of your project. Sometimes all footnotes are numbered the same way, consecutively, but you may also number simple footnotes to sources while using symbols like "#" for explanatory notes.

10.11. Annotating a Bibliography

An annotated bibliography adds comments of some kind to each source. If you are assigned an annotated bibliography, your assignment should specify exactly what kind of notes to add, as well as give you a guideline on how many sources you need to find. If you are not given such an assignment, make an annotated bibliography anyway as a way of organizing your research for use in the essay you are working toward.

At a minimum, a useful annotated bibliography should include, after the citation for each source, a brief statement of its main argument or purpose in your own words—for example, "a first-person account of the treaty negotiations." Do not confuse this with the topic (what the source is about), which is usually obvious from the title ("The Treaty of Versailles"). If the topic is not obvious from the title, add a statement explaining this as well, and perhaps also some notes about what geographical or chronological areas are covered or excluded.

In addition, note for yourself how the source might be used in your essay: is it a primary source you'll use as evidence? Add what you think it might show, or what questions it can answer. Is it part of a "conversation" of secondary sources that helps you explain how your own contribution will fit in? Summarize the conversation, and how your contribution will fit, briefly in your own words ("Adds another case to support Warren's argument, which helps fill in the gaps from my case").

11

The Research Essay

Research essay assignments ask you to identify your own primary and secondary sources and construct an argument from them to answer some question of historical significance. They often require you to formulate your own topic or question.

A research essay incorporates all the skills you practiced in smaller assignments that have been described in earlier chapters. You will need to define concepts (as in a short-answer exam essay), distill secondary sources (as in a response paper), and explain how they relate to each other (historiography). You will develop your own question and identify and evaluate sources (research). You will analyze primary sources (as in a stand-alone primary source interpretation) and construct and support an argument (as in an analytical exam essay). Stitching all these pieces together is a new task, requiring you to juggle more information and synthesize it all into a more complicated whole.

In some undergraduate history programs, a full-scale research essay may not be required until a capstone course at the end of the program. Research essays are more common in graduate coursework, where they may be called seminar papers. Most research essays are expected to be at least 10 pages long, though they can be much longer, even as long as 100 to 150 pages for a bachelor's or master's thesis. Some require you to turn in some preliminary work, such as an annotated bibliography (section 10.11) or a research proposal (section 11.6).

11.1. What's Your Goal?

When you write a research essay, you are replicating on a smaller scale the process professional historians go through, from exploring a topic to developing a question to researching sources to developing your own argument and presenting it to other scholars for feedback.

As the culmination of all the skills historians, and history students, practice, a successful history essay demonstrates that you can do all of the following:

- Formulate a research question that is contestable, specific, and substantive
- Explain how your research question arises out of larger questions significant to existing historical scholarship

- Identify appropriate and relevant high-quality sources
- Articulate a logical series of claims that represent your answer to your research question
- Support your claims with evidence (often by interpreting primary sources)
- Explain the reasoning that connects your evidence to your claims
- Consider and respond to possible counter-arguments

11.2. Topics and Research Questions

When you ponder what to write about, it is natural to think in lists of nouns: people, events, or ideas that you find interesting. However, you're not writing a report, where you simply describe everything you know about a topic. Research essays are argument-driven. An argument answers a question that is of interest and significance to some community of scholars. So your starting point needs to be a question, not a noun. If you're interested in the Triangle Shirtwaist Fire, read about it until you can identify a question that you can pursue with your own research, such as "How did different New York City newspapers react to news of the fire, and what can that tell us about the development of support for the labor movement?" As you're trying out ways to formulate your question, remember the core goals of academic history: to understand change over time. Your research question can't be a "What if?" question or aimed only at drawing attention to a problem, as in, "Why isn't X better understood?" Instead, use the following criteria to test whether your question is workable:

- **Contestable.** If your question already has a clear and provable answer, you have nothing left to argue about: you have identified a fact, not a research question. Your question should invite debate and speculation and not be answerable with a simple yes or no. If you're not sure whether your research question is contestable, ask, "Could reasonable people disagree on the answer to this?" The answer should be yes.
- **Substantive.** A question and answer are substantive when they are of interest to many people, because something is at stake. In history, we can look at this criterion as saying that the question and answer must teach us something about cause and effect over time. If you ask, "Why did Soviet leaders alternate between those who were balding and those who were not balding?" you may amuse yourself looking for an answer, but you will not be addressing anything of substance in historical scholarship, because hairlines were not actually a factor in who led the Soviet Union or how leaders acted.

- **Specific.** A question must be narrow enough to answer with available evidence within the scope of your essay. Asking, "Was Alexander Hamilton more charismatic than Aaron Burr?" may be interesting, but it cannot be demonstrated in any convincing way because no one can agree on what "charismatic" means or how to measure it, especially in people who are long dead. But if you alter that question slightly to "How did Hamilton and Burr each use personal networks and reputation to achieve political power or attack political opponents?" you have a more specific question you can answer with historical evidence that sheds light on significant mechanisms of cause and effect.

(These criteria are from *The Craft of Research* by Booth, Colomb, Williams, et al., where you can find further explanation and examples and instruction on larger-scale research projects.)

Developing a question. The most common way many professional historians develop a topic of interest into a contestable, substantive, and specific research question is to turn to the sources.

First look at what has already been written by scholars. You might address the same question historians have already written on by answering it using different evidence or explaining a different approach to or interpretation of the same evidence they used. But for a relatively short undergraduate essay, it's usually more feasible to identify some smaller point you notice in a secondary source that you can pursue with the resources available to you. Look for claims that seem inadequate, wrong, or tangential, or questions authors raise as an aside (such things are often relegated to a footnote/endnote). Then consider what kinds of evidence you would need to answer your question.

Another way you might develop a question is to begin with primary sources. If you come across a particularly interesting document, think about what questions it could help you answer, and then identify secondary sources that relate to the same question in ways that help you explain your interpretation and its significance.

In short, develop your question at the same time that you begin your research. You may need to read a number of sources before even beginning to formulate a question, and as you refine it you will do further research to see what sources are available to help you answer it. Go back and forth between sources and working out your question, rather than completing one task and then the other. If you find yourself unable to think of questions or areas that are open to further exploration, refer to section 3.1 and ask those questions in relation to aspects or portions of your sources.

Beware of topics that seem easy at first glance. When you can already see the whole answer at the start, you may find as you move further into the project that there isn't enough material to work with. Instead, look for questions and subjects that interest you because they seem strange, confusing, or contradictory. Look not just for topics you enjoy, but topics that make you wonder. Then think about what kinds of questions they raise. Questions such as "What was it like?" prompt you to describe rather than analyze. Can you rephrase such questions to something that begins with "why" or "how"? These questions prompt you to explore, test, and ask more questions, thereby fulfilling assignment goals and learning much more.

Scope. As you refine your research question and explore sources, your other consideration will be scope. How many sources can you read in the time you have, how many sources can you distill or analyze within the page limits of your essay, and how big a question can you satisfactorily resolve within those limits? You can't figure this out at first glance. Narrow your sources down gradually as you get to know them and refine your question along the way.

Your instructor will usually provide some limit. For example, you might be asked to assemble a bibliography of five to ten scholarly sources and then be told to whittle those down to three to five that are most useful. Or you may be asked to focus on one primary source document while also consulting a set number of related secondary sources. If you are given no such parameters, ask for advice. These kinds of restrictions guide you toward an organic process of identifying what you need in order to meet your goal of practicing the historian's craft, as bound by the confines of a course and the available sources. Having too much freedom makes it hard to focus, too much constraint leaves little room for original thought. Professional scholars are similarly bound by and benefit from external constraints.

There is an interrelationship between your research question/thesis and the number and kind of sources you need to formulate an argument effectively. You need sufficient evidence to support your claims and enough basic knowledge of how historians have asked and answered related questions to frame your own argument around them.

- When the amount of relevant source material becomes overwhelming, narrow your research question.
- If your research question is too narrow to resolve with available sources, revise it to more closely reflect what can be accomplished with what you can access.

Remember that a proper analysis will likely be much longer than the text you are analyzing. You may try for a very broad research question out of fear of being unable to fill the required pages or not being able to "prove" an answer. But, ironically, this often leaves you with a question so general that there isn't much you can do to address it, leaving your essay full of repetition and vagueness. If you start with a narrower question that is contradictory or otherwise knotty, you have much more to do to fully explain it. When you explain a complicated problem, explore what answers are possible using specific words, and make clear your reasoning throughout (even if you can't fully resolve the problem, because it's unresolvable), you will find you are fulfilling assignment expectations and really learning.

11.3. Writing Process

The nonlinear nature of the writing process becomes even more dramatic as you write longer essays. A traditional understanding of the writing process for a research essay may look like this list of steps:

- Choose topic
- Find sources, read them
- Outline
- Draft
- Fix errors
- Print

However, an effective process will actually look more like this:

- Ask questions
- Find out what sources are available

- Refine questions
- Choose sources, read
- Refine one question still more
- Add more sources, reject some

- Read more, take notes
- Brainstorm
- Draft
- Brainstorm
- Draft
- Revise, discuss with others
- Draft more

- Revise for ideas
- Reread sources
- Revise for accuracy
- Outline
- Revise for organization
- Revise for style, word choice
- Revise for flow and clarity
- Get feedback
- Revise to respond to feedback
- Correct errors
- Print
- Correct errors again
- Remember to add title, date, page numbers, etc.
- Print again

Even within each of these steps you may need to spiral your way in to completion. For example, when you write a draft, there's no reason you must begin with the introductory paragraph, which is often the most difficult. Start wherever you feel you know what to say, continue as far as you can, and then go back to fill in blanks at a later point, perhaps restarting a fresh draft.

11.4. Argument Types

The core goal of a research essay is the argument. Some students find this intimidating, because they assume they are being asked to think of completely new ideas without the training professional historians have had. Obviously, an undergraduate student—and even most graduate students—do not have access to primary sources that no one else has ever worked with. It is also not possible for a student to master the entire literature on a significant historical problem, let alone the primary evidence that literature is based on. In any case, there is not sufficient time within a semester-long course for even the most prepared scholar to produce that level of work. When you are assigned a research project in a history course, you are not being asked to produce original research in the sense that professional academic historians do it for publication.

However, your instructors may talk about your work needing to be "original," or perhaps criticize your work for "just rehashing" what other historians have said (or being "just a book report"). They are asking that your essay demonstrate your own thinking. It must go beyond a summary of what you've read and take into account the sources you have available to you, while not ignoring obvious ones. You are being asked to chip away at some reasonably sized problem that has not yet been fully resolved and explain what you learned from the process. Problem-solving of this kind is a form of critical thinking.

Your "original" contribution to an essay can take several forms. You might reframe a question or theory to suggest a better way to approach it (without actually having to come to a definitive final solution). You might borrow a term from one context and apply it somewhere else in ways that shed some light. You might suggest a way of refining the definition of a controversial concept. You might combine interpretations from one set of documents with your own reading of another document and notice some interesting commonalities. You might suggest that some event that is generally considered a big breaking point could also be looked at as a continuity if we shift our focus a bit (that doesn't make the original, dominant perspective untrue; it just offers an additional angle). You might point out that while the several currently recognized causes of X are all important, there's at least one other factor involved as well. Review chapter 3 and sections 6.5–6.9, 8.2, and 8.5–8.6 to consider the many ways historians ask questions and formulate arguments.

The following are four broad forms of argument that each offer different ways for you to contribute your own thinking. Choose an approach (or some combination of them) that reflects what you are seeing in your sources. Your approach should inform the structure of your essay and help you to decide what to include.

Conversations. Historiography is one way of forming and distilling a "conversation" among several secondary sources (see section 8.2 for the full definition).

You can similarly use a conversation already created by scholars to frame a problem to which you will also contribute your own reasoning and interpretation of sources. In other words, you are writing a historiography essay but adding your own voice—your argument—to the existing conversation. You might contribute to the conversation by using another primary source (or set of sources) that was not included in any of the studies you are considering, or you could offer your own take on the evidence or reasoning already presented. Either way, your essay goes beyond historiography by not just assessing and critiquing the other works, but offering your own resolution to a question they all address.

For example, you can present a "conversation" among several of the most important works that explore how some European intellectuals resisted colonialism in the postwar period. To add your own contribution, you might read a memoir by one such resister from a different country than the ones considered in your secondary sources, and explain how that new source and the context it came from adds to our understanding of the overall resistance movement.

Another way of joining a conversation is to present each secondary source as part of a chain, each link introducing a new point or adding evidence that leads finally to the claim you want to add. Still another way is to use secondary sources to raise questions that you answer using evidence (primary sources) that you identify yourself. Finally, a third way of entering a conversation, known as "revisionism," is to present an interpretation or set of interpretations that are generally accepted and then propose your new way of looking at the same evidence (depending on the scale of your project, it may be enough to simply explain the new approach without following through with new evidence).

One important consideration when adding your voice to a conversation is to remember to distill each of the other voices on their own terms, relating their argument accurately before you add your own critiques or additions. You have practiced this already in response papers and historiography essays, but the temptation as you add your own argument of equal weight to those of others is to include only the points from other scholars that help you or to overstate the weaknesses of other arguments in an attempt to strengthen your own. This book has described the process of distilling other arguments as "selective"—you choose the most important points to convey for your purpose (sections 4.4 and 5.5). This can be misunderstood as choosing only those points that help you. But that is not what a fair distillation does. Our purpose is to come to a greater overall understanding, not to make ourselves look better or right. Choose details based on what is most relevant to the research question, not on how those points affect your claims. Anything that can shed light on your research question is relevant, even if it forces you to refine or limit your claims. In fact you *want* information that helps you to narrow and qualify your claims.

Compare and contrast. When you structure your essay around comparing and contrasting, you find two sources or situations that are parallel in some way. Perhaps they address the same theme in two locations or at two times; two primary sources argue for the same position by authors from different contexts; you contrast the different causes of two seemingly similar events; two historical figures explain the same event or question in different ways; and so on. Your contribution is to find, explain, and analyze the reasons for the differences and similarities between two cases.

For example, you could compare how both North Korea and North Vietnam became separate entities in 1945 and how they later got into war with South Korea and South Vietnam, respectively. You would consult primary and secondary sources on each case, and your original contribution lies in combining the two cases and explaining what we can learn from their similarities and differences (consult section 6.9 on "weak analogies" to avoid comparing apples to oranges).

Lens. When you take a concept, term, or interpretation from a secondary source and apply it to evidence from another setting, one way to describe that process is to say that you're using the borrowed concept as a lens to help you see the new setting more clearly. Taking an idea from one context and applying it in another is an act of original, critical thinking.

For example, you might read Benedict Anderson's influential book *Imagined Communities* about how nationalism developed and see if Anderson's explanation helps us to understand an atypical case that he does not cover, such as Jewish nationalism, Zionism, and Israel. Your contribution would be in analyzing how Anderson's theories do and do not apply to your new case and exploring what implications that suggests for how historians should understand and use his theories.

New angle. Finally, you can add a fresh angle to material you find in a secondary source by pushing it a little further in some direction it was already heading. For example, you could choose a published primary source document that was mentioned in passing or only partially discussed in a secondary source, and do your own deeper close reading of it, or consider parts that were left out of the historian's discussion. Similarly, you could take a claim or explanation made by a historian and, by giving it more attention and researching more context, explain it further and suggest new approaches. Or you could consider a term whose definition was debated in several readings and suggest your own way to redefine it that, you argue, better reflects the evidence.

11.5. Brainstorming Argument

When you're brainstorming something as complicated as a research essay, try all the methods of brainstorming in your toolbox. For example, after taking notes on your readings as you find them, the next step might be to generate a mind map (see section 7.5). Go over your notes on the sources and think about how they might connect, points you found interesting or strange, parts you didn't understand, or other questions you had. Put these all on paper or into your mind-mapping software. Ideally, this process will help you to develop your research question and begin to think about the general direction your answer might take. Try annotating your mind map or writing up some separate lists to see what your argument might look like based on this preliminary research question(s). Make a list of claims and the evidence you could use to support them. Make a list to represent the conversation you're joining, then add your own claims to it. If you're comparing two situations, make a list to distill the most important factors from each context. Then make a list of differences, and another list of similarities. If you're learning toward a lens-style argument, make a list that defines the concept or idea you're borrowing, then a list of the aspects of your new context you think that lens might apply to.

This process of listing may clarify that your research question is too narrow or too broad. Revise your research question and proposed solution to it accordingly, then try mind-mapping and listing again. Repeat this process until your brainstorming starts to look like a workable early outline for an argument containing all the parts you need (a research question and an answer to it, consisting of one or more claims, which you can support with evidence and reasoning).

This is a good stage to get feedback. Sometimes we can come up with a seemingly neat and workable plan only to find that it falls apart under questioning. You don't want that to happen later, after you have put a great deal more work into your project. Often a research essay assignment will require that you turn in a paper proposal at this point for exactly this reason. Talk over what you have in mind with a friend, classmate, or relative. Speaking out loud will allow you to notice problems you missed before. Ideally, talk with someone who will ask you to explain anything that isn't clear and ask you questions to push you further in your thinking.

In addition to, or instead of, talking through your plan with someone, try free-writing: put pen to paper (or hands to keyboard) and write without pause for a certain set period of time, such as ten or twenty minutes. Write whatever enters your head without editing. Include stray thoughts like "I don't know where this is going but . . . " Just keep writing continuously until your time is up. Then read what you have and choose only one best or most interesting point. Then set a timer for the same interval and start again, using that one interesting point as your starting idea. Repeat as necessary.

11.6. Research Proposals

Some assignments for a research essay will require that you turn in a proposal or plan at an early stage, so you can get feedback on how you are formulating your research question, how you propose to answer it, and what sources you will use and how. Typically proposals include most, if not all, of the following elements:

- **Research question.** You need a full sentence ending in a question mark, not a noun or noun phrase like "the colonization of Africa." Your question needs to be contestable, substantive, and specific (see section 11.2).
- **Answer / thesis statement / main claim.** The answer or resolution to your research question is the same as the "thesis statement" or "main claim" of your argument, and some instructors might call it the "motivation" for your essay or your "contribution." Like the question, your answer or main claim needs to be contestable, substantive, and specific. At this proposal stage, it is assumed that your statement is provisional. It shows where you think your sources are leading you.
- **Sources.** Your assignment might ask you to include only a list of full citations or an annotated bibliography that describes each source and possibly adds a statement on how you will use each one in your essay (see section 10.11). Always include the full citation for each source in correct formatting, so your instructor can see what kind of sources you have. This is how your instructor can catch if you are using a source that is inappropriate or unhelpful for your essay or that will need to be read especially carefully. That important information can determine your chances of success for the final essay, so you want to hear about it now, while you still have time to change direction.
- **Outline/plan.** In some cases your instructor may ask for some further statement about how you plan to use your sources to frame your research question or to support your main claim. Depending on what you are asked for, you may find it useful to describe your argument as one of the types defined in section 11.4. Be sure to explain your plan using the terms for the three elements that make up any argument: claims, evidence for those claims, and reasoning. For example, you might write: "I will use [source] to support my claim that X because Y." Primary sources are nearly always used only as evidence, and "because" indicates that you are explaining the reasoning that connects your evidence to your claim. You might also do this in outline form, like this (or the fuller version in section 6.8):

Claim 1:
Evidence:
Reasoning:

Claim 2:
Evidence:
Reasoning:

11.7. Drafting: Incorporating Sources

To turn your brainstorming into a first draft, you need to incorporate your sources. You will probably use sources in all of the following ways. Remember that *every* use of a source requires attribution and citation, no matter how you are using it (see sections 5.9 and 10.10 for the mechanics).

- **Reference.** Mention a text without describing its contents directly, such as: "Historians who take an optimistic approach (Chazkel, Daniel, and Rossabi) emphasize..."
- **Distillation.** Selectively summarize the contents of a text, or part of a text, in your own words (section 5.5).
- **Paraphrase.** Put a statement or idea made by your source into your own words (section 5.9).
- **Quote in passing.** Quote a word, phrase, or short sentence without analyzing it, like this: "As historian Sheila Fitzpatrick remarked, 'Never underestimate the Russian peasant'" (see also section 5.9).
- **Quote sandwich.** Explain the context a quote comes from, quote a significant passage, and then explain why it matters in your essay (see section 9.15).
- **Close reading.** Thoroughly examine the subtext of a quote or series of quotes (see section 9.11).

As we saw in chapter 9, primary sources are evidence to support our claims, and so we often analyze them closely, presenting lengthy passages as a "quote sandwich" or close reading whole documents or sets of quotes. Since secondary sources are used only to frame a "conversation" and explain the importance of your research question and main claim, they are usually referred to, distilled, paraphrased, or occasionally quoted in passing, but rarely analyzed at length. The only likely occasion where you might need to quote a secondary source for more than a phrase is if you are using a concept or specialized definition from that source as a "lens" to examine some other context, and you need to quote and explain the way the concept was originally used.

11.8. Drafting: Joining the Conversation

If you have trouble finding a way to place your own ideas within the conversation made up of your secondary sources, try identifying the points of concession in the texts you are analyzing. Points of concession are places where the author qualifies her claims, admits to limits or exceptions, acknowledges questions that haven't been fully answered or evidence that is still not entirely clear, or responds to counterarguments. Write a dialogue between yourself and the author, in which she attempts to convince you of her idea, while you are as skeptical as possible. Refer to the places throughout her essay where she cedes points to the opposition and use them to argue for some contrary claim. This is a way of brainstorming to find your own point of view. You may end up agreeing with the author in the end, but still find a way to clarify and expand on the point of doubt raised in her text. Or you may find yourself supporting a strong argument against her. Either way, once you have identified claims, evidence, and reasoning of your own from this exercise, go back to building your draft around them.

Thesis statements. Your main claim needs to meet the same criteria as research questions: it must be contestable, substantive, and specific. The following thesis statement is not contestable:

> Herbert Hoover was an ineffective US president.

Hoover is universally understood to be one of the least successful presidents based on abundant evidence, so there is no case to be made here. If you could find a reason to argue the opposite—that Hoover was more effective than has been acknowledged in some way—while still accurately accounting for the significant evidence of his failures, that would be a workable basis for a research essay. The following thesis statement is not specific:

> The US Bill of Rights and the French Declaration of the Rights of Man have both similarities and differences.

There's nothing to support here, since any two things in the world have some similarities and some differences. Instead, name some ways they are similar or some ways they are different. Even more effectively, you could explain some way we can better understand these documents because of a similarity or difference you identified, as in this example:

> The different ways the US Bill of Rights and the French Declaration of the Rights of Man treat religion and defense reveal fundamental differences in the way American and French intellectuals defined the individual and his role in society.

Consider the following example:

> This paper will discuss Franklin Roosevelt's New Deal, which was a controversial event in history.

While it is arguably possible to contest this statement and it does refer to a specific policy, the claim is not substantive: almost any policy is controversial to some degree. Deciding whether this one was does not help us to understand it better. The statement needs to be revised to make a substantive claim about the policy, such as:

> Franklin Roosevelt's New Deal had greater symbolic importance than the concrete policy changes it introduced by rebuilding a sense of hope and possibility during the Depression.

Finally, your argument also needs to be unified around a single main claim, not a series of disconnected contributions, as in this unsuccessful example:

> The peasants of medieval France were surprisingly prosperous, and also had many different cultures, which is a contradiction of certain myths about peasants.

This statement would have to be narrowed down to be supported even in a very long essay, but the author first needs to decide which of the two claims it makes is the most significant, and either discard or subordinate the other. For example, the author could choose to compare a nineteenth-century speech by a French nationalist that refers to medieval French peasant culture to a series of medieval legal documents that give us clues to what those peasants were really doing and saying. In that case, the question of prosperity might be dropped if it is not addressed in either primary source. The revised thesis statement might read:

> Medieval French peasant culture as documented in trial records contradicts the image created by nineteenth-century French nationalism.

To support that thesis, the author would break the thesis statement (main claim) down into dependent parts (subclaims) such as "Real French peasant culture was diverse." Each subclaim is a part of the main claim and will be supported by a certain piece of evidence or line of reasoning. All the subclaims together support the main claim (see section 6.8 for more on subclaims and argument structure).

11.9. Revising: Ideas

As you draft out your argument, you are likely to run into what seem to be dead ends. This is a typical part of the process. Don't be discouraged if you run into one or more of the following common problems:

The authors I'm reading have already said everything I wanted to say. So the question you started out pursuing has been convincingly answered already. You can't keep writing as if that's not true: it's intellectually dishonest. If your readings have fully answered your research question, you need a new question. The good news is that you're in a good position to find one, having familiarized yourself so thoroughly with the subject. Focus on something smaller or slightly tangential to your original question. What do the authors admit is still not clearly understood? What aspects of the problem do they not address? What parts of their arguments didn't sit right with you, or didn't make sense? These are flags pointing to new questions.

I convinced myself that I'm wrong. This may feel like a bad sign, but actually it's good news, or at least not really a dead end. Now you can revise your main claim and do so knowing that you're right, because you've gone through all the evidence and now know what it's really saying. Revise all your claims to reflect your new knowledge, and rearrange your discussion of evidence and reasoning to follow from these new claims. Things should go much faster from this point, because you're moving in the right direction: the evidence is pushing for you instead of against you, and you're more knowledgeable. You will probably find that the reading, brainstorming, and drafting you've already done still help you, but revising will suddenly go very smoothly because the puzzle pieces fit together. There is no advantage in continuing to argue for a thesis you know is wrong. A quick reset in a direction that is supported by evidence will be both faster and likely to lead to an effective, convincing essay. Remember that it doesn't really matter what "side" you end up on. It matters only that you demonstrate your critical thinking by supporting contestable, substantive, and specific claims with valid evidence and robust reasoning.

I can't explain my evidence and reasoning completely, because that would take fifty pages and I only have ten. This is a sign that you need to narrow the focus of your essay. It is fair to tell your reader that "X is beyond the scope of this essay" as long as X is not logically critical to the main claims of your essay. When you articulate your main claim, you are staking out the territory you will cover. Do so honestly, limiting it as needed for the length of essay required, and then follow through on your promise.

My claim isn't completely true. Most claims aren't, because you are arguing about a messy reality with necessarily incomplete evidence. This is the nature of historical scholarship. Be honest with your reader and state exactly in what circumstances your claim is true, and in what circumstances it is not true (and what the difference is, and why). This actually makes your claim more convincing and improves your essay in many ways (see section 5.10.8 on precise word choice). It may also be a good idea to directly state the kind(s) of counterarguments you expect a reader would raise and explain why you still find your argument the most convincing way to account for the available evidence, even though it's not complete (see sections 6.7 and 11.10 on handling counterarguments).

The following are general troubleshooting principles to keep in mind as you read over your drafts to clarify your claims, evidence and reasoning.

- When in doubt, look at the evidence again. What is it telling you?
- The more specific you are, the more space it takes to explain your reasoning fully. It is better to support a narrower thesis thoroughly than to support a broad thesis inadequately. Narrower, more specific questions are easier to answer well than broad questions.
- Be honest with your reader. Don't try to hide flaws in your argument. Explain them. No argument can account for every case in every way.
- If your evidence doesn't support your claims or your claims aren't contestable, there is no path to an essay. Start over with a new main claim.
- Don't sweep the knotty problems under the carpet. Bring them front and center and try to unravel them. Never generalize, never simplify.
- All troubles are actually opportunities to improve your essay. You are graded on how closely the final version meets expectations, not on how closely you kept to your initial plan. Don't be afraid to make big changes.

11.10. Revising: Expressing Uncertainty and Limits

As a student, you are by definition new to your subject, and that means you are likely to feel uncertain about it. At the same time, anyone doing scholarship—which is by definition the exploration of new knowledge—is working with and through uncertainty. Uncertainty is uncomfortable. Popular myths about academia tend to make students think academic writing needs to be forceful, all-knowing, and certain, but that's the opposite of the truth. Academic writing should be an accurate, precise rendering of what we do know and what we don't know. It is almost never possible or advisable to express total certainty or absolute "proof," since it is rarely possible for evidence to support any claim so completely. At the same time, as we write about a subject that is new to us, we sometimes err the other way and fill our sentences with unconscious hedges that seem to tell the reader, "I don't really have any idea what I'm talking about. Please forgive me." What we should aim to do instead is to express uncertainty only where it really exists in the evidence or reasoning, not as an expression of our internal emotional state. (See section 5.10.8 for common hedge terms and section 6.7 on addressing counterarguments, which is another way to address doubt in your essay.) Compare the following examples:

Midwestern farmers were probably interested in quite different aspects of populism than industrial workers in the East were.

Midwestern farmers were interested in different aspects of populism than industrial workers in the East were.

The first sentence uses words of uncertainty—"probably" and "quite"—that are not needed. They are filler (verbal tics; see sections 4.7 and 5.11). We can be sure of this because when they are taken out, in the second sentence, the statement still accurately describes what we can know from evidence. Now compare these:

The Declaration of the Rights of Man proves that Frenchmen did not care about women.

By applying its principles only to propertied men, the Declaration of the Rights of Man suggests that the idea of equal rights was more limited when first formulated than we understand it today.

The first sentence uses forceful language—"proves" and "did not care"—that is not warranted by the evidence (we can't know what people really "cared" about and no reading of a document's subtext can yield absolute proof). The second sentence introduces uncertainty—"suggests" and "more limited"—that reflects the real state of our evidence.

The following words and phrases are commonly used to express (un)certainty, listed from most to least certain on each line. We use these to accurately and honestly reflect evidence that is limited or incomplete, or the fact that we are drawing conclusions from subtext (defined in section 9.9) or that we cannot be certain of the accuracy of our source. If you're not sure whether you should be using qualifications or hedges, look to your evidence: what exactly can it show or not show?

- Definite, consistent with, probable, suspicious, possible, suggestive, conceivable
- Demonstrate, imply, indicate, suggest, hint
- Does, should, might, could
- Exactly, approximately, roughly
- Very, quite, maybe/perhaps

Another way to express uncertainty is to make relative comparisons rather than absolute judgments. We see this in the earlier example where the Declaration of the Rights of Man is described as "more limited"—that is, compared to something else—or as absolutely "not" caring about women.

Defining your own terms. A related way to grapple with ambiguity or uncertainty is to define your own terms to create categories or distinctions that describe the evidence you are seeing more precisely than established terms can capture. A useful definition accounts for all like cases and distinguishes those from unlike cases. The most common way to form a specialized definition is to take an existing definition—either a dictionary definition or a specialized term already defined by a scholar—and adjust it in some way that, you argue, more closely reflects the evidence, as in this example:

> The women in this study were radical but not socialist, feminist but not liberal. They may best be defined as "liberationist anarchists," my own term that I use to capture their goals of . . .

Similarly, you might impose clarity on an ambiguous existing definition by adding your own clarifying terms. If your sources all discuss the concept of a "failed state" but disagree on what exactly qualifies a government to be in that category, you might handle this with a statement like, "For the purposes of this essay, a 'failed state' exhibits each of the following characteristics," followed by a list from your sources to reflect what is most applicable to your case (with a citation to each source you employ).

11.11. Revising: Structure

The traditional five-paragraph essay model that you may have been taught was developed as preparation for longer, argument-driven essays and is therefore a closer model for the structure of a research essay than other common history assignments. However, the model should still be adapted and made specific to the length, argument, and sources you are working with in any essay, as well as to the general expectations for academic argument, in contrast to general-interest essays.

Introductions. Since you are not trying to entertain or attract a reader who would not otherwise approach your essay, you don't need to worry about starting with a "hook" to grab the reader's attention. If your research question is significant and you have something of your own to say about it, your essay is already interesting for the academic reader. If you happen to have a strange fact or fascinating quote from a source that captures the crux of your research question or argument, that of course can serve well as an opening, but don't search for a hook for its own sake.

The way we let the reader know what the essay will accomplish and why it's important is to explain both the research question and the main claim:

- A statement of research question or problem (often explained in light of what we know so far, by naming specific historians, theories, or outlining known facts or narratives)
- Your main claim / thesis statement / answer / resolution / motivation / contribution (stated as a "promise" pointing to the direction your argument will take)

Some research questions have inherent significance, requiring little elaboration in the introduction. If you are writing about causes of colonialism, for example, you don't need to tell your reader that colonialism was important because it was one of the most transformative processes in history, affecting the whole globe (if you are not sure whether the significance of your question is obvious, try the "twelve-year-old test" in section 5.12).

If your research question is about an obscure subject, however, or you plan to argue that what most readers know about the subject is misleading, you will need to use your introduction to explain more, including some factual background details. Whereas you can assume a reader knows who George Washington was, you would have to describe Thomas(ine) Hall as an intersex individual who lived in the American colonies in the first half of the seventeenth century, who presented at times as a woman and at times as a man. You could then go on to explain that Thomas(ine) is significant because the issue of their sex was taken up by a community and a court, whose reactions have much to teach us about understandings of gender in early America. The more prominent your subject, the less you need to describe, but in many cases the amount of explanation needed is a judgment call; getting feedback from an actual reader will be your best guide.

When you state your research question in the introduction, you don't have to put it in the form of a question ending in a question mark. You can simply explain that there is something historians don't know on some subject of interest. This could be described as the subject of a debate among historians you name, or just as "a debate among historians," leaving their names to appear later in your discussion. Your description of the question should indicate what is not known and what is at stake in finding out more (if the significance is not obvious). You may want to lay out what historians have found out so far or the nature of their debate, or you might want to explain why the question has not been answerable or addressed yet. How much you explain in the introduction versus the body of the essay can be determined by answering these questions: Does your reader need this information to understand why your question is worth pursuing? Put it in the introduction. Does this information play an important role in your evidence and reasoning to support your main claim? Leave it for the body. Or begin with a short preview of this information in the introduction, and expand on it in the body. Or try it each way to judge which flows most easily.

Your main claim must be stated in your introduction because that's what your reader needs to follow the rest. Writers often resist this basic premise of academic writing. It feels more interesting to leave the biggest piece of information for the end. But you're not writing a mystery novel. The reader came here to see an argument that attempts to resolve some historically significant question or problem. She doesn't want to waste her time if she suspects you might not have anything to add to what she already knows (and as a practical matter, you don't want the person grading you to wonder whether you have a thesis statement).

If you begin with something other than your main purpose, the reader expects whatever is in the position where the main claim is expected to actually be the main claim, and can waste energy throughout the remainder of the essay looking for what you promised in the introduction. Readers find this experience confusing and unpleasant—it's the sensation of being cheated. At the same time, they can miss or misunderstand your evidence and reasoning because they don't yet know what it's supposed to be supporting. In contrast, when you begin with a promise ("I will show X") and each subsequent point follows through on the promise (by showing how and why X is true), the reader is more likely to follow your thinking and be convinced by it.

The other reason many writers hesitate to state their main claim in the introduction is that a solid, evidence-based claim is hard to articulate when you haven't yet had a chance to explain the evidence. Think of this first formulation of your main claim as a promise: it needs to tell the reader that you have a resolution and indicate which direction you are going. It does not yet need to be convincing by itself. When you later "restate" your main claim in the conclusion, you aren't repeating yourself. Your concluding thesis statement is the fulfillment of the promise. After going through all the evidence and reasoning in the body of the essay, you will be able to state your claim more concretely, probably with some hedges or limits, and your reader will be better equipped to understand and be convinced by it.

Of course, one final reason students sometimes fail to put their thesis statement in the introduction is that they don't figure out what it is until they finish writing the essay. This is normal and appropriate at the drafting stage. You *should* figure out how to refine your main claim through the process of discussing the evidence. However, it is a crucial part of revising to put that main claim into the introduction for the benefit of the reader.

There is no set rule on what order the necessary elements of an introduction must appear in. Because it is logical to ask a question before answering it, we usually see that order, but even this is not strictly necessary. You could begin with a claim, then explain how it responds to a gap in our understanding (a form of the question). Whatever background information and description are necessary to clarify your question and answer may come wherever they most effectively address the reader's need. Because readers expect to start from a place of familiarity and then add new information to that solid base, the typical order for an introduction is to begin with an orienting statement. This explains what context (who, where, when, what) you'll be addressing and what might be interesting about it. This orienting information can then lead to your research question, and then your main claim in answer to it.

Body organization. The body of an academic essay contains discussion and analysis of sources. It is where you break down your main claim into subclaims, analyze evidence, and explain your reasoning. It is also where you define terms and explain background information as necessary to make your claims, evidence, and reasoning clear to your reader. If you did not sufficiently explain the main existing interpretations of your question in your introduction, the body of your essay will probably also contain some amount of historiography, or distillations of what historians have discovered or argued so far in answer to your question.

In some other disciplines, the body of an essay is often broken down into separate sections, each with a heading, for "literature review," "methods," "discussion," and so on. Historians rarely do this. The elements contained in the essay body and the order they appear in can vary widely, depending on what you have and how it can be most convincingly presented. The only rule of thumb is that the argument (claims, evidence, and reasoning) must determine the structure and remain always at the foreground. Other elements, such as historiography or background explanations, appear only as needed to clarify claims, evidence, or reasoning. Sometimes the reasoning that supports a claim appears in chronological order, like a narrative ("John did X and then Y because of Z"), but the reasons ("because") are emphasized and facts are included as necessary to make those reasons clear.

You might alternate distillations of what historians have written so far with your own contributions, or cover everything historians have showed so far at the outset to frame your own argument and use the remainder of the essay to lay out your claims, evidence, and reasoning point by point. You might define specialized terms as you use them, or begin your essay with a discussion of such a term and how it was used by others so that you can use it freely throughout the rest of the essay. There are as many ways to structure the body of your essay as there are original contributions to make. But that does not mean that you can throw your material onto the page in random order. Look for an internal logic that will determine how your material should be best presented. This is part of the original thinking the task requires of you.

You may well find that you try a certain structure but end up repeating yourself. This tells you to adjust the organization so that each piece of new information gets added it is first needed. One way to revise structure that is surprisingly effective is to print out your draft and cut it up with scissors (this can feel quite satisfying). Cut it into paragraphs or sentences so that each piece of paper represents only one idea. Lay them all out on a clear surface. You may find some repetition: paper-clip these together. If you find ideas that are tangential to your main argument, crumple them up and throw them away. Arrange and rearrange the pieces in as many ways as you can think of until you find a structure where each piece falls into place in a way that should seem natural to a reader. (You can do the same thing digitally using Scrivener software.)

There are several ways writers signal to the reader when they are moving to a new subject. You might separate your body text into sections and put in a subheading that describes the topic of each one. More commonly writers use transition words like "furthermore" or signposting language such as "it follows that . . . " to mark a change from one idea to the next. We can also simply explain what we're doing (this is called metadiscourse), as when we write something like this:

> This essay will first explain the optimistic and pessimistic views that have so far dominated historical interpretations, and then consider how a shift in perspective can indicate a third approach to the problem.

If you find yourself needing a lot of metadiscourse, signposting, or subheadings, consider whether you need to change the order of elements in your essay. A logical structure should ideally flow from one sentence and paragraph to the next without explanation. The shorter your essay or simpler the ideas in it, the less you need to walk your reader through the structure. Long texts of one hundred pages or more are divided into sections, and sometimes the structure is explained at the start because they are rarely read in one sitting and they ask readers to connect abstract ideas across long passages. An essay of ten to twenty pages should not require such explanation.

Another way to work out a logical structure is to make an outline of your draft. Write a brief summary of the main idea of each paragraph in the margin. These summaries, read in a row, serve as an outline of what you already have on paper. Does that outline provide a sensible overview of what you wanted to present that anyone could follow, or is it repetitive, circular, or otherwise potentially confusing? Try making a new outline from scratch that reflects the nature of your argument. Rather than numbering points from beginning to end, label each part by its purpose. You could outline by the parts of the argument (claims, evidence, reasoning, etc.) as shown in section 6.8. Or consider the following alternative outline schemas, depending on what best fits your material and goals. Expect to try several outlines in the process of organizing a long essay.

Outlining a compare/contrast argument. If your argument is based on comparing and contrasting two cases (call them A and B), there are four logical ways to approach this. You could go back and forth between A and B throughout the essay, comparing them point by point, like this: AB AB AB AB AB. Or you could consider the A case on its own, then devote a second section completely to the B case, and discuss their similarities and differences in a third section, like this: AAA BBB ABAB. A closely related structure would begin with a comparison of what A and B have in common, then go into detail on A, then detail on B, then consider their differences last, like this: AB AAA BBB AB. Finally, you could compare two cases with unequal emphasis. For example, if you are primarily interested in understanding the A case but use the B case as a contrast to highlight the points of interest in A, your structure might be more like this: AAB AAB AAB.

To build a detailed outline of any of these structures, you might label each point in this way:

A point 1:   A point 2:   A point 3:
B point 1:   B point 2:   B point 3:

Outlining a lens argument. A lens essay could also be described as a compare/contrast essay where you take one element of the A case to shed light on each element of the B case. This looks like ABB ABB ABB, where A represents the concept you borrow from a source and B represents ways it can apply to a new context. You could also represent this structure as A B_A B_A B_A. In other words, your essay would begin by distilling the lens (what does it mean and what original context did it come from), followed by a series of claims about how applying A to the new context, B, teaches us something.

Another way to represent the structure of a lens essay is to label its parts as various aspects of the "lens" versus the "case," which refers to the new context you are using the lens to explain. Your outline might look like this:

- Lens: (defined)
- Lens source: (its original use explained)
- Case: (new context defined)
- Claim 1: (first claim about what looking at this case through this lens can show)
- Explanation 1: (evidence and reasoning to support the first claim)
- Claim 2: (second claim about what looking at this case through this lens can show)
- Explanation 2: (evidence and reasoning to support the second claim)

Outlining a "new angle" argument. A new angle or addition that you build onto an argument made by one or more of your secondary sources means that once again you are moving back and forth between two elements in your essay: in this case, from what your sources say to what you want to add. You could represent this structure with A as the source argument and B as your addition, and organize it as AB AB AB AB AB or AAA BBB.

Or instead of A and B you could label the elements like this:

Source point 1:	Source point 2:
My addition point 1:	My addition point 2:

Other ways of outlining. You might also consider dividing your material between "large" points that are most significant and "small" points that fill in the details. You could move from small points to large or vice versa. You could also organize your essay around what "they say" in contrast to what you say, as shown in section 8.8. If your claim is particularly provocative or surprising, you might begin with the obvious counterargument(s) your reader is likely to think of, and follow with each point of your own that refutes a counterargument. Or you could label all the parts of your essay in terms of "questions" and "answers"—to see how much of each you have and what else is there on the page that may not be contributing to explaining your research question or supporting your answer to it. This can be an especially helpful way of outlining "conversation"-led arguments, where you have the questions and answers supplied by each of your major sources as well as your own central question and its answer.

Conclusions. The introduction and conclusion of an essay should mirror each other, like bookends. Where the introduction oriented the reader and promised that you would have something to say while pointing to the direction you would go, a conclusion pulls together all the detailed claims made throughout the body into a single, precisely stated, and appropriately limited main claim that fulfills the promise of the introduction.

The conclusion also brings the reader back to the wider conversation of historical scholarship. Where the introduction proposed how you could add to the conversation, your conclusion can state what you added in more detail and ask what questions should be posed next.

You might consider the overall structure of your essay to be represented by the shape shown in figure 11.1.

The beginning and end of the essay reach out to a broad audience and refer to ongoing discussions. Both come to a point around your main claim: the motivating purpose of your essay. The body is hemmed in by this purpose, with each element adding something to the reader's understanding of your argument.

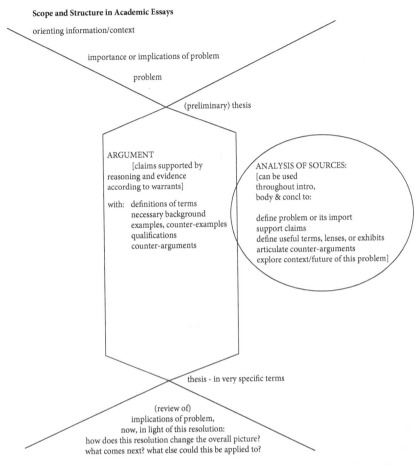

Figure 11.1 This schematic drawing represents visually the content, order, and scope that readers expect in formal academic essays.

11.12. Revising: Getting Feedback

An essay of this length and complexity should not be written without feedback from readers. Professional historians present their works in progress to readers both informally and formally in order to refine the clarity and effectiveness of their arguments, and you should do the same. If you are required to turn a draft in to your instructor or teaching assistant, submit your best effort: the version of the essay you would turn in for a grade if you did not have this opportunity for feedback. If you can do this, you will receive comments that help you push the essay beyond what you can do by yourself. Contrast that to turning in a messy early draft, where the feedback is likely to tell you what you already know (this draft is messy) or be otherwise unhelpful because the reader doesn't have substance to engage with.

In addition to instructor feedback, ask classmates, friends, family members, and possibly a tutor from your campus writing center to read and comment on your draft. Every reader brings something different to your text. People who are not taking your class are more likely to notice where you have not fully explained your terms or ideas; classmates and your instructor are most likely to see where your evidence or reasoning are unconvincing.

Remember, though, not to simply react to every piece of feedback mindlessly, as if following orders. Doing this is likely to set you running in circles, and it is also a problem because you are the author. Your essay needs to reflect your own ideas and goals. Feedback helps you to see how readers react so that you can adjust your words to get the reaction you want. It is up to you to take that information about your readers and decide what adjustments to make. See section 8.10 for ways to direct your readers to pay attention to the parts of your essay that most worry you, and to frame their comments in ways that will be most helpful.

11.13. Revising: Style and Clarity

If you have worked through this book from the beginning, you already have a virtual toolbox full of ways to revise your word choice and sentence structures to make them clearer for your reader. As you become a more experienced writer, you will develop more effective habits and learn which mistakes to watch out for in your own work and which tools best help you to identify problem areas and resolve them.

No amount of experience can get you to a point where you don't need to revise for clarity, however, because being clear is not a matter of rules alone. Being clear is about translating our thoughts from the form and order they occurred to us into a form and order that readers can follow. In other words, clarity is the result of a relationship between you and your audience. That relationship will be slightly different each time you write, as you communicate new ideas for new readers. Turn to your toolbox of strategies for revising each time, and consider which strategies are most appropriate for you, personally, for the purpose of the current assignment, and for the current intended reader.

As you revise a long research essay, the biggest problem you may face is the sheer scale of having to revise a greater quantity of material. Plan extra time to go through a late version of your draft sentence by sentence at least once, and preferably twice. Revising a long and complicated essay is in many ways a matter of cutting. The more you research and the more you experiment and develop ideas, the more likely you are to discover original ideas and the more you will learn. But to convey your ideas clearly to a reader, you need to hack away at that mass of material, continually cutting and reorganizing. What began as a record of your learning process transforms into a forceful, well-supported argument.

Previous sections have addressed word choice (sections 4.7, 5.10–5.11, 6.6, 8.5), sentence-level clarity (section 8.9), and paragraph organization (sections 6.10, 6.13). Two sections offer specific strategies for diagnosing and resolving problem sentences (sections 5.12, 6.12). In addition, there are at least two problems with clarity that may appear for the first time as you write at greater length, while other, already-familiar problems can come back in new ways because of the scale of your project.

Topic strings in long essays. Section 8.9 showed how to identify and revise "topic strings" by marking up the nouns and verbs in each sentence. This exercise is even more critical for longer essays. However, as essays become more complex, the topic strings will reflect this complexity. You still want to see a consistent string of "main characters" or core ideas throughout your essay. If, for example, your main claim is that medieval French trial records show a peasant culture that contradicts nineteenth-century nationalist portrayals, you should expect to see words such as "trials," "peasants," "France," "nationalists," "medieval period," and "nineteenth century" in your topic string. However, in an essay of ten or more pages it is unnecessary and probably not advisable for the subject of every sentence to adhere closely to only one idea. Instead aim for a clear development of your "main characters" over the course of your essay. The early part of your essay may focus on the names of historians who discuss your problem, while each subsequent section might focus on a different document or example that supports your main claim, with words referring to that document or example dominating the topic string in that section. The main characters for one part might be "nationalists," "nationalism," and "the nineteenth century" as well as "peasants," while in the second part you would expect to find "peasants" appearing with "medieval" and "trials," as you contrast this evidence with the later accounts.

Verbal tics revisited. Another clarity problem that is more likely to appear in longer essays is that you may subconsciously overuse some words or rely on verbal tics such as "very" or "quite" in ways that are more distracting for the reader in a long text, while they are harder for you to identify when you are scrolling up and down through many pages. One way to identify this problem is to ask a reader to keep an eye out for it when you are getting feedback. Technology offers a faster and more reliable solution: you can submit your draft into an app that turns it into a "word cloud," or a pictorial representation of your text that represents the frequency of each word by its size. Words you use often are larger than words you use less often. Ideally, the word cloud for your essay will show the "main characters" as the largest words and words with no clear connection to your subject or substantive meaning, such as "very" or "however," as small. Once you are aware of words you tend to overuse, find and revise them using the search function in your word processor.

Vagueness and redundancy revisited: Although you have tried to become better at avoiding vague or generalizing language like "peasants think . . . ," longer essays can reintroduce this problem as an artifact of juggling many sources and ideas. Consider the following sentence:

> Citing old documents, Petronelli argues that Nixon did not expect the rupture with China.

"Old documents" is vague. Either we need to know exactly which documents the historian Petronelli is basing his argument on, or the details of the documents are not important and we can simply write "Petronelli argues" with a note to the source so that an interested reader could identify the sources this claim was based on if necessary. It's up to you to make a judgment about whether the specific sources Petronelli used are relevant to your discussion, but if you do mention them, it must be specifically:

> Citing internal government memos, Petronelli argues that Nixon did not expect the rupture with China.

As we write in depth about complicated historical events, sometimes involving disturbing or upsetting material, a sense of awkwardness can manifest itself in excessive adjectives, redundancy, or belaboring the obvious, as in this example:

> Being an enslaved field worker was very rough and they had to attempt to overcome adversity due to all of the hostile acts that were committed towards them.

Being a slave was more than "rough" and more than "adversity" (and those terms are rather vague). Slavery was not just as series of "hostile acts" but a massive and complicated system of oppression. The sentence is about twice as long as it needs to be: "enslaved worker," "attempt to," and "acts that were committed" are all redundant. The awkwardness of the sentence is probably a reflection of the writer's discomfort with difficult material, as in this similar example:

> Some colonizers committed acts of excessive brutality.

The word "brutality" already means an act is "excessive," but this writer is trying to give the brutality its due emphasis by using more words. This is how emphasis works in ordinary speech: we repeat phrases or add redundant filter to help get our message through to listeners who can't go back to check what we just said. But reading is different. Fewer and more carefully chosen words convey emphasis, especially when we put the most important words toward the ends of sentences and paragraphs. The sentences above could be revised as follows:

> Field slaves faced terrible conditions, such as . . .
> Some colonizers were brutal.

11.14. Revising: Grading Yourself

As the classic genre of all academic writing, a research essay shares certain standard expectations. It will be graded on structure (does it have an appropriate beginning, middle, and end and a logical flow from each piece to the next?); style (is the language clear, accurate, specific, relevant, and appropriate for an academic audience?); use of sources (does it incorporate, attribute, and cite sources appropriately, and use them to frame and support the argument without missing obvious connections?); and mechanics (formatting, grammar, spelling, and punctuation). But most importantly, your grade will be based on how effectively you constructed an argument. Did you articulate a main claim that is specific, substantive, and contestable? Did you explain the implications of your claim for broader academic discussions? Did you support it with evidence? Did you fully explain your reasoning throughout? Did you consider counterarguments and qualify your claims appropriately?

In American universities, essays are usually assigned letter grades from A to F, and each letter grade has a numerical equivalent as points out of a hundred, or a percentage. The point where each letter maps to a percentage can vary slightly from one institution to another. And some institutions, as well as institutions outside the United States, use entirely different grading systems. Table 11.1 offers a ranked list of descriptions from the most successful essays to the least successful, each showing the relationships between argument and other expectations and how different strengths and weaknesses can balance or outweigh each other. Try reading your essay in order to place it in one of the following ranks (if you can have a friend do so as well, your collective efforts might be the most accurate). A blank column has been provided so you can insert the grading system in use at your institution. This process should reveal

Table 11.1 Grading Rubric and Expectations for Argument-Based Essays

Letter grade	Percentage (pts/100)	Alternate grading units	Essay demonstrates the following knowledge and skills
A A-	93–100 90–92		Facts and concepts from the course are correct. Writing is clear, grammatically correct, and organized (there is a clear beginning, middle, and end, and each paragraph has a coherent point). There is a thesis (main claim) supported by several points of evidence, each explained with clear and original reasoning, and counterarguments are addressed. Essay demonstrates creativity or original thinking. All sources are cited correctly, and fully incorporated into the essay. All instructions specific to the assignment have been followed.
B+ B B-	87–89 83–86 80–82		Facts and concepts from the course are mostly correct: any errors are minor. Writing is reasonably clear and has an overall structure (beginning, middle and end), but paragraph organization may be less consistent. A thesis is present but is not completely supported (only one or two points are given in evidence, reasoning is incomplete, and/or obvious counterarguments are ignored). Creativity or original thinking is either absent or underdeveloped. All sources are cited correctly, but not all of them are fully incorporated into the essay. All instructions specific to the assignment have been followed.
C+ C C-	77–79 73–76 70–72		Significant factual or grammatical errors are present. Writing style or organization inhibit a complete understanding of the text. Thesis is absent or not successfully supported by evidence or reasoning (or both reasoning and evidence are present, but not connected to each other or to claims). All sources are cited correctly, but only a few are incorporated into the essay, or too few sources were consulted. Instructions specific to the assignment have not been completely followed.
D	60–69		Significant factual and grammatical errors are present. Style or organization inhibit a basic understanding of the text. There is no original argument. Sources are either not used or are cited correctly but never developed or interpreted. Instructions specific to the assignment have not been completely followed.
F	0–59		Accurate factual material is inadequate, and/or grammatical errors or style problems make the text unintelligible. No argument is present. Use of sources is non-existent, inappropriate, or incorrect. Instructions specific to the assignment have not been followed.

areas in your essay where what was in your head did not make it onto the page. Revise to address these problems.

11.15. Proofreading and Formatting

Proofreading a longer text takes greater time than you may be accustomed to, but it involves the same steps as with shorter texts (see sections 5.13, 6.14, and 8.12). Research essays may require special formatting. A title page should have the essay title (see section 8.7) in the center, with your name, the instructor, course, and assignment names and date centered toward the bottom of the page. Separate this page from the rest of your essay by inserting a page break in the file, not by making a separate document. The essay will begin at the top of the second page, and page numbering begins with 1 on that second sheet (when you insert a page number, you can set it to begin where you like). Insert another page break between the end of your essay and the "Works Cited" sheet. See section 10.10.3 on how sources are formatted differently in your "Works Cited" list than in your notes.

Research essays that are submitted as a special degree requirement, such as a bachelor's or master's thesis, often need to adhere to other requirements for spacing, fonts, and the exact language on the cover sheet. Inquire about this with your adviser or department secretary early enough to make changes before your deadline. In some cases, you might need or want to print your essay and put a protective cover on it or submit it to a campus service for professional binding.

11.16. Writing an Abstract

An abstract is a brief summary of a research project that is often attached to the text when it is published in a journal or included in databases to help researchers identify what the text is about and how it relates to broader research questions. They are rarely required of undergraduates, though they may be a useful exercise.

An abstract states the research question, briefly outlines where the main existing interpretations stand in answering it, explains what you contribute in concrete, full form (like the version of your main claim you put in the conclusion of your essay), and distills what kind of sources you use to support your claims.

The length required for the abstract will probably be given to you, but they are usually no more than one dense paragraph. The greatest difficulty is fitting in all the required elements. For this reason, abstracts are stylistically similar to a short-answer exam essay. You need to "pack your sentences" and use precise words, eliminating any that are not directly contributing to your goals.

Acknowledgments

I started writing the earliest versions of what became this book in 2001. It went through countless versions and in the end owes its existence to many people. First among them is Chris Pickering, who made me pay attention to words and use them precisely from a young age, and Dan Pickering, who talked with me about teaching since I was old enough to talk. Most of all I thank both of them for making me a reader, which is the best way to become a writer.

Second are those who taught me how to think about writing and gave me a language for talking about it with others: Joseph Williams, Larry McInerney, and the teaching assistants of the "Little Red Schoolhouse" writing course at the University of Chicago in 1997.

Third are my first writing students: employees of Arcadia, Inc. in St. Petersburg, Russia, 1998–1999, who taught me that I liked teaching writing.

Fourth is Julia Kraut, now a colleague but in 2001 an undergraduate taking a course at Columbia where I was a teaching assistant. When everyone in the class except Julia bombed an exam, I responded with a crash course on how to approach exam essays. Julia not only suggested I institutionalize this talk and expand it into a much broader workshop, but made it happen as chair of the Undergraduate History Education Committee—it was the rising of the UndEd. I also owe an enormous thanks to the grad student colleagues who helped to build that workshop and vastly expanded my notion of what it could do—especially Aline Voldoire, Giovanni Ruffini, Jennifer Foray, and Molly Tambor—as well as to the Columbia Department of History for supporting the workshop and several of the faculty for taking the time to speak at it.

Fifth are the people who opened the world of composition studies literature to me and who taught me how to teach writing properly: Joseph Bizup, Nicole Wallack, and the Columbia University Writing program. The scales fell from my eyes and I can only hope I've been keeping them off.

Sixth are the many colleagues across Queens College with whom I have discussed the teaching and assessing of writing while hashing out our new disciplinary writing requirement, and the colleagues in my department with whom I have developed our course on writing history. I am so lucky to have such brilliant and dedicated people to work with.

Seventh are the colleagues elsewhere, especially online, with whom I have shared tips, tricks, gripes, and thoughtful musings about writing, history, and teaching for many years. They have all shaped my teaching in many ways that I can no longer trace.

Eighth are my students over the past nineteen years. They have taught me a great deal, and if they wondered why it sometimes took a long time to get their papers back, it was because I was taking notes. I am especially grateful to the students who gave me permission to use their anonymized work for teaching purposes and in this book, and to those who responded to polls or calls for comments and suggestions, and otherwise gave me their feedback on the manuscript while it was still in revision.

Ninth is Nancy Toff, who suggested I do the project for Oxford University Press and thought to organize it around the different kinds of assignments. I thank her and everyone else at Oxford University Press who made the book a reality at last.

Tenth are the anonymous reviewers who gave me their time, comments, and in all but one notable case their goodwill, as well as the additional readers who generously shared their suggestions to make the book better: Heather DeHaan, Jennifer Foray, Diane Miller Sommerville, Anatoly Pinsky, Lisa Ramos, Giovanni Ruffini, Alison K. Smith, Susan Smith-Peter, Aline Voldoire, and the generous graduate students of Jennifer Foray's historiography seminar. Deficiencies that remain despite everyone's best efforts are of course my responsibility. I also appreciate the several colleagues who responded to my urgent calls for examples, especially Jennifer Tammi, Deirdre Cooper Owens, Warren Woodfin, and Bob Wintermute. The late Satadru Sen not only provided examples at need but also gave me his enthusiastic encouragement for the project over several years and shared the company of his delightful family to help keep me and mine sane through some tough times. He is very much missed.

Finally, there is my family, who put up with all the hours of writing and revising and revising and revising, not to mention the years of sleeplessness and teeth-gnashing over delays. Sergei, Anya, and Marina might have preferred I do other things with this time, but they supported me anyway.

Quick Reference

It may seem that rules about writing are arbitrary or intended only to please your instructor, perhaps even to demonstrate your obedience. On the contrary, most writing rules are essential to communicating effectively. Your reader interprets your text according to expectations formed by such rules. If we break these rules, our readers can't follow our ideas (and may look down on us for not having mastered such basic knowledge). Other rules are not essential to the functioning of a language, but do help writers and readers to communicate more easily by creating and maintaining common ground. Still other "rules" *are* just traditions we follow because we were told to follow them, though they may serve little real purpose. These (and only these) rules may be ignored if they make our writing less effective, though in most cases they do no harm and following them may be worthwhile to satisfy the expectations of readers.

The following sections offer brief reminders of important, real rules that most often trip up history students. For fuller explanations refer to a dedicated guide to the appropriate area of usage. The *Bedford Guide for College Writers* by Kennedy, Kennedy, and Muth (New York: Bedford / St. Martin's, 2016) offers a full range of reference material for most purposes. *A Pocket Style Manual* by Hacker and Sommers (New York: Bedford / St. Martin's, 2017) is briefer. *The Complete Sentence Workout Book with Readings* by Fitzpatrick, Ruscica, and Fitzpatrick (New York: Pearson, 2003) and *Dreyer's English: An Utterly Correct Guide to Clarity and Style* by Benjamin Dreyer (New York: Random House, 2019) are good resources for improving your grammar and punctuation. For a deep workout on style for writers who have already mastered the basics, refer to *Style: Lessons in Clarity and Grace* by Williams and Bizup (New York: Pearson, 2016). For more emphasis on the rhetorical conventions of academic argument in any discipline, explore *They Say / I Say: The Moves That Matter in Academic Writing* by Graff and Birkenstein (New York: Norton, 2017). For a full guide to any non-fiction writing, see John Warner's *The Writer's Practice: Building Confidence in Your Nonfiction Writing* (New York: Penguin, 2019). For a full reference on research and citation, get a copy of *A Manual for Writers of Research Papers, Theses, and Dissertations* (Turabian and Booth, Chicago: University of Chicago Press, 2018).

A1.1. Sentences

A sentence is defined as a subject and a verb. Some verbs also require objects. Any phrase that does not have both a subject and a verb is a *sentence fragment* (if punctuated as though it were a complete sentence) or a *dependent clause* (a phrase that is dependent on another, complete clause to make a sentence, separated from the main clause by a comma). Verbs must *agree* with their subjects in number (a plural subject requires a plural verb).

A1.2. Parts of Speech

If a word can have an article (a/an/the) in front of it, then it's a **noun**: "*The* professor read *a* book." "Professor" and "book" are both nouns.

If a word describes a noun ("The *red* book"), then it's an **adjective.**

If a word conveys an action and is not a noun (it can't have an article in front of it), then it's a **verb**: "The professor *read* a book." But: "Reading the book was fun." / "*The* reading of the book was fun." "Reading" is a nominalization, a kind of noun made out of a verb, and the verb here is "was."

If a word describes how an action was done, it's an **adverb**: "The professor read the book *quickly*."

A noun that represents the doer of the action contained in the verb is the **grammatical subject**: "The *professor* read a book."

A noun that is on the receiving end of the verb's action is the **grammatical object**: "The professor read a *book*."

Conjunctions: and, or, but, yet, for, nor, so

Articles: a, an, the

Pronouns: he, she, it, they, you

Possessive pronouns: his, hers, its, their/theirs, your/yours

Prepositions: to, from, around, through, over, under, by, with (etc.)

A1.3. Punctuation

Between each grammatical sentence you need a **period, question mark, exclamation point, semicolon, or a comma *plus* conjunction.** When you use only a comma to separate two independent clauses (two grammatical sentences), the mistake is called a "comma splice." Clauses that are not complete sentences by themselves are *dependent* on the main clause and are separated from the rest by **commas**, as are *appositives* (phrases that rename what came before it):

The professor read a book. (Subject verb object.)
The professor read a book; it was good. (Subject verb object; subject verb object.)
The professor read a book called *Stalinism*. (Subject verb object, *dependent clause*.)
The professor, a very boring person, read a book. (Subject, *appositive*, verb object.)

Apostrophes have two functions:

1. To add possession to nouns: "The professor's book." (The book belongs to the professor.) *Possessive pronouns* (his, hers, theirs, its) are already possessive and therefore don't need an apostrophe.
2. To indicate a contraction: "*They're* better writers than they were." (*They are* better writers than they were.) "*Who's* going to turn in the course evaluations?" (*Who is* going to turn in the course evaluations?)

In formal writing you spell out contractions, leaving only one reason to use an apostrophe in your essays: to add possession to a noun (not a pronoun).

Hyphens combine two words into one:

In the nineteenth century, writers . . .
Nineteenth-century writers . . .

In the first example, "nineteenth" modifies "century." In the second, "nineteenth" and "century" *together* modify "writers." The hyphen indicates that "nineteenth" and "century" are functioning like one word. Compare:

A man-eating shark has been spotted near the beach.
A man eating shark was spotted in a local restaurant.

Dashes can be used to separate a dependent clause from the rest of the sentence instead of commas. This adds emphasis to the interjection of the dependent clause.

The professor, a very boring person, read a book.
The professor—a very boring person—read a surprisingly interesting book.

A1.4. Capitalization

Capitalize *only* the first word of sentences and all proper nouns. Proper nouns refer to a single person, place, or thing, not the category, so you capitalize the title and name of a specific person, like "President Roosevelt" but not the title as a category, as in "presidents are also commanders-in-chief." We capitalize "Brazil" but not the category it is an example of, as in "the country of Brazil." "God" is a proper noun, so it is always capitalized. Foreign proper names are usually capitalized according to the convention of the language spoken there, as in "Rio de Janeiro." Never capitalize a word to give it emphasis! Titles have special capitalization rules (see section A1.6).

A1.5. Quotation Formatting

Quotation marks are used in four instances:

1. **Direct quotes** that appear within the main body of your text (not block quotes)
2. **Titles** of articles, chapters, stories, songs, or short films
3. When referring to **a word as an example**, as in, "When it is appropriate to use 'I' in an academic essay?"
4. **Scare quotes**—quotation marks used to question the meaning or usage of a word. The quotation marks imply that this word may or may not mean what it purports to mean. For example: "I apologize if anyone was 'offended' by my remarks."

Never use quotation marks to indicate emphasis.

In American English, **commas and periods go inside quotation marks, and question marks and exclamation points go outside** (unless they're part of the quote):

The professor said, "Don't forget to do the reading."
The professor said, "Don't forget to do the reading," as we went out the door.
The professor asked, "Did you forget to do the reading?"
Are you familiar with the term "orientalism"?

Note the comma before the quote, as well.

Quoting inside a quote: When you quote someone who quotes someone else, or who uses quotation marks around an example word/phrase or scare quotes, the inside set of quotation marks should be single quotes to avoid confusion: "The professor used the word 'distillation' to describe a particular kind of summary." Use **brackets** to mark off any text that is not part of a direct quote:

> Historian Sheila Fitzpatrick suggests that "[we] should never underestimate the Russian peasant."

When you leave out a passage from the middle of a quote, or stop a quote before the original text reached a stopping point (like the end of a sentence or paragraph), mark this omission with an **ellipsis**:

> The professor advised that we "be more specific. . . ."

Any quote that is longer than three lines should be formatted as a **block quote or extract**: single spaced, indented on the left or both sides, with a blank line above and below, without quotation marks.

A1.6. Title Formatting

Titles are always presented in title case, which requires that you capitalize the first letter of the first word, and of all subsequent words except for articles, prepositions, and conjunctions. In many word-processing programs you can highlight a title and click a command to auto-format it to title case (usually under a "Format" menu). The title on your own paper must be in title case, is usually centered at the top of the page, and may be in bold. Book or film titles that you mention in your text are italicized or (in handwriting) underlined as well as put in title case. Article, story, or other short titles are put in quotes and title case:

> Read *The Essential Guide to Writing History Essays*, especially "The Short-Answer Identification Essay."

A1.7. Conventions

The following rules of usage are conventional in most academic contexts.
Numbers for **monarchs and wars** are in Roman numerals:

Queen Elizabeth II
World War I

No apostrophe is inserted in **dates**, unless the date appears in all-caps (as it may in an essay title):

The 1920s
THE 1920'S

Countries, boats, and ships are referred to with the pronoun "it," never "she," as used to be conventional.

Pronouns or collective nouns referring to people of mixed or unknown **gender** should not exclude women. Use "humanity" or "people" instead of "mankind" or the general "man." Alternate "he" and "she" or use "they" to refer to a singular person of unknown gender. Some contexts encourage "ze" and "hir" as gender-neutral singular pronouns, but these are not widely recognized at this time. The adjectives "male" and "female" are usually restricted to biological contexts ("female anatomy") while gender is described using the terms "masculine" or "feminine" (as in "assumptions about feminine dress") or "man" or "woman" (as in "Women professors became more common" or "Men who ran for office were more likely to get raises"). Refer to people as "men" or "women," not "males" or "females."

Spell out **numbers** up to and including one hundred; use figures for 101 and above. Use "percent," not "%"; "dollars," not "$," for amounts under 100; and "and," not "&."

Spell out **contractions** ("cannot," not "can't").

Foreign words are sometimes used in English texts when they are difficult to translate, as in the Russian word *korenizatsiia*. Foreign words should be italicized and formatted according to the conventions of their language, including diacritical marks or capitalization rules (such as capitalizing all nouns in German). Languages that are written in other scripts or alphabets are usually transliterated into Latin characters according to standardized transcription rules that you can find online.

A1.8. Common Spelling Errors

Effect/affect

- To effect a change ("effect" is a verb, "to bring about")
- The effects of the war ("effect" is a noun, "results")
- To affect people's attitudes ("affect" is a verb, "to change or have an influence on something")
- The victim's affect ("affect" is a noun, meaning the impression created by someone's expressions and behavior).
- Is her accent real, or affected? ("affected" is an adjective, meaning put on, learned)

Lose (no longer have something) / loose (not tight)

- To lose your money
- Because your pocket is loose

Whether (expresses uncertainty) / weather (as in clouds and rain)

- I don't know whether to take this class.
- The weather forecast predicts rain.
- I don't know whether the weather will clear by tomorrow.

Then (a given time) / than (comparison)

- I will meet you then.
- I would rather meet you than any of my other friends.

There/their/they're/its/it's

- If "its" can be spelled out as "it is," then spell it out.
- If "its" is possessive ("the structure of an essay should reflect its goal"), leave it alone.

- If "their" or "there" can be read as "they are," then it's the contraction. Revise to "they are."
- "There" refers to a location, as in "over there."
- "Their" indicates possession, as in "their car."
- If something belongs to someone, you need a *possessive pronoun*: their, your, its. These are possessive by definition, and need no apostrophe.

Who (grammatical subjects) / Whom (grammatical objects)

- I mentioned my friend, who also lives in New York. (subject = "who," verb = "lives")
- I mentioned my friend, whom I will call tomorrow. (subject = "I," verb = "will call," object = "whom")

Bias (noun) / **biased** (adjective): "He is biased," or "He has a bias."
Notion/notation: A notion is an idea; a notation is when you jot down an idea.
Should of: Misspelling of "should've," which should be spelled out as "should have."
Idea/ideal: An idea is something you think up, an ideal is a value you try to live up to.

- Teddy Roosevelt promoted the idea of conservation through national parks.
- Roosevelt's ideals included environmentalism and fairness.

Succeed / secede: "If you work hard, you will succeed" and "A king succeeds his father on the throne," but "The South seceded from the United States."
Tenet/tenant: tenets are basic principles, but tenants are people who pay rent in order to use someone else's property. "My first tenet is never to be a tenant if I can help it."

A1.9. Chicago Citation Reminders

Footnotes:

1. Firstname Lastname, *Title: Subtitle* (Place: Publisher, date), pages.
2. Firstname Lastname, ed., *Title: Subtitle* (Place: Publisher, date), pages.
3. Firstname Lastname, "Chapter Title," in *Title: Subtitle*, ed. Firstname Lastname (Place: Publisher, date), pages.
4. Firstname Lastname, "Article Title," *Journal Name* volume (year): pages.

Works Cited:

Lastname, Firstname. *Title: Subtitle*. Place: Publisher, year.
Lastname, Firstname, ed. *Title: Subtitle*. Place: Publisher, year.
Lastname, Firstname. "Chapter Title." In *Title: Subtitle,* edited by Firstname Lastname, pages. Place: Publisher, year.
Lastname, Firstname. "Article Title." *Journal Name* volume (year): pages.

Further Reading and Future Writing

The principles and methods described in this book also apply to many other tasks related to your coursework, to more advanced historical work, and to many common professional endeavors. Much of what this book teaches is about being specific: identify the goals for each piece of writing, choose the words that most closely convey your meaning, and support each claim with details of evidence and reasoning. The other principle to remember is that writing is a process of revising and refining that rarely follows a straight line. This appendix offers a few suggestions on how to apply principles from this book to other contexts in and after the history classroom as well as suggestions for further reading.

A2.1. Digital, Visual, and Public History

In some history programs, you may have opportunities to explore less traditional or newer ways of doing history, such as exclusively analyzing visual sources or digital history projects. Some courses or programs may also devote attention to public rather than academic history; that is, they emphasize presenting and explaining history for general audiences more than constructing arguments from primary sources. Each of these ways of doing history builds on the traditional historical methods and skills, but applies them in new directions and adds new skills. In some cases, such as when you are assigned a response paper based on a podcast, exhibit, or exploration of a digital tool, you can follow the guidance for a traditional response paper, because the goals for your written product are very similar. But your instructor will offer the most relevant resources. If you are considering whether to branch out into these areas or are having difficulty connecting this kind of work to the rest of your history major, you may be interested in the following general resources.

On digital history, the essay collection edited by Jack Dougherty and Kristen Nawrotzki, *Writing History in the Digital Age* (Ann Arbor, MI: University of Michigan Press, 2013) offers a variety of perspectives and examples of ways that digital history can be done and its impact on the discipline.

If you are devoting your attention to visual sources or historical objects in a significant project or as a central course theme, you will benefit from the extensive exploration of the special problems posed by such sources in Sarah Barber and Corinna M. Peniston-Bird, eds., *History Beyond the Text: A Student's Guide to Approaching Alternative Sources* (New York: Routledge, 2009).

If you are pondering the role of history in society and how historians can speak to the broader public, you will be stimulated by Nigel Raab's *Who Is the Historian?* (Toronto: University of Toronto Press, 2016), Sarah Maza's *Thinking about History* (Chicago: University of Chicago Press, 2017). and Lynn Hunt's *Writing History in the Global Era* (New York: Norton, 2015), as well as the variety of materials on the website of the American Historical Association, especially its Tuning Project, which works to articulate how history works and why it matters.

A2.2. Course Evaluations

The evaluations that you are asked to fill out at the end of a course are a form of critical analytical writing. The principles of good academic writing and feedback still apply: use the most specific possible words to convey your meaning, support claims with evidence (examples), show your reasoning, be both skeptical and constructive. Filling out course evaluations critically and substantively makes them more likely to have an effect: evaluations that say an instructor "rocks" or "sucks" will be ignored because they don't give the instructor anything to act on. But if you can explain your reasoning about specific ways the course could have been more effective, your evaluation is likely to be taken seriously.

Think about some of the things you found useful or frustrating in your course. Consider the degree to which the course fulfilled its stated goals, not whether it was entertaining, easy, or hard. If you did not fully engage in parts of the course for personal reasons, you should decline to evaluate those parts. Whenever possible, name specific assignments, readings, lectures, or activities. Give examples ("Expectations weren't always clear, as in the primary source assignment, where I wasn't sure how much to incorporate other readings"). Qualify your claims appropriately ("This course was less effective for me because I was already familiar with a lot of its content," not "This course taught me nothing" unless the latter is literally true despite your sincere effort to engage). Consider what can reasonably be addressed by the instructor ("This textbook was confusing," not "I don't like history" or "Tuition is too high"). Give concrete suggestions for improvement ("I don't think anything would be lost if the textbook were dropped, because other readings and lectures covered the same ground").

A2.3. Job Search Cover Letters

When you apply for the kind of job that requires a college diploma or higher credential, you usually submit both a résumé and a cover letter. The résumé provides an overview of your work history and education. The cover letter makes a case for why the employer should hire you. In other words, a job cover letter is an example of persuasive, non-fiction formal writing, much like an analytical or research essay.

Use the cover letter to highlight a few key points from your résumé that you most want noticed, making a case for how well you fit the position advertised. Make concrete, specific claims ("My experience running a silent auction prepares me for this position," not "I'm the best marketing professional you'll ever meet") and support each claim with evidence ("I interned at X Company, Y Company, and Z Company" is better than "I have a lot of experience"). Rather than "telling" the reader that you are enthusiastic about the position, "show" it by listing the experiences or accomplishments that demonstrate your real interest in related activities.

Frame the letter in terms of what your reader needs, rather than what you are looking for. Show you researched the prospective employer by naming specific qualities of the company. ("My experience studying abroad in Istanbul in 2010 prepared me to contribute to Company X's global outreach program," not "Company X is the best in the world, so I am very enthusiastic about working there").

Find out what the expectations are in this field, for this level of position. What degrees, skills, and experience do successful applicants have? This information may be made available by the company or discernible from a website like LinkedIn, or you may need to interview people who already have the kind of job you want. Read sections 2.8 and 3.3–3.5 to find ways of explaining how your history education has prepared you for this opportunity.

If some part of your background may be considered a weakness for this position, address it directly toward the end of the letter as you would handle a counterargument in an essay: explain why you still think you should be considered and support that claim with evidence and reasoning ("Although my degree was in history rather than marketing, the critical thinking and communication skills I developed in my major help me think creatively about how change happens").

A2.4. Personal Statements

If you are applying for fellowships or graduate programs after finishing your bachelor's degree, you will likely need to compose some statement of intent that explains how your background has prepared you for the challenging program ahead. This is a crucial component of your application that needs to demonstrate that you have the extraordinary mastery of historical research and writing skills necessary to succeed in graduate studies and that you will enrich the program with your original ideas and dedication to a greater degree than other competent and motivated students.

Begin your statement with a specific claim that describes what you hope to do if you are admitted to the program or awarded the fellowship. Not "I would be delighted to join your prestigious program," but "I will research X using Y resources in the hopes of being able to demonstrate that Z." Follow this with claims about how your plans are a good fit for the program you're applying for, showing you understand the program and its offerings well. Use the rest of your statement to demonstrate how your activities, responsibilities, work, and education have prepared you to handle what is being offered.

A chronological story of your life or repetitive declarations of enthusiasm are not convincing, so look at your biography for evidence of your skills and drive. Work or activities may have given you organizational or interpersonal skills, travel may have inspired ideas for research, extracurriculars may have taught you time management. A course you did not do well in may have taught you about the value of failure as a learning tool (if you can show how you overcame it). Think creatively about connections between your experience and the demands of the program you're applying to.

A2.5. Moving Forward with Historical Research

If you are considering further research in history, you should explore the website of the American Historical Association (historians.org), especially the profiles of historians who work in a broad variety of jobs. As you develop your writing and research, you should also move on to more advanced texts such as *The Craft of Research*, by Wayne C. Booth, Gregory G. Colomb, Joseph M. Williams, Joseph Bizup, and William T. Fitzgerald (Chicago: University of Chicago Press, 2016) and Walter Prevenier and Martha Howell's

From Reliable Sources: An Introduction to Historical Methods (Ithaca, NY: Cornell University Press, 2001). For a more extensive exploration of the nature of history and historical inquiry, your next steps should include *Historians' Fallacies: Toward a Logic of Historical Thought* by David Hackett Fischer (New York: Harper, 1970), *Historical Evidence and Argument* by David Henige (Madison, WI: University of Wisconsin Press, 2005), *Telling the Truth about History* by Joyce Appleby, Lynn Hunt, and Margaret Jacob (New York: Norton, 1995), *Historiography: An Introductory Guide* by Eileen Ka-May Cheng (London: Bloomsbury, 2012), and John Lewis Gaddis's *The Landscape of History: How Historians Map the Past* (New York: Oxford University Press, 2004).

Index

Numbers in bold indicate the primary definition of a term.

Tables, figures and boxes are indicated by *t, f* and *b* following the page number

For the benefit of digital users, indexed terms that span two pages (e.g., 52–53) may, on occasion, appear on only one of those pages.

CPSIA information can be obtained
at www.ICGtesting.com
Printed in the USA
BVHW040528130521
607209BV00001B/4